Creating a Culturally
Enriched Curriculum
for Grades K–6

Related Titles of Interest

100 Ways to Enhance Self-Concept in the Classroom, Second Edition
Jack Canfield and Harold Clive Wells
ISBN: 0-205-15415-8 Paper   0-205-15711-4 Cloth

126 Strategies to Build Language Arts Abilities: A Month-by-Month Resource
Cathy Collins
ISBN: 0-205-13025-9

Language and Literacy Learning in Multicultural Classrooms
Leslie W. Crawford
ISBN: 0-205-13922-1

The Crosscultural, Language, and Academic Development Handbook
Lynne T. Díaz-Rico and Kathryn Z. Weed
ISBN: 0-205-15048-9

100 Ways to Enhance Values and Morality in Schools and Youth Settings
Howard Kirschenbaum
ISBN: 0-205-15489-1 Paper   0-205-16411-0 Cloth

A Green Dinosaur Day: A Guide for Developing Thematic Units in Literature-Based Instruction, K-6
Patricia L. Roberts
ISBN: 0-205-14007-6

Celebrating Diversity: Building Self-Esteem in Today's Multicultural Classrooms
Frank Siccone
ISBN: 0-205-16175-8 Paper   0-205-16390-4 Cloth

Creating a Culturally Enriched Curriculum for Grades K–6

CATHY COLLINS BLOCK
Texas Christian University

JO ANN ZINKE
Educational Research Dissemination
Fort Worth, Texas

Allyn and Bacon
Boston   London   Toronto   Sydney   Tokyo   Singapore

*This book is dedicated to you,
The Teacher*

Copyright © 1995 by Allyn & Bacon
A Simon & Schuster Company
Needham Heights, Massachusetts 02194

All rights reserved. No part of the material protected by this copyright notice may be reproduced or utilized in any form or by any means, electronic or mechanical, including photocopying, recording, or by any information storage and retrieval system, without written permission from the copyright owner.

Library of Congress Cataloging-in-Publication Data

Block, Cathy Collins.
    Creating a culturally enriched curriculum for grades K–6 / Cathy Collins Block, Jo Ann Zinke.
    p. cm.
    Includes bibliographical references.
    ISBN 0-205-14691-0
    1. Multicultural education—United States—Curricula. 2. Social sciences—Study and teaching (Elementary)—United States.
3. Language arts (Elementary)—United States. I. Zinke, Jo Ann.
II. Title.
LC1099.3.B56 1995
370.19'6'0973—dc20
                                                                               94-29669
                                                                                CIP

Printed in the United States of America
10 9 8 7 6 5 4 3 2 1   98 97 96 95 94

Contents

Preface   viii

Acknowledgments   xv

About the Authors   xvi

Assessing Students' Understanding   1

1   **Appreciating Individual Differences**   5

2   **Being Yourself**   10

3   **Building Friendships**   17

4   **Creating**   24

5   **Developing Honesty, Respect, and Manners**   35

6   **Developing Positive Attitudes**   42

7   **Eliminating Excuses and Correcting Mistakes**   49

8   **Eliminating Misbehavior**   56

9   **Exhibiting Enthusiasm and Happiness**   67

10   **Following Directions: Rules and Guidelines**   73

11   **Getting Along with Others**   79

12   **Giving Kindness**   86

13   **Improving Myself**   91

14   **Learning to Listen Better**   97

15   **Making Decisions and Taking Responsibility**   104

16   **Overcoming Fears**   111

17   **Persevering, Trying, and Working Hard**   117

18   **Quarreling Less**   127

19   **Reading Better**   133

20 Setting Goals   141

21 Smiling   147

22 Solving Problems   154

23 Standing Up for Myself   160

24 Succeeding   165

25 Thinking and Learning   170

26 Understanding Ecology and Nature   177

27 Understanding Science and Health   186

28 Valuing School   195

29 Venturing   203

30 Verifying What Is Real through the Senses   209

Blackline Masters

1. Conducting Successful Interviews   217
2. Learning to Appreciate Individual Differences   218
3. Strategies for Overcoming the Negative Effects of Peer Pressure   219
4. How to Make an Easy "Slit Book"
5. How to Make Personalized Bookmarks   221
6. Bookmark Designs   222
7. My Friend the Author   223
8. Learning New Words by Rhyming   224
9. Thinking Processes That Build My Creativity   225
10. Please and Thank You Records to Improve Manners   226
11. Adding to My Train of Knowledge   227
12. Individualized Instruction to Eliminate Excuses   228
13. Game Board   229
14. The Spinning Game   230
15. Parents' Strategies to Overcome Mistakes   231
16. How to Write a Play   232
17. Using a Venn Diagram to Compare and Contrast   233
18. Creating Words Game   234
19. Room Floor Plan   235
20. Your Room Furniture   236
21. School Room Furniture   237
22. School Time Diary   238
23. After School Time Diary   239
24. Webbing to Learn New Concepts   240
25. Writing Evaluation Form   241
26. Telephone Etiquette   242

27	Six Steps to Improving Listening Skills	243
28	Native American Symbols	244
29	Learning to Make Good Decisions	245
30	Map of Africa	246
31	I Persevere	247
32	Methods of Resolving Disagreements as Depicted in Literature	248
33	The Reading Wheel	249
34	Story Map	250
35	Map of the World	251
36	Puzzle Me	252
37	Finger Puppet Pattern	253
38	Block Puzzle	254
39	What Do You See?	255

Preface

This book provides a multicultural curriculum that can be used alone or as a supplemental program for language arts and social studies instruction in grades K–6. This curriculum is unique in that it uses pluralistic values found in our country's heritage to develop students' social and problem-solving abilities. Each of the thirty units contains quotations, lists of selections from children's literature, and activities addressing a societal, educational, and content area goal. Each unit incorporates the human values, social skills, and knowledge that students need to live successfully and meet challenges both in and outside of school, now and in the future. The units in this book will help elementary school teachers enable students to:

- Appreciate the differences and similarities between cultures
- Learn strategies for resolving conflicts and problems that exist in their lives
- Develop their self-management skills and self-esteem
- Build stronger bonds between home and school

Goals

Creating a Culturally Enriched Curriculum for Grades K–6 is designed to help educators reach the following goals.

GOAL 1. Introduces students to the commonalities and distinctions between thirty cultural groups as they influence students' communication and social skill development.

This multicultural emphasis was deemed important because educators need a curriculum that helps them develop students' understanding of the multicultural nature of their learning and of the society in which they live. This curriculum demonstrates not only how cultures share similar values and concerns, but also how students can develop positive classrooms and communities in which many cultures are represented.

This book will help teachers create a democratic classroom atmosphere—a forum in which multiple perspectives are valued. Such a forum enables students to acquire the skills and abilities they need to examine conflicting knowledge claims and perspectives throughout their lives. *Creating a Culturally Enriched Curriculum for Grades K–6* will benefit students by helping prepare them to function in the diverse world of tomorrow by developing bonds between their cultural values and will provide a broad multicultural knowledge.

Moreover, educators have called for a curriculum that helps them use common cultural values to build a caring classroom community. As our world becomes increasingly complex and competitive, students' success in life will depend more on their abilities to develop partnerships in a multicultural world by using reason and critical thinking abilities. Such a multicultural emphasis is also important because students are becoming increasingly diverse in their culturally based cognitive background experiences. To increase students' understanding of their own and other cultural backgrounds, each unit strengthens students' knowledge of contemporary and historical aspects of each of the thirty cultural groups included in the book. As one teacher, involved in the field-test of this book, stated, "*Creating a Culturally Enriched Curriculum for Grades K–6* is the first curriculum I've seen in which multiple cultures are 'placed inside each student.' Students learn that we have so much to be proud of in our unique cultures, and that similar values comprise all people's heritage."

Many activities encourage parents to become involved in the language arts and social studies program by sharing their personal experiences about specific multicultural topics. Parents are empowered to become partners in the education of their children through specific activities within the book, and by helping teachers present culturally appropriate material concerning language, beliefs, and traditions represented in their children's cultural heritage.

Material in this book can also be used by teachers who are trying to expand their units of instruction with multicultural concepts.

GOAL 2. Provide curriculum that develops students' conflict resolution abilities, social skills, self-esteem, and self-management abilities.

Through this curriculum, students develop skills to address common problems they face in life, and then discover that there are multiple strategies useful in solving problems. This curriculum can be used when specific problems arise in the classroom because, in addition to the 30 unit themes, there are nearly 100 specific problems referenced in the books and quotations we have cited. When an individual student or class needs instruction in an area of a diagnosed weakness, information that enhances students' positive growth and understanding is readily available.

This curriculum responds to the new requirements for recertification in New Hampshire (and corresponding movements in Texas, California, and other states) in which a minimum of five clock hours a week in character and citizenship education must become a part of public school instruction. Specifically, *Creating a Culturally Enriched Curriculum for Grades K–6* contains seven units that help students:

- Respond to individuals and groups in positive and productive ways
- Mend disagreements effectively
- Overcome the peer pressure elementary students often experience to accept false goals, appearances, dialogues, and demeanors
- Discern deceptively shallow from deeper, more meaningful aims

Many children today are living with violence. They experience life as events that happen to them rather than things over which they can exert control. Before such students can function in an educational environment that assumes individual responsibility and control over life choices, they must be taught strategies to affect what happens to them. This book will help you prepare students for the increased demands society is placing on them.

Included in this book are activities designed to help develop students' self-concept, identify their talents, and establish their personalities. These units strengthen skills such as the following:

- Overcoming the negative effects of anger
- Learning to take calculated risks and to venture into appropriate learning opportunities
- Establishing new challanges for themselves
- Increasing students' ecological awareness and their understanding of the personal responsibilities they hold to nature
- Understanding the causes and overcoming the negative influence rational and irrational fears have on their learning
- Persevering when difficulties and obstacles emerge
- Increasing reading abilities as well as their value for and use of reading as an important self-selected leisure pursuit in which they gain information, a sense of escape, and alternative points of view
- Focusing students' aims and increasing their abilities to complete their objectives successfully

GOAL 3. To present an integrated curriculum for elementary school programs.
Many elementary programs follow an integrated curriculum or use thematic instruction. As these programs evolve, we see an increasing need for a curriculum that scaffolds instruction for students at different levels of ability. *Creating a Culturally Enriched Curriculum for Grades K–6* provides such a curriculum because each unit contains many activities and selections of literature at numerous levels of difficulty. The goal is to teach the whole child through authentic learning experiences using literature, multiculturally based activities, and insightful quotations. Through this instruction, students are encouraged to live vicariously as they learn how to solve problems that exist in the outside of school.

Special Features

Several features make this book unique.

- More than 300 brief quotations are included. These quotations reflect common human values in our world in a form that students can read and memorize easily. They can (1) become a part of daily language arts and social studies instruction; (2) begin each day's work; (3) serve as starter sentences for "morning message" activities; and/or (4) stimulate students who finish work early, throughout the day, to write (and reflect on) their own thoughts about the unit theme and individual quotations.

- Thirty cultures are integrated into the curriculum to increase students' appreciation and understanding of their own and others' cultures. Many Spanish-language selections are also cited throughout the book.

- All units contain Blackline Masters and opening of the day, journal writing, cooperative learning, reading response group, individual, paired, and whole class activities. These activities support new philosophies of instruction, such as writing workshops, whole language, and parallel scheduling. One reviewer who used this book in her class stated: "The high caliber of journal writing activities really pleased me. They couple critical thinking with thoughtful writing tasks. The one about friendship especially comes to mind."

- The literature in every unit has been reviewed, annotated, and rated as either (I) for K–2, introductory; (E) easy reading; or (M) medium reading. In this way, students of different reading abilities can find books at their reading level that relate to the unit theme, can participate fully in all activities, can select individual titles to read at home, can develop interests in specific topics within units, and can experience bibliotherapy.

- Thirty-nine Blackline Masters contain high-quality graphics that help students learn and reduce teachers' preparation time. These are located at the end of the book.

- Each unit can stand alone. The curriculum need not be sequenced alphabetically or as designated in the Contents. Instead, teachers can use units in the order that best addresses individual classroom and student needs.

- Prior to publication, 54 teachers field-tested units in this book. Some of their own and their students' specific comments appear on pages xiii–xiv. The most common feedback they provided was that the activities in this curriculum are realistic, easy to implement, and inspiring to teachers and students alike.

- This book contains several methods of assessing students' learning through dynamic and authentic performance-based experiences located on pages 1–3.

How to Use This Book

Creating a Culturally Enriched Curriculum for Grades K–6 can be used in many different ways by classroom teachers, curriculum directors, school administrators, and college professors.

1. Teachers in individual classrooms or in whole schools can establish their own literacy and social studies goals reflecting special capabilities and dispositions they wish to develop. Then, individual units can be taught based on the level of priority established. Instructional time spent on each unit can be based upon students' speed of learning.

2. Classroom teachers can teach all units if used in this way; educators can introduce a different quotation each day and engage students in thematic activities for a one-to-two week period per unit.

3. Selected book lists, Blackline Masters, and activities can be duplicated for individual student home or school use or as methods of promoting home–school partnerships. The curriculum can also be used in a variety of other social skill, alternative discipline, guidance counseling, health, character education, and after-school programs as well as in home-based instruction.

4. Within individual classrooms, teachers and students can select a unit and establish a thematic center and/or bulletin board. As one reviewer described it: "I would have my students write the quotations on the board after we finished learning them."

5. Students can select activities within individual units that they want to study.

6. Principals can use the curriculum by incorporating quotations and passages from individual books into daily thoughts, or establishing schoolwide, needs-based themes. For example, administrators can select quotations to announce over the public address system and can use thematic activities in before- and after-school extra-curricular prrograms.

7. Curriculum directors and supervisors can use the book for inservice training programs concerning social, cognitive, and affective development of students in grades K–6.

8. This curriculum is valuable for developmental, cooperative learning, and ungraded classrooms.

9. College professors can use this book in courses such as curriculum, language arts/social studies methods, children's literature, multicultural education, social skills development, and character education for undergraduate and graduate teacher education.

Description of the Book

The book is divided into two sections: thirty instructional units and assessments of students' understanding. All units follow the same format. On the first pages of each unit are the thematic learning objectives and several quotations that exemplify the concept under study. Before beginning the first unit, you may want to define *quote*: "something that someone else said; to reproduce or repeat a statement of a person considered an authority; or to cite or refer to an authority's exact words."

The second section of each unit contains lists of books that can be read orally to the class, used with specific activities, or read by individual students in school and at home to learn more about each theme.

The third section contains activities that teach the concepts and objectives of the unit. Each activity is designed to engage students in individual, paired, small group, and whole class instruction to increase their ability to use the unit's concept in their own lives.

The fourth section contains multicultural activities, information, and extensions of the concepts under study. This section of each unit can be shared with students and then used as the basis for their further research into topics of interest to them, and/or to learn more about the value and interpretation each unit holds for their culture. Students can also interview adults from their culture of origin and combine this new knowledge into a culminating classroom discussion for each unit. This discussion can promote students' abilities to build partnerships between cultures.

The 39 Blackline Masters at the end of the book can be used with several different activities to enhance students' learning. There are also symbols in the left margins to designate activities that can be used for Journal Writing Experiences (JW), Reading Response or Cooperative Learning Groups (RRG), and Blackline Master accompaniments (BLM).

The book offers 20 methods for assessing students' development of social educational strategies, and applying reading, writing, and content area knowledge in their lives outside of school.

Comments Concerning This Curriculum from the 54 Field-Test Teachers

Here are some comments that teachers and students made concerning the unique benefits they received from using the book:

"Using quotations in the units provided a good introduction to each day's lesson as well as a vocabulary and word bank extender."

"The beauty and fun of the lessons is that they give the teacher, as well as the students, an opportunity to be as creative as possible."

"The quotations helped me bring a sense of unity into the lessons and gave direction in planning."

"I liked having many related quotes each day because different quotes related to different students. The quotes gave the students a chance to express themselves."

"My class needs quotes like these to make their sometimes difficult nontraditional lives happier. Activities like this are what they need to build their confidence as far as reading and writing go."

"The successes I had in teaching my lesson were exciting. I think my main success was that everyone walked away from this lesson with some sort of new knowledge, even if not on the same level. I believe I must have tailored the lesson to different abilities when the need arose, and modified throughout the lesson."

"I especially enjoyed teaching units from quotations that dealt with life skills and growing up, because I felt like the units truly had a purpose."

". . . I did the lesson on friendships. I asked the students if they thought they would treat their friends better or do more things to show them that they appreciated them. They responded by saying 'yes' and that they realize how important their friends are to them. They also said that they felt good inside when they did things for others. I thought it was funny that even the "too cool" boys in the class were agreeing with the girls. . . . [T]he students said that they liked the lesson and that it was a good change from the things they usually did during reading."

"I feel that the students like to think that the teacher is also just like them. I put myself on their level throughout the lesson. I feel that I felt comfortable doing this because I enjoyed the quotations myself. The only addition I would like to incorporate into this unit is having students write their own quotes. I would love to base lessons on their own quotes. I feel this would be fun and enjoyable for the class."

Students said:

"I can use it because the lesson relates to my real life."

"It was fun."

"The quotation helps you get into the lesson because it's like the main idea and because it helps me understand the lesson better."

"It helps me understand what the lesson is going to be about."

"It explains things better."

"I'd like to start every morning with a quote because it makes me feel happy."

Acknowledgments

We wish to acknowledge and thank the reviewers of this book for their enlightening comments and helpful suggestions: Patricia L. Roberts, California State University, Sacramento; Margaret M. Naughton and Janice McKenna, both from the Winter Hill Community School, Somerville, Massachusetts; Karen Lindh Boettcher, Beech Street Community School, Manchester, New Hampshire; and Phyllis Sunshine, Maryland State Department of Education. We also want to thank Rick for all he has done on the graphics.

About the Authors

Cathy Collins Block, professor of education at Texas Christian University, earned her doctorate at the University of Wisconsin–Madison in Curriculum and Instruction and Educational Psychology. She has taught at Southern Illinois University–Carbondale, served as research assistant at the Wisconsin Research and Development Center for Cognitive Development, and taught kindergarten through high school–aged students in both private and public schools. She has served as consultant for curriculum development and teacher training in more than a hundred school districts in many states. Dr. Block recently served as a citizen ambassador to Russia and Hungary to assist in curriculum development in those nations. She is author of several college textbooks and has written more than fifty articles for various publications.

Jo Ann Zinke is president of Educational Research Dissemination, Fort Worth, Texas. She has taught elementary and secondary students as well as adults in Texas and California. She has also served as a consultant for inservice training programs for school districts, community colleges, and universities. Her company is dedicated to the translation of research into classroom practices, and her materials have been used across the United States and Canada.

Assessing Students' Understanding

The following activities and forms can be used and modified to assess students' knowledge. These evaluation strategies are presented as a special section of the book because you can select one or more to assess students' understanding of concepts (1) in each unit, (2) during a single grading period, and/or (3) from the total curriculum after you have ended your study of all units. You may use the following assessment activities whenever you need to evaluate students' growth.

1. You can review all quotations and activities introduced in one week, one grading period, or one year. Following the review, ask students to complete a letter to you, similar to the following, to report how much they have learned and why:

DEAR TEACHER,

WHAT I LIKED BEST WAS _____. WHY I LIKED IT WAS BECAUSE _____.

WHAT I LEARNED THE MOST FROM IT WAS _____. WHY I LEARNED THE MOST FROM THIS WAS BECAUSE _____.

THANK YOU FOR _____.

WHAT I STILL WANT TO LEARN IS _____.

2. You can conduct an oral assessment immediately following a unit by stating: Now that we've thought about [topic of the unit], what will we do in the future? You can merely listen for individual students' depth of understanding, or you can list all the responses to refer to at a later date.

3. You can create individual written assessments after a unit in which students draw or finish incomplete statements with a few words. For example, at the end of the friendship unit, you can write the following statements on the board and have students complete them individually with drawings or writings:

I got a good idea from my friend about _____.

Once an idea of my friend was right for them but not for me. That time I _____.

4. Use wraparounds, where students sit in a circle and respond in turn to your assessment questions. Each student has the right to pass. Students who pass know they can earn their evaluation points by summarizing what other students have said or by pointing out differences between ideas voiced by classmates.

5. Students can choose to complete a telegram to anyone they want to tell how much they have learned about specific concepts. Once you have approved their telegrams and used them to assess how much the student has learned, you can return the telegram to the student to deliver to the appropriate person.

>To: _____
>
>From: _____
>
>Message: I learned . . .
>
>Signed: _____

6. At the end of a unit, several units, or the entire book, students write a description of all that they have learned. They also write one or more questions about areas they do not think they understood. Students give their papers to a classmate who attempts to answer the question if possible and to add another question about the material they have learned. The paper is returned to the original student, who answers the peer's question and writes another question for him or her. This cycle continues for as long as desired.

7. Introduce a unit as you normally would, but on the opening day ask the class if they understand the major concept to be taught in the unit. Students will likely respond that they do not because you will have diagnosed in advance that they needed instruction in that unit. Once the unit is complete, ask the class: "Do you remember when we began this unit and you told me that you did not understand _____? I believed you earlier when you told me you did not understand _____. I still believe you do not understand. What can you do to prove me wrong?" Now it is the student's job to dispel your misconception by creating his or her own demonstration of how much he or she has learned.

8. Give students several options of how they want you to evaluate how much they have learned. The options you may suggest include the following:

- Make a miniature state in which students present two- to ten-minute dramas to explain what they have learned.

- Make a poster describing the most interesting and valuable information they have learned. Display the poster and give a two-minute talk explaining why you found the information interesting.

- Broadcast a "review" of the topic as if you were on a television newscast. Tape-record the oral comments you make, or write them if you prefer not to stand before the class.

- Construct a diorama to illustrate an important piece of information learned. Display the diorama at a center and allow students to come and ask questions as an artist might display and explain a piece of work.

- Make a mural in a group or alone to illustrate the information you considered most valuable. Display the mural and answer questions that may arise.

- Make a time line or diagram depicting important dates and events.

- Write a song including the most important information you have learned. Sing the song in person or on tape for others.

- Make a crossword puzzle and let other students try to complete it. Check and return their papers to them.
- Write a script for a television program; then produce and participate in the program.
- Analyze two points of view concerning a topic you learned.
- Study all that you wrote or drew in your journal concerning a topic or topics. Analyze how much you learned and what you learned.
- Describe how you learned a concept, where you began in your thinking, and how your thinking changed. Ask three other classmates to do the same and share your reactions to each other's reports of learning.

1 Appreciating Individual Differences

Learning Objectives Through this unit, students learn to appreciate the differences between themselves and peers. Quotations, activities, and books in the unit describe methods students can use to respond to individual differences in a positive way.

Resources *Select a different quotation to discuss and write on the board each day of this unit's study.*

There is something to learn from all people.

Every individual has a place to fill in the world,
and is important in some respect whether
he chooses to be so or not.
—Nathaniel Hawthorne

Nobody is a nobody.
Everyone is a somebody.

Learn the differences the world has to offer.

Everyone has their own personality,
Only you can choose the one you want.

Remember, labels are hard to remove.

If everyone is thinking alike
then somebody isn't thinking.
—George Patton

To live is good.
To live vividly is better.
To live vividly together is best.
—Max Eastman

One of us may be smarter
than another of us;
But none of us are
smarter than
All of us working together.

Being different makes us special.

Be sure you can be responsible
for that which you create.

Actions speak louder than words.

A contrary mind listens to no one.

Finding the Right Book Concerning Appreciating Individual Differences to Meet Students' Needs

Difficulty code: I = Introductory; E = Easy; M = Medium

		Book
E	An interesting perspective on prejudice	*Billy the Great* by Rosa Guy
E	Discerning differences positively	*Hooper Humperdink, Not Him!* by Dr. Seuss
E	Wanting to be like others	*Alexander and the Wind-Up Mouse* by Leo Lionni
E	Trouble for someone who looks different	*Big A* by Andrew Clements
E	Buford uses his differences to be the star of the show	*Buford the Little Bighorn* by Bill Peet
E	Humerous adventures of unique individuals	*Gregory Griggs & Other Nursery Rhymes* by Arnold Lobel
E	The immigrant experience	*We Come from Vietnam* by Muriel Stanek
E	A Jewish child and Christmas	*There's No Such Thing as a Chanukah Bush, Sandy Goldstein* by Susan Sussman
E	Recognizing and accepting differences	*Why Am I Different?* by Norma Simon
E–M	Prejudice	*Black Like Kyra, White Like Me* by Judith Vigna
M	Passing judgment without facts	*The Witch of Blackbird Pond* by Elizabeth George Speare
M	Helping people with handicaps	*You're Somebody Special on a Horse* by Fern G. Brown
M	Expectations of others	*The Way of Our People* by Arnold Alfred Griese
M	Making judgments about others	*Crow Boy* (film) by Taro Yashima
M	Prejudice and lack of consideration; Indians teach a boy survival skills	*Sign of the Beaver* by Elizabeth George Speare (video)
M	Having a closed mind about others	*The Great Gilly Hopkins* (video, film, record) by Katherine Paterson
M	Feeling different	*The Difference of Ari Stein* by Charlotte Herman
M	Accepting people with handicaps	*Head over Wheels* by Lee Kingman
M	Understanding handicaps	*Chloris and the Weirdos* by Kim Platt

1 APPRECIATING INDIVIDUAL DIFFERENCES

Activities to Use with Quotes and Books

Opening the School Day Discussion

Discuss the unit objectives and write a new quotation each day. Ask students to discuss how its meaning relates to their lives.

(RRG) *There are many types of differences.* Make a photocopy or overhead transparency of the books listed for this unit. Let each student select a book to read about one type of individual difference. Divide students into groups to read the books of their choice. Then ask groups to discuss what they learned about methods of appreciating individual differences and then to report this information to the class.

Remove the label. Discuss the quotation "Remember, labels are hard to remove." Ask students to bring labeled jars to class and have them try to take off the labels. If the labels on some jars cannot be removed completely, or if any adhesive remains, use this as an analogy to discuss the implications that labeling holds for people (i.e., some labels remain with a person forever and cannot be removed). Last, place all the jars that have had their labels successfully removed side by side on a table at the front of the room. Have students discuss how similar these containers become when they do not have labels—and how the same is true for people.

Learning from giants of old. Discuss the quote, "There is something to learn from all people." Then ask each student to choose a biography about a famous person. After reading, have students engage in the following activity and the culminating large group activity.

1. *Individual:* After students have read about their famous person, ask them to write a letter to that person mentioning specific events in the person's life that were important to the student. Next, ask students to read their letters in class and to ask classmates if they have any questions to ask this famous person. Have students conclude their presentations by reporting what they learned that helps them appreciate individual differences.

(BLM) **2.** *Small group:* Form pairs of students who have read different biographies. Ask students to describe their biography to their partner. During the interview, have them identify how their main characters accepted individual differences. You may want students to follow the interview guide on Blackline Master 1 (see the Blackline Master section of the book). Last, ask students to write a paragraph about what they have learned from this activity about accepting individual differences.

3. *Culminating large group:* Have the whole class gather and reread the quotation for the day. Discuss what they learned from each other during the activities.

(JW) *Journal writing.* Have students select the quotation they like best in this unit, describe why it is their favorite, and tell how they can apply it to their lives.

(BLM) *Learning to appreciate differences.* First, have students divide into small groups to discuss a situation in which differences existed between people. List these situations on the bottom of Blackline Master 2 (see BLM section). Next, ask each group to choose a quotation that could be helpful in each of the situations. Last, ask small groups to role-play a positive response to each situation.

Multicultural Emphasis: Concepts about Appreciating Individual Differences That Come from Other Cultures

You may want to teach the following information about individual differences between languages. After sharing the information, ask how increasing communication with people who are different from themselves can increase people's ability to accept individual differences.

(BLM) *Native Americans.* Individual tribes and groups of Native Americans have their own methods of communicating. In North America alone, in the early fifteenth century, there were more than a thousand different Native American languages in use. In addition, each tribe used symbols to show the human qualities they valued. One way of communicating symbols was by using smoke signals, created by using a blanket to cover and uncover a smoky fire at specific intervals. The intervals between smoke signals sent a message to members of the tribe who were far away.

The following words that come from Native American languages have been adopted into the English language: *adobe, powwow, buffalo, tipi, canoe, totem, desert, wampum, forest, wigwam, plains, woodlands, pottery.* Introduce the symbols on Blackline Master 28 (see BLM section) that were used to communicate in one Native American language, and have students write stories for classmates to decipher.

France. The French language was once used by all the rulers and nobles in Europe and Russia. Today, French ranks second to English in prominence as an international language. Some believe that French is so highly valued by people from a variety of cultures because it is beautiful, harmonious, and flowing to hear.

There is another possible explanation for the popularity of French. France is sometimes referred to as "the hexagon" because of its six-sided border. Three sides of the country interface with water, but France's other borders adjoin three different countries. Because of their proximity to several countries, French borders have been moved many times as a result of wars. Moreover, languages, ideas, and customs were easily shared between France and its neighbors. For example, people in northeastern France speak a dialect mixed with German; in southern France, the dialect is influenced by the ancient Roman language; and many French people speak Breton, a dialect related to that of southwestern England. Although many French people use one of these dialects, all of them also speak the purer form of French. Some speculate that this adherence to standard French and the dispersion of French throughout Europe has led to the prominence of French as an international language.

(RRG) *African American.* Read or have students read Mildred Taylor's books about the travels of the Logan family: *Roll of Thunder, Hear My Cry; Let the Circle Be Unbroken;* and *The Road to Memphis.* After they have read these books, form four small groups (each of which has read one of the books, if possible).

1 APPRECIATING INDIVIDUAL DIFFERENCES

Ask students to report on and compare the appreciation and rejection the Logan family felt from others during their long journey. Last, discuss how the journey could have been altered if the people in the book appreciated individual differences more.

Your Own Additions to the Unit

2 Being Yourself

Learning Objectives Students often have difficulty seeking their identities, recognizing special talents, and developing strong personalities. In this unit students learn to establish their own voices, points of view, beliefs, and knowledge.

Resources *Select a different quotation to discuss and write on the board each day of this unit's study.*

Be able to laugh at yourself.

It really brings pride when I know I tried.

Character is who you really are.
—Dan Zadra

If you hide your feelings to keep the peace, you'll never have any.

I am as big for me as you are big for you.

If you like yourself, you can be yourself.

*Feeling positive about yourself
Brings out the better in you.*

You must have great expectations for yourself.

One must know himself before he knows or understands life.

If you can't be yourself, you have nothing.

We could be cowards, if we had courage enough.
—Thomas Fuller

Your worth is not what you have, but what you are.

*Reputation is what others think of you;
character is who you really are.*

No one can make you feel inferior without your permission.
—Eleanor Roosevelt

*Some people will like you; some people won't,
but always be able to like yourself even when others don't.*

*Do what you can,
with what you have,
where you are.*
—Theodore Roosevelt

*If I am not for myself, who will be for me?
But if I am only for myself, what am I?*
—The Talmud

*His own image was no
longer the reflection of a
clumsy, dirty, gray bird,
ugly and offensive.
He himself was a swan.*
—Hans Christian Anderson

Finding the Right Book Concerning Being Yourself to Meet Students' Needs

Difficulty code: I = Introductory; E = Easy; M = Medium

		Book
I	Poor self-concept	*Why Am I Different?* by Norma Simon
I	An error in a toy dog	*Sniffles* by Robert Larranaga
I	Feeling inadequate	*Titch* by Pat Hutchins
I	Feeling special	*Rackety, That Very Special Rabbit* by Margaret Richards Friskey
I	Accepting yourself	*A Color of His Own* by Leo Lionni
I	Feeling as if you are inferior	*How I Faded Away* by Janice Udry
E	Wishing to be someone else	*The Whingdingdilly* by Bill Peet
E	Having your own opinions	*I Know What I Like* by Norma Simon
E	Biography of a female artist	*Georgia O'Keefe* by Robyn Montana Turner
E	Liking yourself	*The Long Haired Boy* by Shel Silverstein (poem)
E	Finding your own importance	*Time Flies* by Florence Parry Heide
E	Insight into what makes a kid pretend to be tough	*Summer Wheels* by Eve Bunting
E	A speech-impaired boy learns to improve	*Growl When You Say R* by Muriel Novella Stavek
E	The importance of being yourself	*Big Orange Splot* by Daniel M. Pinkwater
E	Maintaining your own identity	*The Art Lesson* by Tomie de Paola
E	Finding out what your talents are	*Will I Ever Be Good Enough?* by Judith Conoway
E	Five cats who imagine being something else but end up glad to be who they are	*Copycats* by Nicola Bayley

		Book
E–M	Growing up	*When I Was Young in the Mountains* by Cynthia Rylant
E–M	A girl who wants to play the role of Peter Pan but feels she can't because she is black finds she can do anything she sets her mind to do	*Amazing Grace* by Mary Hoffman
M	Self-realization	*The White Horse Gang* by Nina Bawden
M	Native American racial identity	*A Girl Called Wendy* by Beverly Kathleen Butler
M	A boy who wants to fly like a hawk	*Hawk, I'm Your Brother* by Byrd Bayton
M	Getting to know yourself	*Shelter from the Wind* by Marion Dane Bauer
M	Identity	*Glass Slippers Give You Blisters* by Mary Jane Arech
M	A boy who learns that his actions can be successful	*Farm Boy* by Douglas W. Gorsline
M	Attitude toward oneself	*Doug Meets the Nutcracker* by William Hooks
M	Effects of group pressure (Japanese folklore)	*The Wave* by Margaret Hodges
M	Becoming aware of individuality	*Big Orange Splot* by Daniel M. Pinkwater
M	Overweight harassment	*Dinah and the Green Fat Kingdom* by Isabelle Holland
M	Growing from a klutz to a confident, mature sixth grader	*The Biggest Klutz in Fifth Grade* by Bill Wallace
M	Understanding yourself by appreciating what's within	*Zeely* by Virginia Hamilton
M	Peer pressure	*Kathleen, Please Come Home* by Scott O'Dell
M	Feeling different	*The Difference of Ari Stein* by Charlotte Herman

Activities to Use with Quotes and Books

Opening the School Day Discussion

Liking oneself. Discuss the students understanding of "Being Yourself"; set the class objectives for this unit. Read the quotation for the day from the board. Then ask students to spend about ten minutes describing in writing what this quote means to them. Any words from the quotation that students do not know can be discussed and placed into their personal word banks.

What makes me special. Have students write a description of a character they would like to be or a character they admire from one of the books listed for this unit. Then have them compare this character's traits to their own by listing the traits in two columns, one describing their character's traits and one describing themselves. Next, ask students to read other students' lists. Last, after all students have had a chance to contrast many character traits, ask them to write about the traits that make themselves special and unique.

(BLM) *Overcoming peer pressure.* Select the quote, "If you hide your feelings to keep the peace, you'll never have any," and read one of this unit's books on peer pressure. Then divide students into small groups and discuss the pros and cons of peer pressure. After this discussion, ask students to read one of the books for this unit and make a chart listing strategies used by the characters in their books to overcome the negative influences of peer pressure. Next, have each group answer these questions, either orally or in writing:

1. What would have been different if the characters had not used a strategy to overcome peer pressure?
2. Do they agree or disagree with their character's actions? Why or why not?
3. What are some options that the character overlooked?
4. How will they respond if they face a similar situation?

Last, have students analyze the extent to which peer pressure influences them. Emphasize the importance of each person's individuality of thought and, as a class, list strategies to use in situations where peer pressure is exerting a negative influence. Blackline Master 3 in the BLM section is to be used with the activity.

Cultural emphasis. Have students choose, and read one of the multiculturally oriented books from *The Visual Geography Series* or one listed in this unit's book list. Then have students relate real-life situations in which they have had difficulty sustaining their personal identity. Last, ask students to share any strategies they learned from books that could help in these situations.

(RRG) *Accepting our weaknesses.* Ask your students to think of the silliest situation they have ever experienced or seen. Ask them: "What did you do? Were you scared? Embarrassed? Upset? Happy? Sad? Is there something about yourself in that incident that you didn't like?" Ask if they know who Ross Perot is? Say: "People make fun of Ross Perot because he has large ears, but he has learned that if he laughs first, others will laugh with him, not at him. The next time you feel you are being laughed at, remember that if you start laughing, they can only laugh *with* you, not *at* you." Then, ask students to get into groups of four or five to share their interpretations of this unit and an event or personal trait about themselves that they can now better accept. Or have each group select a book from the list of books for this unit in which main characters experience personal turmoil that affects their daily lives. After students have read the book, ask them to write a list of important details from the book and to answer the following questions:

1. What was the main character's problem?
2. How did the main character's problem affect others around him?
3. What special quality, talent, or personality trait did the main character employ to solve that problem?
4. Do you possess that quality? If so, how do you know? If not, what talent do you possess that is of comparable value, and how would you use it to solve a problem in your schoolwork?

Discover what courage could mean. Discuss the quote, "We could be cowards, if we had courage enough." Point out that being a "coward" (by some people's standards) would take courage. (e.g., saying "no" to drugs or to smoking a cigarette or drinking liquor; not doing what others want you to do when you sense danger or believe that an action is not right). You may want students to divide into small groups, create a solution for each situation discussed, and present solutions to the class.

(RRG) *What I tend to value in others.* Place students in groups of two or three and ask each group to choose a library book from this unit's book list. Then ask students to take turns reading one page aloud to their partner(s), or have one student read orally while the other(s) read along silently. After all partners have read aloud four times, tell students to set the book aside and list the admirable qualities the main character possessed. Continue this process until they have about twenty items on their lists. Have students discuss the list of qualities they admire with another group who read the same book. Then have them answer the following questions:

- Why did differences exist?
- What do these differences suggest about the differing values we hold?
- What did this experience teach us about things we value in ourselves and others?

(JW) *Journal writing.* Ask students to select their favorite quote and to discuss how this quote "speaks" to them in their lives. Next, ask students to cite examples of things they know about themselves, in relationship to the quotations discussed, that they can use to relate better to their family and friends. Last, have students write about the value of being themselves and communicating who they are to others.

(RRG) *Onsets and rhymes.* Read the poem "The Long Haired Boy" by Shel Silverstein. Relate this poem to the quote, "Some people will like you, some people won't; always be able to like yourself when others don't." Then discuss onsets and rhymes by focusing on the rhymes that appear in the quote and in Shel Silverstein's poem. An onset is the initial consonant or vowel sound that begins a word. The rhyme is the sound that ends a word. Discuss how rhythmic poems, songs, and chants enable people to practice recognizing onsets and rhymes in new words when they read.

Next, have small groups of students compose their own poem, rap, or song about self-esteem (or liking themselves) using onsets and rhymes with a rhythmic beat. Students can read aloud, act out, or sing their works to the whole class. End the lesson by asking students to make a final journal entry concerning their feelings about the quote and the lesson on onsets and rhymes.

Multicultural Emphasis: Concepts about Being Yourself That Come from Other Cultures

Thailand. Read the following Thai proverb to students: "You don't force a buffalo to eat grass." Discuss its meaning as related to being yourself. (Don't pressure people to follow a certain path.) Also, discuss if the people in Thailand hold a value about "being themselves" that is similar to the value held in North America.

African American. The African-American culture values being yourself. The Swahili word *imani* (ee-MAH-nee) refers to self-esteem—literally, "believing in yourself." Ask if students have ever heard of this term. Ask them how *believing in yourself* helps you to *be yourself.*

Multicultural. Read and discuss the following information about the Irish, German, Italian, and Laotian cultures. Before you share the information, ask students from each of these cultures to share aspects of their heritage that helped them become who they are (e.g., the German culture values being the best that one can be). List students' comments on the board. Then share the following information and ask how these facts help people to develop the conviction to be themselves in difficult situations. Add students' ideas to the list on the board. Last, review the lists and ask students to summarize what they learned about cultural influences on "being yourself."

Germany. The family is very important to the German people, as is a sense of national pride.

Greece. The family is the center of Greek society. They consider an injury or insult to one member an injury to every family member. The Greeks are expressive; they use a colorful form of body language when they are talking. When people watch two Greeks engaged in a discussion, they may think a heated disagreement is occurring when in fact the two people are simply gesturing to better communicate their friendship.

Italy. Read *Enchantment of the World* by R. Conrad Stein. This book depicts how the traditional Italian family shares everything it has with its members. Grandparents, aunts, and uncles quite often live together. The problems of the family take precedence over all other problems in life. The traditional Italian man considers it a sacred duty to protect and defend his family. Italians long distinguished themselves as excellent sailors and fearless explorers; Marco Polo and Christopher Columbus are two good examples.

Laos. Laotian people tend to be unselfish, uncomplaining, and altruistic. The phrase *bo pen ngang* means, "There's no problem; if it is going to happen, let it." Families are very close. As many as four generations may live under one roof, with all members, from the youngest to the oldest, contributing. Success and happiness depend on the family as a whole. Competition is discourage: If someone is best or first, then someone else must be last, an unwelcome feeling in Laotian culture.

Ireland. The Visual Geography Series has books about many nations, including Ireland, that students may want to read. The Irish are known for their songs and wit, their political skills, and their distinctive personalities. The Irish are traditionally devoted to their parents, and the bond between siblings is often very deep. Ask students to conduct a little research on an Irish-American family, like the Kennedys, to identify these traits in Irish Americans.

Your Own Additions to the Unit

3 Building Friendships

Learning Objectives Students with many friends or few can benefit from the quotations, activities, and books in this unit. This unit helps students build closer associations, support groups, and friendly attachments with people.

Resources *Select a different quotation to discuss and write on the board each day of this unit's study.*

Be a friend.

*Trouble one can get through alone,
but it takes two to be glad.*
—Ibsen

Give and receive.

Talking with one another is loving one another.
—African saying

Be a friend to have a friend.

Without trust there is no friendship.

Meet a friend.

A friend remains loyal, even when others turn away.
—Rebecca Barlow Jordan, On Being a Friend

I have a friend in me.

*Time changes in many ways and we with time,
But not in ways of friendship.*

A friend is a present you give yourself.
—Robert Louis Stevenson

A friend is one before whom I may think aloud.
—Ralph Waldo Emerson

*Make new friends and keep the old.
One is silver, the other gold.*
—Traditional children's rhyme

My best friend is the one who brings out the best in me.
—Henry Ford

A friend is one to whom one may pour out all the contents of one's heart, chaff and grain together, knowing that the gentlest of hands will take and sift it, keep what is worth keeping and with a breath of kindness blow the rest away.
–Arabic proverb

Finding the Right Book Concerning Building Friendships to Meet Students' Needs

Difficulty code: I = Introductory; E = Easy; M = Medium

		Book
I	Gaining confidence through friends	*Timothy Goes to School* by Rosemary Wells
I	Helping friends	*Frog and Toad: The Lost Button* and other *Frog and Toad* books by Arnold Lobel
I	Sharing and friendship	*Tico and His Golden Wings* by Leo Lionni
I	Friends in times of need	*A Special Trade* by Sally Wittman
I	Best friends	*Natalie Spitzer's Turtles* by Gina Willner-Pardo
I	A special relationship	*A Visit to Oma* by Marisabina Russo
I	Friends	*May I Bring a Friend?* by Schneck de Regniers
I	Stories about true friends	*Pelly and Peak* by Sally Wittman
I	Best friends	*My Friend John* by Charlotte Zolotow
I	Resolving differences	*Two Good Friends* by J. Delton
I	Playing with friends	*I'm Calling Molly* by Jane Kurtz
I	Overcoming jealousy	*Jealousy* by E. Eriksson
I	Rhyms about friendship	*That's What a Friend Is* by P. K. Hollinan
I	Trouble making friends	*I'm Not Oscar's Friend Anymore* by Marjorie Sharmat
I	Best friends	*Charlotte's Web* by E. B. White
I	Friendships	*My Friend John* by Charlotte Zolotow
E	When a friend moves	*Mitchell Is Moving* by Marjorie Sharmat
E	Friendship with a robot	*Norby the Mixed-up Robot* by Janet and Isaac Asimov
E	Friendship and adaptation	*Alex is My Friend* by Marisabrina Russo
E	Trusting friends	*Danny and the Dinosaur* by Syd Hoff
E	A new neighborhood for field mice	*Nice New Neighbors* by Franz Brandenberg

		Book
E	Learning the value of friendship	*Through the Hidden Door* by Rosemary Wells
E	Overcoming misunderstandings	*The Story of Ferdinand* by Munro Leaf
E	Learning to be a friend	*Meaning Well* by Sheila Cole
E	Kinds of friendship	*Together* by June York Behrens
E	A boy finds that a girl can be a friend	*Everett Anderson's Friend* by Lucille Clifton
E–M	Maintaining friendships by resolving differences and sharing special talents	*Two Good Friends* by J. Delton
E–M	Guide for friendship	*Every Kid's Guide to Making Friends* by Joe Berry
E–M	Making friends	*The Biggest Bear* by Lynd Ward
E–M	Good friends	*Ben and Me* by Robert Lawson
M	As Eliza teaches her best friend, who is deaf, to sing, she learns about courage, friendship, real limitations, and self-imposed limitations	*The Gift of the Girl Who Couldn't Hear* by Susan Shreve
M	Friendship between a boy and dogs	*Where the Red Fern Grows* by Wilson Rawls
M	Short stories about friends	*Friends Are Like That* by Patricia Hermes
M	Friendship emerges from misfortune	*Martin Quiere Leer* by M. Gispert and C. Peris
M	The responsibility of friendship	*The Magic of the Glitz* by Carole S. Adler
M	Friends in large cities and how they face problems	*Julian's Glorious Summer* by Ann Cameron
M	Friends in large cities and how they face problems	*Me, Mop and Moondance Kid* by Walter Dean Myers
M	Making friends in a new neighborhood	*Chester* by Mary Shura
M	Friendship helps make progress in individual struggles	*Words of Stone* by Kevin Henkes
M	Befriending yourself and others	*Making Friends with Yourself and Other Strangers* by Dianna Daniels Booher
M	Story of the deep, long-lasting thirty-five-year friendship between Alexander Graham Bell and Helen Keller	*Dear Dr. Bell . . . Your Friend, Helen Keller* by Judith St. George

Activities to Use with Quotes and Books

Opening the School Day Discussion

Discuss the unit objectives and write a new quote on the board. Ask students to discuss how its meaning relates to the friendships in their lives.

What is friendship? Read a book from the list in this unit that the class selects, discuss the book's definition of friendship, and ask students to list the kinds of things they like to do for their friends and why. Then have students write a want ad for the perfect friend, and post these ads on the bulletin board.

(JW) *Journal writing.* Read the quotation, "You must be a friend to have a friend," and ask each child to make a list of the qualities they would like their friends to possess. Afterwards, have them describe their own personalities and compare the two lists. Last, ask them to consider ways that they could become a better friend.

(BLM) *My guide to making friends.* Read *Every Kid's Guide to Making Friends* by Joe Barry or another book from this unit. Then, ask student to make their own eight-page books or skits using the following directions:

1. Have students copy a quote for each of the first seven pages of a book, and describe how they will use that quote to become a better friend.

2. On the last page, ask students to write their own quote (using their own idea or an idea gleaned from the unit list of books) to develop better friendships. Have them describe what their quote means to them.

Use Blackline Master 4 (in the BLM section) to make the blank books students will use.

Martian friends. Have students divide into groups of six to consider the following scenario: Students are playing on the school grounds when a spaceship lands nearby. The occupants appear at the entrance of the ship. Have students divide into Earthlings and Martians and create a play. The Earthlings describe things that are not yet perfected in friendships on earth. The Martians describe how those problems are overcome on Mars by using their favorite quotes as examples of actions or laws followed on Mars. The resulting plays can be presented to the class, to other classes, or at parent meetings.

(BLM) *Books are friends.* Ask the entire class to participate in a discussion of how a book might become a friend. Chart their answers on a long piece of butcher paper, which is to be displayed in the hallway for schoolmates to read. Next, discuss how books can be used to change a person's mood. Last, distribute slips of cardboard for students to decorate as bookmarks. On the bookmarks, students list the "friends" they have gained who are main characters in the books they have read. Blackline Masters 5 and 6 (BLM section) can be used as patterns for students' bookmarks.

(JW) *Many types of friendship.* Have students read the book *Friends Are Like That,* or read it to them. This book contains more than a dozen types of friendships and students' concerns have about friendships. Then, ask students to write in their journals what they have learned about their own friendships through the information in this book.

Treasured friends. Have students, working alone, think of their most treasured friend and write ten ways they value that friend. Then, compare and tally students' lists to see whether people value similar things in friendships. Last, ask students to select a book or quotation from the unit that best depicts the friendship they share with their best friend.

New friends. Have students form groups of four (preferably, of students who do not know each other very well). Within groups, have students choose partners and tell a little about themselves to their partner. Next, have each recommend or loan a book to his or her partner as an act of friendship. After books have been read, have students discuss what they enjoyed about meeting a new friend.

(BLM) *My friend the author.* Read a book from the list in this unit. Discuss the book, the author's background, and the author's style of writing. Then have students construct a list of qualities that make the author their friend. Blackline Master 7 (see BLM section) can be used for this activity.

Friend begins with "F." For younger students, this unit can focus on learning the letter *F*. Discuss how *F* depicts the /f/ sound, and ask students to write the capital letter *F* with a lower-case *f* next to it. Practice saying the /f/ sound and reading words that contain /f/.

(RRG) *Frog and Toad are friends.* Have groups of four take turns reading pages from *Frog and Toad Together* or other *Frog and Toad* books, and discuss, write, or draw one quality they found about friendship. Have students make a poster reflecting their thoughts on how to be a good friend and hang it up in the classroom.

The principal is our friend. Tell the class to write a letter or draw a picture to their principal about how they would like to be a friend to the school, schoolmates, or the principal.

Pen pals. Working with another class or teacher, match students with another from each class. These students send anonymous letters or drawings about themselves to their "across the hall" pal. Students write or draw what subjects they enjoy, what they like to do, and so on in their letters or drawings.

Buddy system. Start a buddy system and have students go everywhere with one buddy for a day. Then ask students to discuss the positives and negatives of working and playing in pairs.

You can join in. Present this situation: "There is a child by themselves in the playground. What could you do to become a friend to that person?" Then this situation: "You are going out to play. There are several children playing, what can you do to join them.

Class pals. Read *Pelly and Peak* by Sally Whitman or another book from the list in this unit. Students make their personal mailboxes for "class pals." They write three names of fellow classmates to whom they will mail letters or drawings. Beside each name, students write or draw about qualities they consider this person to have as a friend.

Troubles making friends. Read one of the books from this unit list and emphasize how the main characters experience the same feelings they themselves have about friendships. List various ways friendships are formed from your discussion with the class.

(JW) *Journal writing.* Have students draw a picture or describe their pet. It might be an animal, a book, or a toy. They can write about how they are friends with their pets and how their pets might have friends also.

Multicultural Emphasis: Facts about Building Friendships That Come from Other Cultures

Multicultures. In many cultures, students have similar difficulties "becoming friends" with siblings, and problems with being the youngest, the oldest, or the middle child in their families. Read *A Lion for Lewis* by Rosemary Wells and *Much Bigger Than Martin* by Steven Kellogg. Have students compare how the main characters in these books learned to become friends with siblings. Rosemary Will's book *Stanley & Rhoda* also can be used; it contains three different stories about ways brothers and sisters help each other. Ask students from various cultures to share how they help their families and develop friendships with siblings.

Italy. If you read *Harlequin and the Gift of Many Colors,* students will discover the high value Italians place on friendship. This book is set in fourteenth-century rural Italy during the Italian Carnival time. When Harlequin's friends discover that he has no costume to wear to the carnival, each friend cuts a piece of his or her own costume to give to their beloved friend.

Mexican American. Arnold Lobel has written three beautiful books in Spanish about friendship. Read them or have an older student read them to bilingual students to introduce the value of friendship in Mexican-American culture: *Sapo y Sepo Son Amigos* is a delightful book about the friendship between a frog and a toad. *Sapo y Sepo Son Inseparables* is a hilarious story about the friendship between the frog and the toad. Another story is *Sapo y Sepo un Ano Entero.*

For students who enjoy reading books in Spanish, the following books will increase their understanding of friendship:

> Broger, Achim. *Buenos Dias Querida Ballena.* Spain: Editorial Juventud, 1978. This charming story is about a friendship between a sailor and a whale that follows him home.
>
> Broger, Achim. *Adios, Querida Ballena.* Madrid: Editorial Juventud, 1985. Children will truly enjoy this sequel to *Buenos Dias Querida Ballena.*
>
> Cantieni, Benita, and Fred Gachter. *Elefantito y Gran Raton.* Mexico City: Editorial Trillas, S.A., 1984. In this well-illustrated book, two

friends discover the difference between the words *small* and *big* and between *far* and *near*.

D'Atri, Adriana. *Asi Son Nuestros Amigos.* Madrid: Editorial Altea, 1977. This book describes Clara and Enrique's daily experiences with their friends.

El Amigo Nuevo. Spain: Editorial Altea, 1980. The neighborhood children welcome a new Japanese boy and become great friends.

Heuer, Margarita. *Chipil y Macanudo.* Mexico City: Editorial Trillas, S.A., 1984. This is a story of two friends who are very different when it comes to making new acquaintances. Together, they learn the value of friendship.

Greece. Explain to students that the Greeks are known as very friendly people, who often invite outsiders to join their extended family. Ask students to research Greek culture and find examples of the value placed on friendship in ancient as well as modern Greek history.

Vietnam. In the early history of this country, the Vietnamese people were influenced by both the Chinese and the Indonesian people. Although Vietnamese culture is predominantly influenced by Chinese culture, Indonesian influences are evident even today in the country's language, literature, art, theater, music, and architecture. Ask students for examples of other countries they have studied in which various cultures influence the people, and ask them which country in the world today most influences other countries.

Your Own Additions to the Unit

4 Creating

Learning Objectives *Creativity* involves bringing into being, making, originating, producing, giving rise to, risking, portraying for the first time, and/or investing with a new idea. In this unit, students uncover aspects of the creative process for which they have the greatest aptitude.

Resources *Select a different quotation to discuss and write on the board each day of this unit's study.*

Know how to create and the fun of it is yours.

Real creation is enjoyed by all.

A good imagination is creation at work!

Creativity comes from an absence of the fear of deviation.

Your only limitations depend on the number of your ideas.

If you can imagine it, you can achieve it.
if you can dream it, you can become it.
—William Arthur Ward

Almost all really new ideas have a certain aspect of
foolishness when they are first produced.
—A. N. Whitehead

Instead of relying on recall—CREATE.

Minds only function when open.

A mind is most alive when it is creating to improve.

Creativity is so delicate a flower
that praise tends to make it bloom,
While discouragement often nips it in the bud.
Any of us will put out more and
better ideas if our efforts are appreciated.
—Alex F. Osborn

Finding the Right Book Concerning Creativity to Meet Students' Needs

Difficulty code: I = Introductory; E = Easy; M = Medium

		Book
I	Imagining a singing cow	*When Bluebell Sang* by Lisa Campbell Ernest
I	Cat has all kinds of fun	*The Cat in the Hat* by Dr. Seuss
I	Things to do with rubbish	*What Can You Make of It* by Franz Brankenberg
I	Bathtime fantasy	*Where Will You Swim Tonight?* by Milly Jane Limmer
I	Using all your senses when the sun sets	*When Light Turns into Night* by Crescent Dragonwagon
I	Bringing unusual shapes into reality	*Spirals, Curves, Fanshapes and Lines* by Tana Hoban
I	Planting apple seeds to bring apples everywhere	*Johnny Appleseed* by Steven Kellogg
I	Good model of drawing and telling a story	*Cherries and Cherry Pits* by Vera B. Williams
I	Trying to count sheep but seeing cows, pig, and other animals	*Sheep, Sheep, Sheep, Help Me Fall Asleep* by Arlene Alda
I	Creating figures with string	*More String Games* by Camilla Gryski
E	Creative story of adventure in fantasy	*The Lion, The Witch, and The Wardrobe* by C.S. Lewis
E	Despite others' ideas, Small Bear creates in his own way	*Small Bear Builds A Playhouse* by Adelaide H. Hall
E	A superb example of the picture book as theater	*Shortcut* by Donald Crews
E	Account of an artist's work	*Morgan and the Artist* by Donald Carrick
E	A first attempt at carving and appreciating one's efforts	*Daniel's Duck* by Clyde Robert Balla
E	Step-by-step approach to imagination and creativity	*Shadow Theater: Games and Projects* by Denny Robson and Vanessa Baily
E	Fourteen illustrations for creating imaginary plots	*The Mysteries of Harris Burdich* by Chris Van Allsburg
E–M	How a girl creates a new father from an old man	*A Private Matter* by Kathryn Ewing
E–M	Conceptualizing the role of the artist	*An Artist* by M. B. Goffstein

		Book
E–M	Slave riddles, trickster tales, tall tales, and slave narratives	*The People Could Fly: American Black Folktales* by Virginia Hamilton
E–M	A collection of African-American folklore	*The Knee-High Man* by Julius Lester
E–M	Scenes rendered in styles reminiscent of Picasso, Rousseau, and Chagall	*When Cats Dream* by Dav Pilkey
E–M	Creativity from the life around you	*The Cartoonist* by Betsy C. Byars
E–M	Creating more than hats	*Hats Off to John Stetson* by Mary Blount Christian
E–M	Stories of our national monuments	*Our National Monuments* by Eleanor Ayer
E–M	Stories of our national symbols	*Our National Symbols* by Linda Carlson Johnson
M	Langston Hughes acting out his life story for young admirers	*Langston: A Play* by Ossie Davis
M	A fantastic tale	*Charlie and the Chocolate Factory* by Roald Dahl
M	Adventures of two runaways	*From the Mixed Up Files of Mrs. Basil E. Frankweiler* by E. L. Konigsburg
M	A young boy buys a dragon's egg	*Jeremy Thatcher, Dragon Hatcher* by Bruce Coville
M	Fun with one's imagination	*Wingman* by Daniel Pinkwater
M	The role of the artist	*Looking at Art* by Alice Elizabeth Chase
M	Creating a written language	*Ahyoka and the Talking Leaves* by Peter and Connie Roop
M	A choice between watching television and real-life writing	*The TV Kid* by Betsy C. Byars
M	What to create when there is no television	*The Week Mom Unplugged the TVs* by Terry W. Phelan
M	A Burmese boy's creativity makes him a hero	*The Boy Who Played Tiger* by Patricia W. Garlan and Mary Jane Dunstan
M	A girl writes about her life	*Dinah and the Green Fat Kingdom* by Isabelle Holland
M	Boys create a cosmic awareness to help others	*The Strange but Wonderful Cosmic Awareness of Duffy Moon* by Jean Robinson

Activities to Use with Quotes and Books

Opening the School Day Discussion

Write a quotation on the board each day. On the first day, discuss the learning objectives of this unit and the definition of creativity. Ask students to identify the aspects of creativity they most often demonstrate. Discuss how students' sense of wonder, their questions, and their curiosity will help them become more creative. You can also discuss the fears and doubts that tend to halt students' creative thinking. Also, discuss the idea that wondering can be the root of invention because it adds curiosity and excitement to the learning process.

Brainstorming to increase creativity. Define *brainstorming* and teach the following chart.

Steps in Brainstorming

1. *All ideas are welcomed.* No suggestion is invalidated. Students shouldn't worry that their ideas are not good enough—all ideas are helpful.
2. *Give as many ideas as you can.* The longer the list, the more likely it will contain a number of workable ideas.
3. *Add to each other's ideas.* People can help each other be creative.
4. *Think of crazy new ideas.* One idea can trigger another useful idea that helps someone else see a problem in a new way.
5. *Record each idea and combine ideas at the end.* After all the ideas have been given, combine and select the best.

Next, ask students to meet in groups of three or four for five to ten minutes to brainstorm and write about one subject they have studied during that day or week. The next day, have students review their brainstorming from the previous day and pick a main subject or topic that interests them. Then ask each group to write a story about the subject. After the story is finished, ask students to share their stories and discuss how brainstorming improved their writing. Last, ask students to list other aspects of their lives and schoolwork that brainstorming or creativity could improve. Once they have practiced using the brainstorming process several times in class, they can contact adults they respect and ask how brainstorming is used in the business world. Students then practice brainstorming silently and alone for a few minutes before they meet in small groups to work on a project. After that small group meeting, ask them why pausing before important meetings to do some mental brainstorming can be a valuable tool for them as adults.

(BLM) *Identifying aspects of creative thinking for which I have the most aptitude.* Teach the following information and strategies that promote creative thinking. Explain to students that many of the factors that increase creativity have not yet been discovered. It has been proved, however, that the ability to sense problems is a crucial ingredient, as is the ability to take care of your own and others' needs and difficulties. To be most ingenious, students must learn to "scramble" ideas. Hence the title of this lesson, "SCRAMBLIN'," which is the acronym for the nine thinking processes that can increase creative thinking:

substitute, combine, rearrange, adapt, minimize, bigger, linking, invention, and newness. Teach these processes to students individually, in as many as nine separate lessons if you desire. Then introduce the activities that follow, in which students can use the mnemonic aid for the acronym SCRAMBLIN' to remember and employ these creative thinking processes interactively. A description of these processes follows, along with the methods students can use to elicit each process, follows:

1. *Substitute thinking processes.* This process helps students be creative by putting one idea in place of another. One method for eliciting substitute thinking is for students to ask someone else for advice whenever their first idea was less successful than they would have liked. In the process, students can use that person's thinking pattern, which is likely to be different from their own. This new thinking pattern will increase their creativity. Another way to use substitute thinking is for students to think about what a person they admire would do if he or she were in their situation. For example, if students are not doing well on their weekly math tests, they could ask three people who do well on their tests to explain how *they* study. Then students could substitute these methods to see if their test grades improve.

2. *Combine.* When new thoughts are not coming easily, students can combine two unlike objects or images to stimulate their thinking. Brainstorming is an example of *combining* thinking and a method students can use to combine unlike ideas.

3. *Rearrange.* Rearranging thinking means changing the sections of a process or reordering the steps in an idea. By using "rearrangement" thinking in areas that students have the power to change, they can create very effective solutions. Ask students to pretend they are sitting beside someone who talks frequently during class. They feel as if they have tried *everything,* but the person keeps right on talking to them. Then they remember the SCRAMBLIN' processes and use it to find a creative solution. They realize that, up to now, they have tried to change another person's behavior (which is out of their control). They reviewed their unsuccessful actions: not answering questions, avoiding eye contact, not initiating conversations very often; trying to look away from the talkative person. They realize that they have not tried the "rearrange" strategy. So they ask you if they can move. You answered that they can't because everyone must sit in alphabetical order during that class period. Next, they think about rearranging things that they *can* control and no longer wasting time trying to rearrange things they cannot change (the other person's behavior, their own naturally friendly nature, or your rule about alphabetical order).

Using the rearranging strategy, they come up with a new idea: suppose the direction in which the desks face in the room can be changed. If the chairs in the room were moved so that two rows were placed at the back, facing the front, and the remaining chairs were at the side by the windows, the entire class would remain in alphabetical order, but they would be across the room from the talkative person. You agree to the suggestion to change the seating. The rearranging strategy has worked!

4. *Adapt.* Adaptive thinking means changing only a small detail of an idea to improve it. Ask students to pretend they want to become better basketball players or improve their hairstyles. They don't like their first solution—only attempting shots they know they can make, or pulling their hair back into a ponytail. By adapting their thinking slightly, they might decide to practice only one new position shot each week, or to cut bangs and seeing how they look. Explain that students can make several adaptations in simple steps until they are pleased with their results.

5. *Minimize.* Explain that students can sometimes change outcomes by making a product smaller or by omitting something. This creative thinking process lets students identify disposable elements and make their ideas more compact. Let them know that one method of initiating minimizing thinking is to ask, "What is something in this idea that I can do without?"

6. *Bigger.* Students can become creative by adding things. They can increase the size, strength, time, or frequency of actions to improve them. One method of using this strategy is for students to write facts concerning a part of their problems about which they want to think creatively. They can ask themselves: (a) What else might be happening? (b) What other things are possible? (c) What if _____? (d) What ideas can I get about _____ by thinking about _____?

7. *Linking:* The principle behind this creative thinking process is that the more responses produced, the greater the chances of coming up with a satisfactory solution. If you have twenty ideas to choose from, there's a greater probability that one of them is a good idea than if you have only two ideas. Students can initiate linking by asking themselves: (a) In what ways might I (we) _____? (b) Make a list of things that _____ _____. (c) How many different examples (reasons, solutions, etc.) can I think of? (d) What comes to mind when you think of _____?

8. *Invention:* Explain to students that inventive thinking means turning their thoughts around. Inventors use this type of thinking process to make extreme rearrangements. Students can initiate this type of thinking by (a) turning objects or ideas upside down and inside out, (b) becoming their own "devil's advocate," and (c) thinking of all the reasons that a new idea wouldn't work.

9. *Newness:* Originality is the creative thinking behavior that produces novel responses. Explain to students that they can invite a new idea by asking themselves: (a) What else, or what more? (b) What is a new, original way to _____? (c) Can I invent a new _____? (d) How can I change _____ to make _____ _____?

Once you have taught these processes, ask students to create a graphic drawing or a design of their own to remind them of methods of creative thinking on Blackline Master 9 (BLM section). Then ask students to practice using these processes interactively by completing one of the following activities or solving a personal problem.

1. Ask students to identify a situation at school that annoys them and to create a change to eliminate this annoyance.

2. Ask students to think of a time in the past when they could have used creative thinking and describe that time as if they were writing a short story. Explain that this time they will change the ending by using one or more parts of the SCRAMBLIN' process for creative thinking. Next, tell them to write down which creative thinking process(es) they used to make this change and when they will use this process in the future.

3. Tell students that they have been told that too much of anything is not good. Then ask them to use their creative thinking to describe two situations in life in which thinking creatively could be detrimental rather than valuable.

4. Ask students to imagine that their parents told them the family was going on a family vacation but the time conflicted with the most important party of the summer. What could they do? Write about the creative SCRAMBLIN' thinking processes they can use to solve this problem.

5. Explain that inventors can sometimes take two objects and combine them to create solutions to difficult problems (e.g., fitting both a washer and a dryer into a small apartment by stacking small washers and dryers on top of one another, or taking away the need to use a footstool with a chair by inventing the recliner). Then ask students to think of something uncomfortable in their own lives and to describe the process they would use to change this annoyance. (See *Small Inventions That Make a Big Difference* by Donald Crump, National Geographic Publishers, 1984, for examples of inventions.)

6. Ask students to improve something they dislike about their appearance or personality and to describe the SCRAMBLIN' process they used to devise the plan.

7. Ask students to think of the last time they felt as if they had tried everything but failed. Knowing what they know now, what would they have done differently in that situation?

Combining creators. Pair two students who have different strengths—for example, one with musical talent and one with science ability. Ask the pairs to create something of value together that uses both their strengths and uses the content from a subject that is being studied—perhaps a painting that depicts a science presentation of the galaxy, or a rap song for learning addition facts. At the end of the week, ask pairs to teach their creations to the class.

Inventing connections. Have students bring objects they value from home. Then, ask groups of four to combine all the objects they brought into a creative (yet believable) story. After forty minutes, ask each group to read their stories to the class. Remind students to use the SCRAMBLIN' process of creative thinking that they learned earlier in this unit as they invent the connections between objects in their stories.

Ideas take wings. Start with reading a book or part of a book that demonstrates the creation of something or describes a freedom that students have (e.g., *Jonathan Livingston Seagull*). Then play a song (with no words) (e.g., the soundtrack of the movie of this book, "Flight of the Gull"). The first time the music is played, ask students to listen. Then play the music a second time and have students draw or write something creative about an image the music elicits in their mind. After about fifteen minutes, end the activity. If students have not finished their art or writing, ask them to do it as homework. Last, have students (a) discuss the relationship of music to creative thinking, (b) hypothesize about why this relationship exists, and (c) explain the relationship between freedom and creativity.

Overcoming the fear of deviation. Put this quote on the board: "Creativity comes from an absence of the fear of deviation." Ask students what it means to act or look different from other people. Then have them describe incidents in which they have felt different than others and to explain the definition of *deviation* (i.e., *deviation* means to go against the grain, to stray from what other people consider normal). Then ask students to write about (or use art materials to depict) something that deviates from normal but would improve a part of our world. After students have finished, have them share the creative thinking processes they used to create their improvements (the SCRAMBLIN' process) and show their creations. Complete the activity by saying that when they have a new way of doing something, they should not hesitate to share that idea, as they alone can improve aspects of our world.

Toy maker. Ask students to pretend they are toy makers. Ask, "What would you create?" List their answers. Expand students' answers beyond brief statements like "a doll" by prompting with questions such as, "Can it walk, drink, sleep, talk?" Continue the discussion until several detailed descriptions have been given. Then ask older students to draw and/or describe their own new toy, and have younger students create one as a class, with each child drawing the final creation independently. Also, younger students can take a field trip to a bakery, manufacturing company, or museum where one emphasis of the trip is to view creations that began as a single person's idea and grew to help others.

Explain that "mental picturing" is imagination at work. If some students have difficulty creating mental images, describe how you create mental images.

(RRG) *Group create.* Ask students, in groups of four, to listen to one of this unit's books that you read without showing the pictures. Then assign each student in the group to draw a different part of an object from that book you read; for example, one makes the face, one the body, one the feet, and one the legs of the main character. Then, each group puts the four parts together, and the whole class votes on the best drawing. Animals can be made out of clay or drawings.

(BLM) *Making rhymes.* This lesson starts by discussing the meaning of the quotation, "Real creation is enjoyed by all!" and what rhyming words are. Then distribute Blackline Master 8 (see BLM section) and ask students to write all the words they can that rhyme with *all* in the left-hand column. Then ask students to think of all the words that rhyme with *eat* and *old* and to record those as well. Last, ask students to tell or write a story that uses some of the words they like best on the Blackline Master that individual students can now read independently. Tell the class to make new words by taking a beginning consonant sound and adding it to the rest of an existing word—for example, *M—eat* and *h—eat*. At the end of the lesson, ask students to describe what they have learned that will help them to read other unknown words in the future.

Multicultural Emphasis: Concepts about Creating That Come from Many Cultures

The following examples demonstrate the value of creativity in many cultures.

Burmese, East Indian, Sri Lankan. In these three Asian countries, bells ring in the New Year. Collect and use an assortment of bells—large brass bells, sleighbells, glass bells, china bells, wooden bells, cowbells—and ask students to note the differences in sounds that these bells would make as they ring in the New Year in these three Asian countries. Next, have students make bells for their wrists or ankles because these are the locations where bells are worn in these countries. Show students how these bells are made by stringing bells on yarn and knotting each in place using the following instructions. To increase the difficulty of the task, you can ask students to use a longer piece of yarn to make a bell-headband, another ancient Asian custom as well. You can use a strip of elastic to make a more durable backing.

Instructions for Creating Asian New Year Bells

Time needed: 20 minutes

Materials: One ten-inch (twenty-inch for a headband) strip of one-inch-wide elastic, and five small bells per child. A needle and thread for your use.

Method:

1. Knot five small bells at regular intervals onto the elastic.
2. Sew the two ends of elastic together.

Before you enact a Burmese New Year's ringing, share the following information about this event.

On New Year's Day, metal bells are hung around cows' necks, and brass dinner bells are used in the home and in churches. On Buddhist New Year, Buddhist priests ring a bell 108 times to summon the New Year. You can make a simple tin bell and use it to accompany songs or to call the children for snack.

(RRG) *Africa.* Some African tribes create masks for special occasions. Leo and Diane Dillon illustrate such masks in *Who's in Rabbit's House?* by Verna Aardema. This book can be used to stimulate students' creativity as they make their own African masks and write a class play in which masks are used to enact the story for parents or classmates. Once the masks are made and the plays are written, divide the class into groups of four and allow each group to embellish the enactment of the play using their own creativity. In this way, all groups can present their enactments before their classmates and can see for themselves the difference individual creativity makes in the world. At the end of the productions, discuss this concept.

Japan. Many students enjoy learning about the Japanese art of origami. Begin this activity by reading *Easy Origami* by Dokuihtel Nakano, and demonstrate a few of the creative paper-folding examples in the book. Because this book contains easy-to-follow, step-by-step illustrations, even younger students can be successful in creating and appreciating origami. You may want to end the lesson by discussing the differences between the creativity needed in Japanese art and that expressed in Western sculptures and clay modeling.

(BLM) *Native Americans.* Native Americans were the first people to create shelters from the weather, means of travel, hunting tools, cooking materials, and toys. Ask students to find samples of these inventions and discuss how each demonstrates the creative thinking of an individual cultural group. Once all the samples have been shared, ask students to hypothesize about which SCRAMBLIN' processes Native Americans used most often. Blackline Master 9 (see BLM section) could be used here.

Multicultural. Share the following information and books with students and ask how they demonstrate the value each culture placed upon creativity:

Hamilton, Virginia. *In the Beginning: Creation Myths from Around the World*. Discuss why students think such myths would be used in different countries.

Woolf, Felicity. *Picture This: A First Introduction to Paintings*.

Kinney, Jean, and Cle Kinney. *23 Varieties of Ethnic Art and How to Make Each One*.

Pettit, Florence. *How to Make Whirligigs and Whimmy Diddles and other American Folkcraft Objects*.

Thompson, Vivian L. *Ancient Hawaiian or Polynesian*. Views of the world in the ancient Hawaiian and Polynesian cultures.

Italy. Leonardo Da Vinci (1452–1519) created the famous painting called the *Mona Lisa*. Viewers have long been fascinated by her enigmatic smile. Leonardo was also an inventor, scientist, architect, and student of astronomy, botany, and medicine. The notebooks he kept of his ideas and his unfinished inventions are studied by scholars today.

Michelangelo (1475–1564), the famous Italian painter, lay flat on his back on a scaffolding for four years to paint the ceiling of the Sistine Chapel. His work is viewed as one of the greatest artistic accomplishments in the world. Many artists had been asked to do the work and declined before Michelangelo accepted. He delighted in the challenge this project provided. Books about Michelangelo will inspire students to become more creative themselves and will increase their understanding of the positive attitude and flexibility that is necessary to become highly creative.

Raphael (1483–1520), another artist whom students may wish to study, is famous for his painting of the Madonna and Child.

France. France has old castles in which knights lived and chateaus dating from the 1490s. The castle at Chinan contains the room where, as a teenager, Joan of Arc first met Charles VII.

Switzerland. In 1679, Daniel Jean Richard created the first Swiss watch. Since that time, the Swiss have used their creativity to invent numerous variations of this basic watch, which people around the world enjoy today. Seven of every ten watches ever made in the world originated in Switzerland.

Disney's Matterhorn ride is named after the Swiss Matterhorn near Zermatt. The Matterhorn's needle-nose peak is 14,692 feet high. A good picture can be found on page 17 of *Enchantment of the World: Switzerland* by Martin Hinte. Many Swiss enjoy hiking. They use a walking stick that is curved like a cane. They decorate the sticks with their own creative badges depicting the different places the hikers have been.

Asian American. These artists have brought the technical and sophisticated artistry of the Orient to the United States. Ed Young's screenlike panels, Allen Say's precision, and Yoshi's fabric paintings are noteworthy examples as shown in children's books such as *The Boy of the Three-Year Nap* by Diane Snyder, illustrated by Allen Say, and *Who's Hiding Here?* by Yoshi.

Jewish-American literature. Many outstanding Jewish artists and authors emigrated from Europe to America during the years the Nazis were in power in the 1930s and 1940s. They promote literary creativity through two book award programs: The National Jewish Book Awards and the Association of Jewish Libraries Awards.

Your Own Additions to the Unit

5 Developing Honesty, Respect, and Manners

Learning Objectives One of the most difficult challenges in teaching is to confront students who have acted dishonestly. The quotations, activities, and books in this chapter are designed to deter such incidents. Also in this unit, students will learn to refrain from lying, cheating, or stealing and to be truthful and fair when they are tempted to be dishonest. The quotations, activities, and books demonstrate how good manners can increase students' respect for others and their self-respect.

Resources *Select a different quotation to discuss and write on the board each day of this unit's study.*

*Mind your manners,
and it will help to bring respect to yourself*

*Understand what respect means;
Respect is a two-way street.*

*A lie is a great multiplier.
Respect is something you have to earn.*

*Hearts, like doors, open with ease
When you say: thank you and please.*

*Clean hands are so fine
When I am ready to dine.*

If you can't respect yourself, no one else can.

When you can respect yourself, you can expect respect.

The truth is more important than the facts.
—Frank Lloyd Wright

Can it ever truly be yours to take someone else's possession?

*Sometimes our classroom's happy,
Sometimes we're in a fuss,
But our classroom's disposition
Always depends on us.*

*A truth that's told to correct an event
Beats all the lies you can invent.*

Finding the Right Book Concerning Developing Honesty, Respect, and Manners to Meet Students' Needs

Difficulty code: I = Introductory; E = Easy; M = Medium

		Book
I	Boy is rude to girl	*Hiccup* by Mercer Mayer
I	Bad manners lead to bad consequences	*Uncle Remus—Br'er Rabbit and Tar Baby* Walt Disney
I	Developing manners	*What Do I Do* by Joe Lasker
I	Cleanliness	*Spiffen, a Tale of a Tidy Pig* by Mary Ada Schwartz
I	Taking advantage of friends	*The Lazy Bear* by B. Wildsmith
I	Greedy friends	*Petunia's Treasure* by Roger Duviosin
I	Table manners	*Dinner at Alberta's* by Russell Hoban
I	Expressing regret	*What Does It Mean? I'm Sorry* by Susan Riley
I	Table manners	*Bread and Jam for Frances* by Russell Hoban
I	Table manners	*Gregory the Terrible Eater* by Mitchell Sharmat
I	Bathing rituals	*No Ducks in Our Bathtub* by Martha Alexander
I	Bathing rituals	*No More Baths* by Cole Brock
E	Not interrupting adults	*Five Minutes' Peace* by Jill Murphy
E	Respecting people's names	*But Names Will Never Hurt Me* by Bernard Waber
E	Greetings and manners from absurd situations	*What Do You Say, Dear?* by Sesyle Joslin
E	The value of cleanliness	*Oh What a Mess* by Hane Wilhelm
E	Lying to get attention	*Wishful Lying* by Rose Blue
E	Behavior toward others	*Drummer Hoff* by Barbara Emberley
E	Actions that earn respect	*Doctor de Soto* by William Steig
E–M	Revenge and truthfulness	*Maggie Marmelstein for President* by Marjorie Sharmat
E–M	Lies about animals	*Lies (People Believe) About Animals* by Susan Sussman and Robert James
E–M	Helping a friend become honest	*I'll Tell on You* by Joan Lexan

5 DEVELOPING HONESTY, RESPECT, AND MANNERS

		Book
E–M	Different kinds of lying	*Ivan the Great* by Isabel Langis
E–M	The emotions felt by a lie	*The Lie* by Ann Helena
E–M	Japanese folktale about a husband who broke his promise	*The Crane Wife* by Sumiko Yagawa
E–M	Poems by African-American children's expressing universal feelings	*Spin a Soft Black Song* by Nikki Giovanni
E–M	Respect between siblings	*We're Very Good Friends, My Brother and I* by P. K. Hallinan
E–M	Respect for family members	*Me and My Aunts* by Laura Newton
E–M	Respect for wildlife	*The Hunter and the Animals* by Tomie de Paola
E–M	Respect through communication of feelings	*The Hundred Penny Box* by Sharon Mathes
E–M	Learning the price of leadership	*Skateboard Four* by Anne Evelyn Bunting
E–M	Respect for nature and freedom	*Amy's Goose* by Efner Holmes
E–M	Respect for all people	*The Whipping Boy* by Sid Fleischman
E–M	Consequences of a lack of respect toward the teacher	*Miss Nelson Is Missing* by Harry Allard
E–M	Respecting nature	*Storm Boy* by Colin Milton Thiele
E–M	Winning a school presidential election, honestly or not	*Who'll Vote for Lincoln?* by Dale Fife
M	Black children's thoughts and feelings	*Daydreamers* by Eloise Greenfield
M	Standing by when your honesty is challenged	*The Case of the Stolen Bagels* by Hila Crayden Calman
M	Learning to trust those who deserve it	*A Tangled Web* by Hamilore Valencak
M	Learning respect for one's heritage and culture (Vietnamese)	*Hello, My Name Is Scrambled Eggs* by Jamie Gilson
M	When adults disbelieve a child	*The View from the Cherry Tree* by Willo David Roberts
M	Shame and the risk of being discovered after cheating	*I Know You Cheated* by Valjean McLeninghan
M	Lying to cover an embarrassment	*Nothing Rhymes with April* by Naomi J. Karp
M	Gaining respect and pride for one's Jewish heritage and upbringing	*Does Anyone Know the Way to Thirteen?* by Stephen Kaufman

		Book
M	Two exchange students in Japan	*Pacific Crossing* by Gary Soto
M	Learning how to recognize lies and humbug	*Humbug* by Nina Bawden
M	A child reacting to a divorce learns that there is freedom in truth	*To Live a Lie* by Anne Alexander
M	Interpretation of truth	*Truth and Consequences* by Miriam Burt Young
M	The trouble caused by lying	*Lizzie Lies a Lot* by Elizabeth Levy

Activities to Use with Quotes and Books

Opening the School Day Discussion

Put a quote on the board each day and ask students to discuss it. Have them set a goal to become more honest and respectful this week and record their progress each day in a learning log. At the end of the week, for the last five minutes of the period or day, ask students to review and share what they did that week to increase their honesty and respect in difficult situations.

A different multiplication. Write on the board "A lie is a great multiplier." Have students list situations in which they have been tempted to lie in the past. Then ask students to form pairs, with one being the "liar" and the other simulating the situations listed on the board that could cause a lie to grow. After three simulations, ask students to write a paragraph about each situation. Then ask students to change roles and, instead of lying in each situation, to face it honestly and, again, write a paragraph about how they felt. Finally, bring the class together to discuss the results of this activity and how each student can face difficulties in the future.

Predict the ending. Read one of the books from the list for this unit. Stop before the end of the book and ask students to predict the ending. Then ask the class what the moral of the story was. After the class reaches a consensus, finish the story and share the author's moral. Relate the book to the quotation studied on that date, and have students create their own quotation to depict what they learned from the book.

(RRG) *Various meanings of respect.* Read one or more of the books listed in this unit. Discuss whether the author's portrayal of respect was subtle or direct, and why. Then discuss which characters in their favorite books earned their respect, and ask each student to write about the qualities of the character that they respect, how that character earned their respect, and how they can apply what they've learned to increase their self-respect.

(JW) *Journal writing.* Have students select one person in their school, home, or community that they respect. Then ask them to write the reasons they respect that person. Have them include a description of what that person first did or what they first noticed about the person that earned their respect. After students complete their descriptions, ask them to share and analyze them in small groups. Instruct each group to write at least two paragraphs to report their analyses: one paragraph describing what people they respect have in common, and the second describing what the group learned about themselves from this journal-writing activity.

Teaching students to give and receive respect. Present this list of actions that generate respect in group settings, and ask students to add other ways respect can be increased when they are doing group projects.

1. Avoid getting into a discussion when you are tired or in a bad mood.
2. Make sure those around you live by the same basic rules.
3. Say you're sorry—and really mean it—when you are wrong.
4. No one is right all the time.
5. If you respect other people's opinions, other people will be more apt to respect and accept yours.
6. Share your thoughts with people who respect and accept you.

(BLM) *Thank you and please.* Plan a time for students to practice saying "thank you" and "please," such as at snack time ("I would like cookies, please"). Then each child should reply, "Thank you." Mimeograph and cut out the four sections of Blackline Master 10 in the BLM section. Give each child a section and have children make a mark every time they say "thank you" and every time they say "please." Gather up the Masters at the end of the day and tally the marks. Ask the students how they felt doing the actions. How did people respond to their manners?

Mother-may-I: Modern version. Select four students to be the "mothers." Classmates divide into four lines. One at a time, each "mother" gives a command like "Take one step forward." The first child in each line must repeat, "Mother, may I please take one step forward?" The "mother" says, "Yes, you may." Then the child must reply "thank you" before stepping forward.

Manners matter. Read one of this unit's books about manners. Discuss why it is important to use good manners. Next, write, "Clean hands are so fine when I am ready to dine," on the board. Discuss how this is related to good manners and the importance of having clean hands before eating.

(JW) *Journal writing.* Each day, read a different book from the unit books list. At the end of the unit, ask students to write in their journal what they have learned about developing honesty, respect, and manners.

Multicultural Emphasis: Respect, Honesty, and Manners as Depicted in Other Cultures

Share the following information and ask students to discuss ways that honesty, respect, and manners are portrayed in their cultures.

Cambodia, Vietnam, and Laos. Traditional Cambodians and Vietnamese write their family name first, middle name second, and given name last. They use first names to address each other. Laotians write their names as Americans do. In these cultures, extra effort is extended to pronounce these names correctly; doing so shows respect.

Indonesia. Indochinese children are not accustomed to asking for help or asking questions. They use nonverbal greetings to communicate "hello" and "goodbye." The most common gesture is to join their hands together and slightly lower the head. Moreover, many children from this culture have been taught that when first offered something, they should refuse politely, but that they can accept a second offer.

The apparent shyness of Indochinese children is a polite way of showing respect.

Hmong. This cultural group came originally from Mongolia and settled in northern Laos. If the Hmong suspect someone of being dishonest, they have the "old ones" put a spell in two glasses of a liquid (tea, wine, or water). Then they confront the suspected person and say that if he or she is honest, the spell of happiness and long life will occur when he or she drinks the liquid. But if the person is dishonest, he or she will have bad luck and die. The "old ones" in this group then invite the person to drink with them. Of course, if the person doesn't drink, it is obvious that he or she is guilty or dishonest.

Mexican American. One Mexican-American custom of the 1800s and early 1900s continues today in some families: Mexican-American men remove their hats as a symbol of respect when talking to former employers and older family members. For example, there are numerous anecdotes about men of importance, such as Mexican generals, who stop conversations in mid-sentence in order to snap to attention as soon as their fathers enter the room. Such respect is often offered to teachers and other adults as well. Another custom in Mexico that shows respect is *pilon* ("a little something extra"). When a customer pays for groceries, it is customary for the merchant to demonstrate appreciation and respect by giving the customer a *pilon,* usually candy for young children, trinkets for older children, tobacco for the father, or something decorative for the mother. *Pilon* is seen today between Mexican-American schoolchildren who may give more than requested to their classmates.

It may be important to point out to students that customs such as these exist in all cultures and that these customs add distinctive qualities to people's lives.

Native American. Native Americans deeply respect the animals, the earth, and the laws of their tribe. For example, the Navajo tribe holds coyotes in special respect for their cunning and ability to survive under many different conditions. They respect Mother Earth because of her kindness to them.

Native American and African American. Traditionally, both Native Americans and African Americans treated dishonesty severely as it was considered to jeopardize group survival. Ask students if they agree with this cultural value and if they think U.S. society holds the same value.

Africa. The government of Kenya in East Africa is teaching its people how important it is to wash carefully and keep their houses clean. At present, of every 1,000 babies born in Kenya, approximately 25 die because of unsanitary conditions.

Japan: The Japanese still have strict regulations about honesty and honor. To dishonor oneself is considered very degrading. In ancient Japan, *samurai* warriors (soldiers of the lower nobility) took their own life (committed *hara-kiri*) if they judged that they had dishonored themselves. Today, it is illegal to commit *hara-kiri* (suicide) in Japan.

Spain. The Spanish book *El Vuelo del Barrilete* (Argentina: Editorial Atlantida, 1981) describes the value of honesty in Spanish culture. You can read it aloud to students. In this book, Nicholas borrows his best friend's special kite and loses it. Then he tries to redeem himself by telling lies.

Multicultural. Ask students to suggest several customs in their families. Then ask them to discuss or write why these customs are important in their families.

Your Additions to the Unit

6 Developing Positive Attitudes

Learning Objectives   Many students are unaware that their actions and thoughts can promote, influence, and stimulate others to become more positive, creative, and effective. The quotations, activities, and books in this unit teach strategies that increase motivation.

Resources   *Select a different quotation to discuss and write on the board each day of this unit's study.*

Wake up each morning feeling this day is important.

Each day holds new beginnings.

Make your memories a joy.

Feel as if your life is very special.

*I am the best one
to make it a great day.*

Starting over can be fun to see the changes when I'm done.

There is always time for a fresh start.

If I think I can, I can.

Easy to do? It's up to you.

*Achievement: A time for looking back
with pride and for looking ahead with joy.*

*Each day is a new invention. We can discover
that there is no end to the good that can be achieved.*

*Negative thinking is a stop;
Positive thinking puts you on top.*

*Write it on your heart that every day
is the best day in the year.*
—Emerson

*Its not who you are that holds you back,
It's who you think you're not.*
—Dan Zadra

Finding the Right Book Concerning Developing Positive Attitudes to Meet Students' Needs

Difficulty code: I = Introductory; E = Easy; M = Medium

		Book
I	Keeping faith	*The Carrot Seed* by Ruth Kraus
I	Keep goals	*The Tortoise and the Hare* by Aesop and Stevens
I	Looking for the good in others	*The Unfriendly Book* by Charlotte Zolotow
I	Strong desire and determination	*Fidelia* by Ruth Adams
I	Achieving what you desire	*Swimmy* by Leo Lionni
I	Looking for your positive side	*The Luckiest One of All* by Bill Peet
I	Changing your mood	*Lyle and the Birthday Party* by Bernard Waber
I	Activities and traits of young children	*Kids* by Lawrence Anholt
E	A boy who knows what he wants to be and appreciates his Hong Kong city	*Our Home Is the Sea* by Riki Levinson
E	Search for identity needs a positive attitude	*The High King* by Lloyd Alexander
E	Positive attitudes toward different types of families	*Circles* by Mendel Sitomer
E	Bear and Lion fight until adventure unites them	*The Happy Lion* by Louise Fatio
E	Being inspired	*The Story of the Flight at Kitty Hawk* by R. Conrad Stein
E	American folk songs representing various regional and cultural sources of inspiration	*Gonna Sing My Head Off* collected and arranged by Kathleen Krull
E	Folktales about inspiring oneself and others	*My Grandmother's Stories: A Collection of Jewish Folk Tales* by Adele Geras
E	Focusing on what can be done	*Grandma Drives a Motor Bed* by Diane Johnston Hamm
E	Youth fantasies	*The Field Beyond the Outfield* by Mark Teague
E–M	An inspirational biography	*Amelia Earhart: Flying for Adventure* by Mary Dodson Wade
E–M	Changing negative attitudes and days into positive ones	*The Happy Birthday Book* by Peter Seymour

		Book
E–M	Changing negative attitudes and days into positive ones	*Fall Is Here, I Love It* by Elaine W. Good
E–M	A Japanese girl who inspired others both before and after her death	*Sadako and the Thousand Paper Cranes* by Eleanor Coerr
M	How African-American cultural traditions and linguistic patterns enrich U.S. society	*The Mouse Rap* by Walter Dean Myers
M	Boy inspired to save a building and finds a great discovery	*Who Goes There, Lincoln?* by Dale Fife
M	Becoming a writer	*How I Came to Be a Writer* by P. R. Nayler
M	Inspiring girls to succeed	*Young and Female* by Louis Haber
M	Determination and resourcefulness	*Where the Lilies Bloom* by Vera Cleaver
M	A cherished place of precious memories	*Good-Bye My Wishing Star* by Vicki Grove
M	A girl determined to improve her family's life	*Sweetly Sings the Donkey* by Vera Cleaver

Activities to Use with Quotes and Books

Opening the School Day Discussion

Discuss the concept students have of this unit and set goals they want to achieve during this study.

I'm positive about me and you. Explain that students are to list ten positive characteristics that describe themselves. Then ask students, in groups of two, to write ten qualities they value about their partners; and to read both lists to each other when they are finished. Last, ask pairs to discuss what they learned from the lists and write a summary to turn in to you. Two samples from students who did this activity follow:

1. Making things
2. Good handwriting
3. Helps people
4. Is kind
5. Is fun to play with
6. Good at baseball
7. Good sportsmanship

1. I am caring
2. I am reliable
3. I am sweet
4. I love people
5. I am kind
6. I am happy
7. I am helpful

Making my day and/or my attitude more positive. Read one or more of the books listed for this unit and the quotations concerning changing negative days or emotions into positive ones. After reading the books, ask students to reflect on the story and on similar experiences in their life. Explain that they have ten minutes to list the personal resources they use when they face negative emotions or events. After some have shared their lists, ask all to select the three resources most available at school for developing positive attitudes and to describe ways they will use these resources more frequently in the future.

Avoiding negative feelings. Discuss times of being sad or angry and times when you had to have self-control in order not to hurt others' feelings. Then discuss a quotation from the unit that helps you have a more positive attitude. Last, ask students to write about three such incidents and tell what they can do to avoid hurting someone else in the future.

(JW) *Journal writing.* Write a quote on the board that relates to making one's own day the best it can be. Then tell students that one of the most important factors in a great day is that they must take steps to begin each day happily and positively. Have students write about ways that the school day could begin more happily and positively or ways that their own days can begin more happily. With each change they recommend, ask them to state why the change would make the day happier. Last, have classmates suggest two methods of implementing a few of the suggestions in their classrooms.

Helping others become more positive. Have some students write a sentence that they could tell to someone to help that person have a great day. Have them place these sentences on the bulletin board, either signed or anonymously. Have students invite the principal, janitor, cooks, and other teachers to contribute a quotation they use to make their days better.

Teaching students to increase positive attitudes. Explain to students that they should avoid saying negative things because their subconscious minds may not hear the negative and may actually do the opposite. Show them how this occurs: If they say, "I can't fail this test," their minds may recall it as "I can fail this test." (This example is taken from *The Secret of the Slight Edge* by Dan Zadar, Creative Education Publishers, page 31.) Then ask students to practice keeping their thoughts positive by focusing directly on what they are doing and concentrating on winning instead of on *not losing*.

(JW) *Inspired times.* Ask students to share times in their lives when they were inspired by someone else, by nature, or by music. Next, have them read a book from this unit's book list or remember a book character or situation that inspired them. Last, ask them to write how this person, natural phenomenon, or musical selection inspired them and what they did because of it. Those who desire can share their writings with the class.

People I admire. Invite community leaders chosen by students (e.g., a local news or sports broadcaster, the mayor, etc.) to class to describe the things that inspire them to do their best. After the speaker finishes, ask students to interview an adult in their life to determine other sources of positive attitudes and inspiration. Do not allow students to tell classmates what they have learned.

Instead, ask each to write a story about these people's strategies and to give the story a title. Compile all the stories into a class book which will be read aloud, discussed, and placed in the classroom library for individual students' reference.

Poetry. Compare Langston Hughes's poetry in *The Dream Keeper and Other Poems* to collections by poets he admired such as Paul Lawrence Dunbar and Carl Sandburg.

Teaching students to value inspiration. Explain to students the "three-bones" philosophy of life:

> *The wishbone:* Your dreams and wishes inspire you to chart your course in life.
>
> *The backbone:* Enables you to have the courage and character to achieve your dreams and goals.
>
> *The funny bone:* Sees you through the hard times and prevents you from taking yourself too seriously.*

Discuss this philosophy and describe how it can be used to help students maintain positive attitude.

Happy memories. Ask students to think about a fight they had with one of their friends: "What was it about?" Now have them recall a time they had fun with one of their best friends: "Which one do you remember the best? Why?"

(BLM) *I can.* Write the quote, "If I think I can, I can." Read the book or see the filmstrip *The Little Engine That Could.* Define positive attitudes. Discuss the benefits of a positive attitude, and list what the group could more easily accomplish with a positive attitude. Use Blackline Master 11 (located in the BLM section) for students to draw or write the things they would like to accomplish. Then have students cut out the number of cars they think they will need to write all the goals they have. Join them to the engine. Last, ask students where they would like to hang their train—school hall, classroom, or at home.

(JW) *Journal writing.* Students begin at the top of the page by writing the sentence "I think I can _____ because _____."
Then they write five more sentences recording new ideas they think they can implement and how they will begin them.

Identifying positive attitudes. Each day for a week, read a different book from the book list for this unit. At the end of the week, ask students to draw their favorite character and write or tell in a sentence why they preferred that character. After all have shared, summarize by listing the qualities children wrote as positive attitudes. Summarize how each of their selected characters' positive attitudes helped the character be successful and better liked.

*Adapted from *The Secret of the Slight Edge* by Dan Zadra, Creative Education Publishers, pages 34–35.

Multicultural Emphasis: Concepts about Positive Attitudes That Come from Different Cultures

After sharing the following information, ask students to compare the differences between positive attitudes in various cultures.

Indonesia. Beginning in mid-May, the countries of South Asia await the heavy rain and wind brought by the monsoon. Its arrival is greeted with joy, however, because people know that despite the hardships the monsoon brings, it also means water for plants, crops, flowers, and grass.

China. Read the following Chinese legend to students and then ask what it taught them about positive attitudes in China.

How P'eng Brought the Rain

In Spring, when the day is as long as the night, a big bird called P'eng flies out of the sea. With his big golden wings he covers the whole sky. He spreads his wings to blot out the sun, and the whole sky darkens. Then he flies faster, and the winds begin to blow. He flies faster, and the waves roll up as high as the trees. The sky is dark, the winds blow, the waves roll, and the people run into their houses. "P'eng is here!" they shout. "P'eng is here!" They stay inside until the big bird flies away. They then go outside to feel the sun and the soft, wet earth. The rains are over and P'eng is gone for another year.

For more information about Chinese people's emphasis on positive attitude, compare two stories. One is *In the Year of the Boar and Jackie Robinson* by Bette Bao Lord, about a Chinese girl who moves to Brooklyn, New York. The other is *Homesick* by Jean Fritz, about an American girl living in Hankow, China. In what way were the girls inspired? How are their difficulties the same or different?

Japan. Japanese authors have used animals symbolically in their tales to inspire people:

- The dragon is the most important beast in Japanese folk literature. Legend has it that the dragon is king of the animals and lives in a palace at the bottom of the sea.
- The fox is a symbol of abundance in some Japanese stories and a mischief-maker in others.
- The cat is a symbol of friendliness, welcome, and prosperity.
- Many buildings and homes are decorated with the monkey because it is believed to protect children.

Thailand. Many traditional Thai beliefs are told through folktales and stories. In this culture, animals are almost human, with each representing specific traits. For example, water buffalos are fierce but trust small children; the rabbit is either a hero or a trickster; and the parrot, with his mimicry, is never himself.

Mexican American. Because the language of a culture conveys many of the values held by its people, reading the following book, or inviting a Mexican-American parent or other adult to class to read it, will teach students about the value Mexican Americans place on positive attitudes. After the reading, ask students what they learned about Spanish people's positive attitudes. The book is *Lanudo,* by Gyo Fujikawa (Buenos Aires: Editorial Atlantida, 1981). As a result of a bad dream, Lanudo becomes a better pet because he learns to have compassion for smaller creatures.

Native American. The following Native Americans inspired many in their culture to reach major accomplishments. Students can select one of these heroes to study. They can report the events in these people's lives and the specific actions they took to inspire others. Vine Deloria, Jr., a Sioux writer; Ella Deloria, a Sioux historian and linguist; Charles Eastman, a Dakota Sioux author; and Madge Skelly, an Iroquois communication specialist who invented Indian hand talk.

French. Share the following books:

> Georges, D. V. *A New True Book: Europe.*
> Hillyer, V. M., and E. G. Huey. *Young People's Story of Europe.*
> Moss, Peter, and Thelma Palmer. *France: Enchantment of the World.*

Explain that the French are very proud of Paris, called the City of Light because of its renown as a sophisticated world cultural center. In its rich history, world leaders came to Paris to establish democracy. Paris also has many displays of art and science. Since 1635, a group of forty appointed scholars, writers, and intellectuals, called the French Academy, have attempted to keep the French language pure and to set standards of good usage. As a result, the French are very precise and clear in their language.

French people love beauty in all things—clothing, food, and manners. French fashion designers and chefs are famous all over the world. Sidewalk cafés are common, as the French love to spend time outdoors.

Your Own Additions to the Unit

7 Eliminating Excuses and Correcting Mistakes

Learning Objectives Some students offer excuses in place of effort. They cry and become depressed when they make mistakes. The quotations, activities, and books in this unit teach students to recognize the negative impact that excuses can have on their productivity. This unit also demonstrates the adverse effects of (1) trying to free oneself from blame, (2) minimizing or pardoning oneself unjustly, (3) persuading others that an offense was unimportant, and (4) releasing oneself from important obligations. Students also must realize that they can learn from their mistakes and that there are several ways of responding productively to errors.

Resources *Select a different quotation to discuss and write on the board each day of this unit's study.*

It is O.K. to make a mistake.

Grow by your mistakes.

When in doubt, think first, then act.

Don't use an excuse as a crutch; it slows you down.

A mistake is only wrong when it is not corrected.

What if I am wrong?
Can I be strong?

Have you ever noticed the numerous
unproductive side effects excuses have?

With the good people, you can see
the learning juices churning around
every mistake. You learn from mistakes.
When I look back, my life seems to be
an endless chain of mistakes.
—Edward Johnson, a millionaire businessman

Not everything that is faced can be changed, but
Nothing can be changed until it is faced.
—James Baldwin

Finding the Right Book Concerning Eliminating Excuses to Meet Students' Needs

Difficulty code: I = Introductory; E = Easy; M = Medium

		Book
I	Making excuses for not playing with friends	*The Unfriendly Book* by Charlotte Zolotow
I	Trouble caused by lying	*The Boy Who Cried Wolf* by Aesop
I	Learning a lesson	*One Fine Day* by Nonny Hogrogian
I	Learning from mistakes	*Amelia Bedelia* by Peggy Parish (available on cassette)
I	Feelings of relatives	*When the Relatives Come* by Cynthia Rylant
I	Things are not always as they seem	*Little Red Riding Hood* by Brothers Grimm
I	The meaning of the buzz. An African folktale	*Why Mosquitoes Buzz in People's Ears* by Verna Aardema
I	Consequence of envy	*The Tale of a Pig: A Caucasian Folktale* by Wallace Tripp
I	A solution that was a mistake	*Too Hot in Potzburg* by Seymour Fleishman
I	Accidents happen.	*Ooops!* by Suzy Kline
I	Little Millie forgets to close the pasture gate, and animals get inside the house	*Parents in the Pigpen, Pigs in the Tub* by Amy Ehrlich
I	Harris, a parrot, has a fun rescue mission	*Theres's Only One Harris* by Frank Remkeswicz
E	Parents make mistakes	*Nobody's Perfect, Not Even My Mother* by Norma Simon
E	Blamed all troubles on starting school	*The King Boy* by Judy Rhodes
E	Anansi wants a fish but is too lazy to catch one	*Anansi Goes Fishing* by Eric Kimmel
E	Not knowing the magic brings unexpected results	*Big Anthony and the Magic Ring* by Tomie de Paola
E	Billy makes up excuses to himself about new shoes.	*Billy's Shoes* by Gen LeRoy
E	A look at vandalism	*We Didn't Mean to* by Sharon Addy
E–M	Success comes from work, not luck	*Where the Goal Luck Was* by Osmond Malarsky
M	Lies to conceal an embarrassment	*Nothing Rhymes with April* by Naomi J. Karp

		Book
M	Things can be good without being perfect	*Journey* by Patricia Mac Lachlan
M	An Indian girl overcomes excuses	*Island of the Blue Dolphin* by Scott O'Dell
M	Running away from problems	*The Runaway Summer* by Nina Mary K. Bowden
M	Superstition as an excuse that affects one's expectations	*Volleyball Jinx* by Bobbi Katz
M	A situation viewed as unbelievable by adults	*The View from the Cherry Tree* by Willo Davis Roberts
M	Adjusting to a new homeland	*Candita's Choice* by Mina S. Lewiton
M	Substituting courage for excuses	*Call It Courage* by Armstrong Perry
M	Frustration leads to lies and theft	*J.T.* by Jane Wagner
M	A family learns that money does not equal success	*Boom Town Boy* by Lois Lenski
M	Excuses for Dad not working	*Give Dad My Best* by James Collier
M	A small boy learns his worth	*It's a Mile from Here to Glory* by Robert C. Lee
M	A broken home makes a child face facts	*The Genesee Queen* by Winifred Madison

Activities to Use with Quotes and Books

Opening the School Day Discussion

Discuss the negative effect of excuses and mistakes and the learning objectives of this unit. Tell about an experience from your life when giving a true reason or making a genuine effort instead of an excuse helped the people involved. Tell how you learned something by making a mistake.

A look at excuses. On the board, list excuses that students volunteer ("I left my homework at home," "I didn't have a pencil"). Then divide students into small groups and discuss one of the excuses from the list and the best way to overcome its use in the future. Next, list the suggested action(s) on the board. The following sample list of excuses, generated in one class, could be used to begin this discussion:

I was asking for paper.	I need a pencil.
I was throwing my paper away.	I forgot.
I'm doing my homework.	I didn't have time.

I was talking to myself.	She or he was in my way.
I wasn't doing anything.	_____ stole my paper.
My papers blew out of my folder.	I wasn't copying.

Easy way out? Pair students and have one partner generate a situation in which excuses are normally made, and the other partners respond to that situation without using an excuse. After twenty minutes of discussion, ask students to write what they have learned. Topics for the situations they create can include school, home, friendships, and the like. You may want students to read one of the reference books for this unit which introduce methods that can be used to overcome excuses before they begin this activity.

(JW) *Receiving excuses.* Have the class discuss times when someone gave them an excuse and how they felt about the person who made the excuse. Then discuss how they can avoid giving excuses to others and help those who give excuses to them. List their ideas on the board. Conclude the activity by asking students to write about what they have learned.

(JW) *Journal writing.* Ask students to write down their most frequently used excuse. Then have them record the results the excuse has produced in the past and answer a few questions:

- Did they grow from its use?
- Where was their attention after the excuse?
- How did they feel?

Next, have students record a specific statement they will say to others in the future each time they are tempted to give each of the excuses they described. Last, ask them to write a thought they will use to counter that excuse whenever they attempt to *give themselves* that excuse in the future.

(BLM) *Individualized instruction.* A few students may need additional instruction to overcome the habit of using excuses. Have these students meet with you individually and list the excuses they frequently use on the left side of Blackline Master 12 (BLM section). This Blackline Master becomes a learning contract. In the middle column of Blackline Master 12, ask students to write the reason they gave that excuse in the past. Next, ask students to describe a positive way to address the reason for each of their excuses in the next column. For example, if excuses are given to avoid uninteresting tasks, they will pause before starting such tasks to create personal challenges that will make those tasks more interesting. At the end of the week, meet with these students again to tally the number of times they used positive strategies to overcome excuses. Last, to reinforce these students' efforts and give the class an opportunity to review this unit, ask students to create a board game using either Blackline Master 13 or 14 (see BLM section). The cards of the game will list past situations in which students or their classmates gave excuses. If students can think of a statement they will make to others instead of an excuse, they can move ahead 1 space (or gain 1 point); if they can add a statement they will make to themselves, they can move ahead 2 spaces (or gain 2 points); and if they can add a statement they will say to help a friend who offers that excuse, they can move ahead a total of 3 spaces (or gain 3 points). Students can decide on other rules of the game and on what the winner receives.

Teaching students to eliminate excuses. The following are two strategies students can use to eliminate excuses. Teach one or both.

Strategy 1:

1. Write down your worthwhile positive dream.
2. Discard the worn-out reasons and excuses that are keeping you from reaching this dream.
3. Listen to the voice of your soaring hopes.
4. Make your plan.
5. Pinpoint your destination.
6. Make actions toward your goal exciting and worthwhile to *you*.

Strategy 2: The **have, be, do** *technique:*

Think of the one thing you would really like to have. Think of something you really want to be. And think of something you really want to do.

1. Visualize these three dreams in your mind's eye as if they have already happened. Do this any time you need to increase your motivation to work toward your dreams.
2. Don't let anyone talk you out of your dream! Only you know whether or not the dream is valuable.
3. Make a list of why you *can* do the things needed to reach your goals. *Don't* concentrate on why you *can't* do them.
4. The last, most important step is: When you have reached a goal, set another.

Correcting mistakes. Give each small group the following mistakes to read and discuss how they can correct them: (1) making a mistake with a peer, (2) having an idea and not saying it to the class, (3) not doing something you were supposed to do, (4) getting angry, and (5) other mistakes they made at school.

(BLM) *Messages about mistakes from parents.* Have students ask their parents what they want their children to do when they make mistakes. Then ask students or parents to list the parental suggestions on a chart (use Blackline Master 15 in the BLM section). The next day, discuss the new ideas students found to overcome mistakes.

(JW) *Journal writing.* Have students find a mistake they've made in a composition in their journals or on a sheet of paper. They correct their mistake and put it in their journals. Then they compare how the two papers look and how they feel when the mistake is gone.

Multicultural Emphasis: Rules and Guidelines Followed in Other Cultures to Prevent Excuses

Share the following information and activities about eliminating excuses that appear in the history of different cultures. Once these are complete, have students discuss how long people have used excuses and how future cultures could avoid the use of excuses.

Native American. Traditionally, Native Americans all knew the rules and guidelines of their tribe. No excuses were allowed in the tribal community. A person who broke any rules might be cast out of the tribe or even put to death. Native Americans felt execution was more humane than imprisonment.

Mexican American. Students from all cultures enjoy learning about the games and rules of previous generations. *Juegos de Ayer y de Hoy* by Maria Claret (Spain: Editorial Juventud, 1983) describes such rules as they existed in the Mexican-American culture. This interesting book compares games that grandparents played in past times and those that children play today.

Multicultural. Discuss the view of historians that dishonesty, deception, and greed have caused more wars between nations than any other factors. Then have students study some past wars and consider whether these qualities were a cause: Discuss World Wars I and II, the Mexican–American War, the Korean War, and civil wars within various nations—Russia, China, Somalia, Vietnam, and our own Civil War.

Africa. Read the following legend and ask students if the water gave excuses.

The Sun, the Moon, and the Water (a Zimbabwean legend)

Once the sun, the moon, and the water all lived in Africa. The sun and the moon shared one hut, and the water lived alone. Now the sun and the moon felt sorry for their friend the water, and invited the water to share their home.

"You wouldn't want me," said the water, "I am too big."

"Nonsense," said the sun and the moon. "You are always welcome."

"But I will take up too much room," said the water.

"Nonsense," said the sun and the moon. "You don't take up too much room. We insist."

"All right," said the water, "If you insist, I will come and stay with you."

So in came the water. All day long the water moved into their home, all day and all night, and all the next day. The water filled the hut right up to the roof, and sent the sun and the moon whirling into the sky. The sun went one way, the moon another high up into the sky, and neither one has ever come back to live in Africa again!

Your Own Additions to the Unit

8 Eliminating Misbehavior

Learning Objectives   The quotations, activities, and books in this unit emphasize the value of proper behavior management and provide strategies for overcoming anger. Students discover that they can become angry as a result of injury, mistreatment, or opposition and that this feeling can surface as the desire to strike out at something or someone else.

Resources   *Select a different quotation to discuss and write on the board each day of this unit's study.*

*I can't help how I feel, but
I can help how I think and act.*

*Weakness on both sides is the
Motto of all quarrels.*
—Voltaire

You mold your character and future by your thoughts and acts.

Love brings joy in stride; hate hurts you inside.

I end up sad when I stay mad.

Bitterness in your heart will only grow if not sweetened.

Harboring a resentment will keep you from sailing.

When I do wrong I don't feel good for long.

When I get mad I can get glad.

*I have a temper.
But . . . (complete this phrase after you model an answer)
And . . . (complete this phrase after your modeling)*

*I was angry with my friend.
I told my wrath, my wrath did end.
I was angry with my foe:
I told it not, my wrath did grow.*
—William Blake

Keep your interest up, not your dander.

He who acts badly ends badly.
—Rosemary Holman

Words can hurt.

8 ELIMINATING MISBEHAVIOR

Let's talk it over, not fight it out;
Our way through it is not to pout.

When angry, count ten before you speak;
If very angry, count to a hundred.
—Andrew Jackson

If you are patient in one moment of anger, you will
escape a hundred days of sorrow.
—Chinese proverb

Finding the Right Book Concerning Eliminating Misbehavior to Meet Students' Needs

Difficulty code: I = Introductory; E = Easy; M = Medium

		Book
I	A main character who misbehaves is resentful, and steals (film and video)	*The Great Gilly Hopkins* by Katherine Paterson
I	A main character who gets into trouble because he misbehaves (film)	*Tale of Peter Rabbit* by Beatrix Potter
I	A bully and a solution	*Benjamin and Tulip* by R. Wells
I	Cheering up a grump	*What Do You Do with a Kangaroo?* by J. B. Moncure
I	Growth of a lie	*A Big Fat Enormous Lie* by Marjorie Sharmat
I	Becoming unbelievable	*Who Will Believe Tim Kitten?* by Jan Wohl
I	Aggression	*Martha's Mad Day* by Miranda Hapgood
I	Teasing	*Am I a Bunny?* by Ida DeLage
I	Isolated child is teased	*Oliver Button Is a Sissy* by Taro Yashima
I	Being angry is a human emotion	*I Was So Mad* by Norma Simon
I	Ladybug is upset, looks for a fight	*The Grouchy Ladybug* by Eric Carle
I	Working through one's anger	*Let's Be Enemies* by Maurice Sendak
I	A child's anger	*That Makes Me Mad!* by Steven Kroll
I	Anger at mother's discipline	*Spence and the Mean Old Bear* by Christa Chevalier
I	Jealous anger	*Feeling Angry* by Sylvia Root Tester
I	Anger	*Monster Birthday Party* by Sally Freedman

		Book
I	Anger is real	*What Does It Mean?* by Susan Riley
I	Throwing a fit of anger	*Don't Throw Another One, Dover!* by Beverly Keller
E	Realizing that anger and jealousy can turn to love	*Stevie* by John Steptoe
E	Family problems	*A Family That Fights* by Sharon Bernstein
E	Don't do their jobs	*Two Bad Ants* by Chris Van Allsburg
E	Boy misbehaves	*Superfudge* by Judy Blume
E	Name calling	*Frog, Duck and Rabbit* by Susanna Gretz
E	Misbehaving by being ignored	*Betsy and the Chicken Pox* by Gunilla Wolde
E	Team discipline	*Miss Nelson's Field Day* by Harry Allard
E	Guilt and fear of lying	*The Lie* by Ann Helena
E	Boy acts up and is sent to bed without supper (video and cassette)	*Where the Wild Things Are* by Maurine Sendak
E	A bad day	*Alexander and the Terrible, Horrible, No Good, Very Bad Day* by Judith Viorst
E	Anger about giving up a pet	*Emma's Dilemma* by Gen LeRoy
E	Describes differences between positive and negative emotions	*Miss Nelson Is Missing* by Harry Allard
E	A rat who constantly gets into trouble	*Rasco and the Rats of NIMH* by Jane Leslie Conly
E	Wanting to win for revenge	*Maggie Marmelstein for President* by Marjorie Sharmat
E–M	Controlling negative behaviors	*Josie Smith and Eileen* by Magdalen Nabb
E–M	An argument between best friends	*Marinka, Katinka, and Me (Susie)* by Winifred Madison
E–M	Have you heard this question before?	*Can't You Make Them Behave, King George?* by Jean Fritz
E–M	Harry, the cat's outrageous behavior and his chicken friend's wise commentary	*Harry the Explorer* by Dyan Sheldon
M	Solution for a quick temper	*Gilly Gilhooley: A Tale of Ireland* by Arnold Dobrin
M	Anger among siblings	*The Pain and the Great One* by Judy Blume

		Book
M	Consequences of tricking other people	*The Boy Who Cried Wolf* retold by Freya Littledale
M	Understanding emotions	*Mad Martin* by Patricia Windsor
M	Dealing with problems	*Peace on the Playground* by Eileen Lucas
M–H	A self-centered, arrogant cat	*Beethoven's Cat* by Elisabeth McHugh
M–H	Realizing that elders got into scrapes when young	*The Chicken Pox Paper* by Susan Dubinsky Terris
M–H	Continual joking brings anger	*Dogs Don't Tell Jokes* by Louis Sachar

Activities to Use with Quotes and Books

Opening the School Day Discussion

Ask students to make a private journal entry describing a behavior at school, at home, or with friends that they want to improve. Ask them to write down a specific action they can take that day to improve the behavior. Then have students seal that entry so no one else can read it. On each subsequent day of this unit's study, during morning message time, ask students to share strategies that worked for them on the previous day, and have them reread their previous day's entry. Finally, introduce a new quote and have students write a new journal entry.

You be the judge. Divide the class into four groups and give each group one of the following types of rules systems:

1. Home rules
2. School rules
3. Public rules (e.g., traffic rules)
4. Friendship rules (e.g., yelling at a friend)

They must analyze their type of rules by answering the following questions:

1. What are the rules of this type?
2. How do these rules get broken?
3. Why was each rule made?
4. How important is each rule relative to the others? (Students should rank the rules.)
5. What would they add or take out of the list of rules?
6. What are the consequences of breaking each rule?

Ask each group's secretary to record group discussions, and have a speaker for each group explain the findings to the class in a five-minute presentation. Conclude by explaining that there are usually consequences for breaking rules. Reassure students that it's O.K. to get mad but that they should channel their strongly negative emotional responses toward positive actions. Explain that if a rule ever seems senseless, students may be able to help change it.

Selecting correct actions. Write on the board: "I can't help how I feel, but I can help how I think and act." Then read aloud to the class *Oliver Button Is a Sissy* by Tomie DePaola or another reference book from this unit. At the climax of the story, stop reading and ask students to brainstorm possible endings. Write their suggestions on the board. Then finish reading the book and see who predicted the ending correctly. Finally, ask students what they learned about eliminating misbehavior.

(RRG) *Name calling.* Read *Frog, Duck, and Rabbit* by Susanna Gretz or another book in this unit. This book describes three friends who disagree so much about a costume project that they began calling each other names. The book demonstrates that friends should put aside their differences, think about how their words could hurt someone else, and stop themselves before saying those hurtful words out loud. In a discussion, you might ask: How did each character feel? What could each person think about before acting or speaking? How did the characters resolve the problem?

(RRG) *Changing negative emotions.* Read *Josie Smith and Eileen* by Magdalene Nabb. Discuss how Josie is angry with her best friend but learns to make up in a surprising way. The story is a good example of controlling oneself even when experiencing negative feelings. After discussing the book, ask students to write how they will change their negative emotions in the future by implementing the messages from this book, other books, and the quotations in this unit.

Never cry wolf unless you mean it. Read *The Boy Who Cried Wolf* as retold by Freya Littledale. On the first day, read up to the point where Tom cries wolf for the third time. Then ask children to write what they think happened next. After hearing a couple of their predictions, complete the story. Ask the students to think about why no one answered Tom's cries the next time. Finally, explain why his continual tricks led people to mistrust him, no matter what he said, and ask students how this story applies to their own lives.

Understanding anger. Write on the board: "Love brings joy in stride; hate hurts you inside." Then explain that liking or loving a person takes less energy than disliking someone. Ask students how liking other people will help them like themselves. How can liking other people make someone happier? When students are mad at someone, how do they feel? Why does it stay on their minds? Then read *Miss Nelson Is Missing* by Harry Allard or another similar book. Explain that while you read students should think about the quote and what it means. Last, discuss students' feelings about anger and the quote.

Testimonials. Ask students to divide into small groups and give a testimonial about applying their favorite quote in this unit to their lives. After each group has shared its best example of an incident in which they experienced the messages of the quotation, have students describe what they learned from the testimonials that will enable them to respond more effectively to anger-provoking situations in the future. You may have to give a personal example to begin this activity.

"I'm so mad I see red." Ask: Is there any reason, from a scientific point of view, that the color *red* was used in this phrase? Have the discussion end with two or more children going to the library and researching the origin of this saying and other associations between colors and feelings: "I'm feeling blue," "blue Monday," "I'm in the pink," "Green with envy," and the like.

(BLM) *Overcoming anger in our world.* Have students create a short dramatic piece and perform it for another class. It can be about a real situation at school, in town, or somewhere else in the world, or a situation they read about in one of the books listed in this unit. The ending must show how anger was brought under control individually and by group actions. Explain to each group that they can use the grid in Blackline Master 16 (see BLM section) to generate ideas for their production.

The anger court. After exploring the emotions of misbehaving and anger, hold an "anger court" where students act out a judicial handling of an emotional situation. In this one-week exercise, students play the following roles: a judge, two lawyers, the accused, the plaintiff, and up to thirteen jurors (name an alternate juror in case a student is absent one day). Ask students to choose a situation to bring before the court—for example, one student teases another or calls another student names; "my mother doesn't understand me"; a class bully breaks another student's locker; a younger child uses an older child's things without asking).

On the first day of this activity, students select the situation and the roles they will play. On the second and third days, the class divides into two groups, excluding those chosen as jurors and judge. (At this point, the jurors and judge can go to the library to work on another project.) One group includes the lawyer for the accused and any others who want to help plan the case or testify. The second group includes the lawyer for the plaintiff and other students to help plan the case or testify.

On the fourth day, the trial is held with the jury present. Each side gets fifteen minutes to present its case.

On the fifth day, the jury presents the verdict. If the verdict is "guilty," the jury also decides on the punishment. Discuss with the class what they learned from this exercise. You might also choose a situation in which something other than a person caused anger. For example, take the case of a child riding a bike. The bike chain catches the pant leg and the child falls, hurting his knee. He becomes angry at the bike. One student could take the part of the bike and try to prove that the child could have avoided the anger had he fixed the chain or taken better care of the bike in the first place.

Helping students to understand their anger. Socially competent, popular children will be involved in fewer conflicts involving anger than children judged to be less socially competent or popular. Ask students to explain why this is so. Does social competence help prevent anger? How? Why or why not? How might popularity help determine the frequency with which one becomes angry? At social functions, what might cause an argument? How might you prevent or stop one?

Time out. Introduce a time-out area where children can go when their temper is out of control, when they become upset, or when they need to be alone.

Ask the class to establish rules for the center—how long students can stay, how many students can be in the time-out area at once, and so on. Preferably, students themselves should control the amount of time they can stay, so that each student can return to the group when he judges that he no longer needs a time out. When the rules are in place, ask a good writer to write them down and post them in the time-out area.

(BLM) *Overcoming anger.* Have students draw a Venn diagram in their journals (or use Blackline Master 17 in the BLM section). Teach that the circles' overlap indicates things the two books have in common, and that the areas within the circles where they do not overlap are places to write things the two books do not have in common. Then, read two books listed in this unit's books that describe different ways of overcoming anger. Ask older groups of students to list items as you read. For younger students, list characteristics of anger that they identify in the books as you read them. When the Venn diagrams are complete, ask students to write below the diagram the most important thing they've learned about overcoming anger.

(JW) *Anger in all of us.* Have students copy a quote into their journal. Then ask them to write or talk about a similar experience or feeling they have had. For younger students, make a class-constructed story that all students copy after the quotation into their journals. Have older students write about their individual experiences.

(RRG) *Sometimes I wish people would not . . .* Divide the class into small groups and have each group meet with you. In the meetings, have each student finish the sentence "Sometimes I wish people would not. . . ." Write their endings on a chart below the opening sentence stem. After all students have shared their endings, ask the entire group to read the completed list and discuss what they can do to overcome situations like these. Rotate the class until all students have had an opportunity to add their items to the chart. Last, select a book from the unit's book list that deals with one of these items, and read it to the class the day after this activity. When the book is finished, ask the class to identify the item on the list that the book can help them address.

Making up. Have students think of an action for which they are sorry. Then have them write a note or draw a picture for the person the action was against. Write the words "I'm sorry" on the board so students can copy those words onto their paper. After school, have students make sure the intended recipients get their notes.

Acting out. Read and discuss a book listed for this unit. For a social studies lesson on how to behave in various social settings, discuss responsibilities in the following settings and ask students to role-play incidents in which they exercise these responsibilities effectively (e.g., learning at school, helping parents at home, playing with friends). After each role-play, display the quotations and ask students to select one that the role-play demonstrated.

The way out. Have the class create a rap or melodious song using as many quotes as they can read and wish to use. Once the song is complete, have students present it to other classes, or have them divide into smaller groups and present it to other members of their class. Here are some examples of rap songs combining quotations that you could use as samples to open the lesson.

What is right	How a person acts
Is what you feel good after	Speaks louder than words;
and what is bad	He who acts badly ends badly.
Is what you feel bad after	So let's talk it over, and
When I do wrong	Not fight it out
I don't feel good for long.	Our way through is not to pout

Younger students can use:

I end up sad	When I get mad
When I stay mad	I can get glad.

Good rewards. Following the discussion of several quotes, have students list rewards they do receive for good behavior, or make a list on a chart of the rewards students suggest. Reread the list at the end of the lesson.

Working it out together. Have students raise their hands if they feel bad, sad, good, or just O.K. Then pair students who have opposite feelings. For example, a student who feels bad would be paired with a student seated nearby who feels good, a student who feel all right with one who is sad. Next, ask these two students to work together on the next activity and, as they work, to talk about how they feel and why. At the end of the activity, have the pairs discuss with you how their feelings changed as they discussed how they felt and worked with someone else. Conclude the activity by asking students what they have learned about changing negative feelings in the future.

Doing good feels good. Begin a discussion by stating: "Imagine that you were asked to do a chore for someone. You started to do the chore, but after only a few minutes you stopped and began playing instead. While you were playing, the person came back into the room and asked you if you had done the chore. You look up at the person. How do you feel?" Allow volunteers to give their answers, and then continue the scenario. "Now, imagine yourself doing the requested chore. When you are done, the person thanks you. How do you feel?" Allow volunteers to answer, and then conclude the activity by saying the following. "What quotation that we've learned will help you the most when you have chores to do in the future?"

(JW) *Journal writing.* Have students discuss or write about what they think *behaving* means and give some examples. After students have written (or drawn) in their journals about a time they behaved very well and what happened to them, allow those who desire to read their stories. Last, discuss any new ideas students have gained from classmates that they want to use in the future to improve their behavior.

"Getting better every day." Draw a big frowning face on the board. On the face, make a list of general misbehaviors that happen in your classroom. Do not use individual students' names. Have the class discuss better ways to act in similar situations in the future. List these actions on the smiling face beside the complementary negative actions. Last, ask students to draw a smiling face and, on it, to tally the times during the rest of the day when they use better actions.

At the end of the day, discuss what students have learned about the habitual nature of good behavior.

(RRG) *Thinking before we act.* Read *Where the Wild Things Are* by Maurice Sendak. Ask students to discuss one message in the book—that once Max realized he knew how to act properly, his dinner was waiting for him—and answer the following questions:

1. What was a misbehavior Max used, and what good behavior could he have used instead?
2. What were the consequences for him?
3. Were they fair? Why or why not?

Conclude by discussing what students have learned from Max's behavior that they will use throughout their lives. Older students can write about what they have learned.

Turning bad days to good days. Ask for a show of hands of students who have ever thought or said, "I can't believe I did that." Then ask a few of them to describe what prompted that remark, and help them understand that everyone has bad days. Discuss ways to change a bad day into a good day. Read *The Terrible, Horrible, No Good, Very Bad Day* in conjunction with this discussion.

The lie. Show how a lie can hurt someone, even if it is not about a person. Ask students to predict the ending of *What Does It Mean? I'm Sorry* or another book from the book list. Then model ways to express regret.

Teasing hurts. Read *Am I a Bunny?* and discuss how name calling can hurt a person's self-concept. Have students share incidents when their feelings were hurt and what they wish the person would have said instead.

Multicultural Emphasis: Facts from Many Cultures about Eliminating Misbehaviors, Anger, and Behavior Problems

Native Americans. Most tribes have a strict code of behavior. Families tend to handle problems among themselves, but problems involving more than one family were traditionally solved by chiefs. Most Indian tribes were peaceful and willing to exchange their customs and share their resources, but some fought other tribes for food or land. The Navajo and Apache tribes were more likely to fight than most. When Anglo settlers broke their promise to the Native Americans and took their land, these tribes tried to force the Anglos off their territory. Much anger and bitterness resulted from the behaviors on both sides.

Next, share a Native-American story about anger. You may read this story to students. In *The First Strawberries: A Cherokee Story,* illustrated by Anna Vojtech, a renowned Native American storyteller, Joseph Bruchac, retells the Cherokee legend of how strawberries came into the world. The most important part of the story describes the role anger played in the creation of strawberries.

Greece. The Greeks have an interesting word for resolving behavioral matters: *philotimo.* It refers to the self-esteem that governs day-to-day behavior. The male Greek should never lose face in public. As a grown man, he must never disgrace family honor but must defend it at all times.

Greece and Switzerland. In some countries, such as Greece and Switzerland, people may argue with other natives of their country but will rally together if someone outside the country makes disparaging comments about their people or their country. Ask students if they believe Americans are like Greeks and Swiss in this way. Then have students think of situations in the United States in which a group of Americans would rally together to promote something they have in common—for example, school friends banding together to promote their friends or their school, family members supporting each other, state pride.

Switzerland. The Swiss, as a "large family," may argue among themselves. Zurich residents mutter about the "thickheaded" citizens of Basel, and Basel citizens joke about the "down sensibility" of the Zurichers. But outsiders had better not try the same thing. The Swiss will quickly band together and confront any attacking outsider.

Italy. Rivalry is common in the Italian family, but the conviction that an injury to one is an injury to all usually handles the problem. The Roman system of law, dating back to 450 B.C., guaranteed Roman citizens certain rights. These rights continued to expand until, in A.D. 527, Emperor Justinian drew up new ones based on Roman law. Here are some points of Roman law:

- No one suffers a penalty for what he thinks.
- No one may be forcibly removed from his house.
- A father is not a competent witness for a son, nor a son for a father.
- In inflicting penalties, the age and inexperience of the guilty party must be taken into account.

The U.S. Constitution, which has governed us for more than two hundred years, was influenced by Roman law.

Multicultural. The United Nations was established so that all member nations would be able to bring their disagreements before an objective audience. The United Nations was also designed to help communicate world problems and bring a peaceful conclusion to situations affecting single countries. Ask students to recall situations in which the United Nations has helped nations resolve their angry feelings.

African American. Read a book or picture book about slavery. Then ask students to imagine being a slave. The year is 1841, and they must work in the fields from sunrise to sunset. They cannot play or leave their farm at any time. Ask older students to write a diary entry describing their feelings on a single day. For younger students, create a class story and have them write the story in their own handwriting.

Additional evidence of anger in our world is seen in civil wars, wars between nations, riots, and hostile acts like the erection of the Berlin Wall. Long after a war has ended, anger and distrust will remain between some of the people concerned. Ask students to think of ways for people involved in wars to overcome their anger and distrust. If you wish, lead the discussion toward situations in students' lives in which they can overcome anger and distrust on the basis of what they have learned from the quotations, books, and activities in this unit.

Share the following information about ways that different cultures emphasize good behavior. Contrast the behaviors that are valued in each culture.

Indochina. In Indochinese culture, more than in other cultures, children are taught to control their emotions and suppress aggressive behavior.

Thailand. In Thailand, children are taught to speak and work quietly. A common proverb in that culture illustrates the importance that Thai people place upon children behaving properly at all times. Before you share the proverb and its meaning, ask students if they can suggest the intended meaning: "When eating, don't use the spoon or fork to hit the plate or you will starve in the future." ("Don't lose your temper and make a loud noise.")

Laos. Laotian people are characterized as unselfish, uncomplaining, and doing good for others. Laotian people also value quiet and will handle disagreements within the family privately.

Ask students to tell some facts they have learned about anger in this unit and how they will use these ideas in their lives. Students can ask parents or grandparents for more information about how anger was expressed in the history of their culture.

Your Own Additions to the Unit

9 Exhibiting Enthusiasm and Happiness

Learning Objectives *Enthusiasm* is defined as intense and eager interest. The quotations, activities, and books in this unit describe enthusiasm and how it can help people achieve positive purpose and happiness. They also demonstrate how luck, pleasure, joy, and happiness are not accidental but under students' control. Students enjoy learning how literary characters obtain happiness.

Resources *Select a different quotation to discuss and write on the board each day of this unit's study.*

Happiness is free.

We cannot be happy and disruptive at the same time.

To get where you want to be, start where you are.

A happy face makes a happy person.

Let's have a happy day.

I love the way I feel when I'm happy.

Nothing great was ever accomplished without enthusiasm.
—Ralph Waldo Emerson

Birds don't fly because they have wings—
they have wings because they fly.

It is easy to be negative,
it is tempting to be neutral,
it is wisdom to be positive.
—W. A. Ward

This world belongs
to the energetic.
—Ralph Waldo Emerson

Finding the Right Book Concerning Exhibiting Enthusiasm and Happiness to Meet Students' Needs

Difficulty code: I = Introductory; E = Easy; M = Medium

		Book
I	Happiness with what you have	*It Could Always Be Worse* by Margot Zermach
I	Acceptance	*Sniffles* by Robert Larranga
I	Bored pigs find happiness	*Pig Tale* by Helen Oxenbury
I	Crying with happiness	*Sometimes I Like to Cry* by Muriel Stanek
I	Happiness through helping	*What Does It Mean? Help* by Susan Riley
I	Celebrating a birthday	*Happy Birthday to Me* by Anne and Harlow Rockwell
I	Learning to be happy with yourself (a lesson on greed)	*The Moon, the Sun, and the Coyote* by Judith Cole
I	Detailed account of a Mexican-American birthday celebration	*Hello, Amigos!* by Tricia Brown
I	A pleasant introduction to math	*Many Stars* by Camilla Gryski
E	Two boys who make valentines for the whole neighborhood	*One Zillion Valentines* by Frank Modell
E	A child's fantasies inspired by an absent father	*My Father Is Far Away* by Robin Ballard
E–M	Enthusiastic thinking	*Nothing Is Impossible* by D. Aldis
E–M	Encouraging students' enthusiasm about radio plays	*WKID: Easy Radio Plays* by Carol Adorjan and Yuri Rasovsky
E–M	A Grandpa who brings happiness	*Song and Dance Man* by Karen Ackerman
E–M	The joy of family reunions	*At the Crossroads* by Rachel Isadora
E–M	Eight tales that could inspire enthusiasm in students	*Hans Christian Andersen Fairy Tales* by Lisbeth Zwerger
M	A stepfamily is enthusiastic about finding a treasure so they can live in a house left to them	*The Treasure Bird* by Peni Griffin
M	A girl's desire to honor her father turns into a tribute to other servicemen	*Hang Out the Flag* by Katherine M. Marks
M	Determination	*The Tennis Menace* by Alex B. Allen
M	A boy's enthusiasm for music	*New York City Too Far From Tampa Blues* by T. Ernesto Bethancourt (pseud.)

9 EXHIBITING ENTHUSIASM AND HAPPINESS 69

		Book
M	A Native American girl is enthusiastic, month by month	*Alice Yazzie's Year* by Ramona Maher
M	Black folklore interwoven with Black history	*The Magical Adventures of Pretty Pearl* by Virginia Hamilton
M	Enthusiasm of people who were subdued	*The People Could Fly* by Virginia Hamilton
M	A boy who goes back in time and gains enthusiasm about history	*Taking Control* by Ann Love
M	A book baseball players and fans	*Sluggers' Twenty-Seven of Baseball's Greatest* by George Sullivan

Activities to Use with Quotes and Books

Opening the School Day Discussion

Have students share times in their lives when they were most enthusiastic or happy, the conditions that created this emotion, and the effects of being enthusiastic or happy.

(JW) *What is enthusiasm?* Read one of the books mentioned for this unit. When a character is enthusiastic, stop and discuss or have students write about the characteristics of this person, what happened to cause the enthusiasm, and the effects of the person's enthusiasm. After you complete the book, ask students to share their insights about enthusiasm and to describe how the ideas in one of the quotations in this unit increased their ability to become enthusiastic and to share their positive emotions with others.

Music enthusiasts. Play or sing the school song or the national anthem, and ask students how they felt during the performance. Discuss what aspect of music causes enthusiasm and why. Finally, list on the board other types of activities that build students' enthusiasm (e.g. having a new idea, planning a new project), and ask students to identify common characteristics between these events.

Campaign enthusiasm. During a national, state, city, or school campaign or sporting event, have students discuss what created enthusiasm in the people involved. Then ask students what they can use to stimulate enthusiasm for projects they value.

(RRG) *Happiness comes in many ways.* Have enough books on happiness for each group to select a book of its own to read. Ensure that they help each other with words that are unfamiliar. Then let students share what they learned about happiness from the book.

(BLM) *The happy table.* Have students work in pairs to make a book about what makes them happy. Ask students to bring things from home that make them happy and add these things to a table with their books. A sample to use in making books can be found on Blackline Master 4 in the BLM section.

Happy birthday. Have several calendars for children to copy. Have them make a calendar of the month of their birthday. They can make it in any shape they desire, but it must show the numbers and days of the week. They should also write "Happy Birthday" on the square designating the day they were born. At the end of this activity, ask students to describe or write about their happiest birthdays and why these birthdays made them so happy.

Enthusiasm at school. Ask students what activity in school they enjoy most. Divide the class into groups according to the activities they mention. Tell them to agree on one exercise they would like to perform. If you have too many in one activity, divide them into several groups—for example, art into painting, coloring, drawing, and clay, or math into addition, subtraction, and so on. They will have a time during the day in which they get into their different groups and do that activity.

Multicultural Emphasis: Concepts about Enthusiasm and Happiness That Come from Other Cultures

Present the following information about ways enthusiasm is generated in different cultures. Then ask students to describe the colors and types of music that increase enthusiasm in their cultures.

Thailand. In Thailand, colors build enthusiasm. For example, a Thai proverb states that if you wear certain colors on certain days of the week, you will be successful and lucky: Sunday—red, Monday—yellow, Tuesday—pink, Wednesday—green, Thursday—orange, Friday—blue, Saturday—violet. Discuss whether colors generate emotions in other cultures.

(RRG) *Native American.* Native Americans value colorful decor and use color to build positive emotions. For example, they use natural clay dug from creek beds to make pottery, and they dye cloth with vegetable coloring. They use colorful feathers for headdresses, decorate weapons and other prizes, and paint totem poles from big trees or rocks. Read *The Legend of the Indian Paintbrush* by Mischa Damjam, which illustrates numerous things about which Native Americans are enthusiastic. Have students research information about several different tribes. Then divide them into small groups and ask them to draw a totem pole of objects they enjoy. Next, have them create a name for a Native American tribe to which they could belong that would share these joys. Then have them write a paper describing where they lived and the activities in which they engaged. Last, have students present their creations to the class and ask students to think of the different ways music can cause enthusiasm—for example, Native American war dances and rain dances, national anthems, football pep rallies, and the like.

Native Americans have traditionally celebrated happiness through verses similar to the one in William Sleator's *Whale in the Sky,* translated by Ann

Siberell. Children can learn this easily, and motions may be added to the farewell:

> Hogooneh ("So be it").
>
> There shall be happiness before us.
>
> *(Arms stretched out in front.)*
>
> There shall be happiness behind us.
>
> *(Arms stretched behind body.)*
>
> There shall be happiness above us.
>
> *(Arms stretched over head.)*
>
> There shall be happiness below us.
>
> *(Bend and touch the floor.)*
>
> There shall be happiness all around us.
>
> *(Turn around with arms spread out.)*
>
> Words of happiness shall extend from our mouths.
>
> *(Touch lips with both hands and stretch arms outward.)*

Korea. A Korean's first birthday is considered an important one. The custom is to put a variety of items on a birthday table. Each item has a symbolic meaning for the future of the birthday child. The item the child picks up first determines the fate that may await the child at adulthood. For example, a book or pencil portends a teaching career, money will bring wealth, and a thread points to a long and prosperous life.

Vietnam. The Vietnamese have two birthdays, the actual date of their birth and a second celebrated at the lunar New Year. They also enjoy poetry and have used it for centuries at times of happiness. As in many other cultures cradle songs are some of the first poetry Vietnamese children experience.

Hispanic culture. Background information on birthday celebrations in Hispanic culture are shown well in Lila Pert's *Candles, Cakes, and Donkey Tails: Birthday Symbols and Celebrations.* If there are Hispanic pupils in class, see if their celebrations resemble those described in this book.

Jamaican. The Chalk Doll by Charlotte Pomerantz will give students a good idea of Jamaican childhood through the stories a mother tells her daughter about events the author experienced as a child. The full-page paintings capture scenes of her Jamaican childhood.

Greenland. Tobias Has a Birthday *by Ole Hertz* not only gives the students a traditional Greenland birthday celebration, but also portrays other aspects of Greenland culture, with a map of a village included. Two more in Tobias's series are *Tobias Goes Ice Fishing* and *Tobias Catches Trout,* both by Ole Hertz.

Your Own Additions to the Unit

10 Following Directions: Rules and Guidelines

Learning Objectives A common complaint among students is that they are "disorganized." The quotations, books, and activities in this unit teach students how to set guidelines and work within rules. This unit can be taught at the beginning of the year to empower students to work with you in creating a classroom community.

Resources *Select a different quotation to discuss and write on the board each day of this unit's study.*

Be safe, not sorry!

Rules help us get along.

*Know how to play by the rules, and
The fun of it is yours.*

*If you can organize,
time will be on your side.*

*Good rules let us
have a happy day.*

*If there were no rules, the
world would be full of fools.*

*Rules are not just for you;
They tell everyone what to do.*

*Guidelines point the way
for all to have a great day.*

*Before proceeding with any difficult task,
stop and think, organize, then remember
to get started again.*
—William Ward

*I've got a problem.
That's good I'll organize first
and then my job will be half done.*

One who loses his aim doubles his efforts.
—Santayana

One way we succeed in life is by having structure.

Finding the Right Book Concerning Following Directions: Rules and Guidelines to Meet Students' Needs

Difficulty code: I = Introductory; E = Easy; M = Medium

		Book
I	Personal space	*My Body Is Private* by Linda Girard
I	Not following rules	*Goldilocks* retold by Ian Paul Robinson
I	Art activity	*Don't Touch!* by Suzy Kline
I	How prejudice effects judgment	*A Look at Prejudice and Understanding* by Rebecca Anders
I	Human differences	*Like Me* by Alan Beightman
I	Rules	*I Dare You!* by Judith Conaway
I	What families should be	*All Kinds of Families* by Norma Simon
I	Being nosey and rude	*Karen's Witch* by Ann Martin
I	The rule to go to bed is OK	*I Do Not Want to Go to Bed* by Astrid Lindgren
I	Denying one's grief	*I Don't Care* by Marjorie Sharmat
E	Disobeying the rules	*Myra* by Barbara Bottner
E	A clever hen who outwits a fox and sees her guidelines used	*Stove Soup* by Tony Ross
E	Problems of being a hostess	*I Do Not Like It When My Friend Comes to Visit* by Ivan Sherman
E	Organizing a mess	*Just a Mess* by Mercer Mayer
E	Poor organizing for a trip	*Not the Piano, Mrs. Medley!* by Evan Levine
E	Putting things in order	*The Queen's Holiday* by Margaret Wild
E–M	Becoming a leader in organizing helps girl realize she is growing up	*Phoebe* by Marilyn Kaye
E–M	Keeping an amusement park operating	*Behind the Scenes at the Amusement Park* by Elizabeth Van Steenwyk
M	How baseball began	*The Story of Baseball* by Lawrence Ritter
M	Father and son searching for a name on the Vietnam Memorial Wall	*The Wall* by Eve Bunting
M	Facts, projects, checklists, and a how-to section on organizing projects	*Save the Earth* by Betty Miles

			Book
	M	Solving things the best way she can, with disastrous results	*Anastasia on Her Own* by Lois Lowry
	M	Buz organizes a soccer team	*Soccer Hero* by Mike Neigoff
	M	The story of a union organizer for the miners	*Trouble at the Mines* by Doreen Rappaport
	M	An eleven-year-old who starts a business needs better organization	*Kid Power* by Susan Beth Pfeffer

Activities to Use with Quotes and Books

Opening the School Day Discussion

Create a new classroom rule or ask students to select an established rule to emphasize throughout the day. At subsequent morning message periods, ask students to read a new quote and to describe how following yesterday's rule made the classroom a better place for everyone. Each day of the unit's study emphasis a new rule for which everyone will pay special attention during the day.

Doing what's right. Read *Karen's Witch* by Ann Martin or another book from this unit. Point out how Karen [or another main character] was scolded for being nosey and rude or disobeyed. Ask questions such as the following: 1. What did Karen do wrong? 2. What was her consequence? 3. What could Karen have done to get her questions answered and still be right?

(JW) *Journal writing.* Students write the class rule they like best and why.

Making playground rules. Have students discuss rules they would like to follow during recess. When each student suggests a rule, ask them to tell why he/she wants that rule. Then have the class vote before the rule is written on the chart. After students implement the rules on the playground, discuss how the rules helped or hindered in making recess more fun.

Rules adults must follow at work. Describe a few of the rules you follow as a teacher. Ask students to tell why these rules help you be a better teacher. Then have students ask family members or workers at school about rules they follow at work. Discuss the answers they receive as a class and why each rule was needed.

You are the teacher. Have students discuss the following scenario: You are a teacher ready to organize a day for your class. Write on the board their suggestions for better ways to organize activities. Then ask students to suggest things to alter or eliminate from the daily schedule and have them defend their suggestions. Prioritize their list by voting, and implement one or more of their ideas. At the end of a month, ask students to evaluate the effects of their suggestions on the class's productivity.

(BLM) *Looking at your room at home.* Have students form small groups and visualize their rooms. How could they organize their rooms to benefit them better? For example, is the light located well enough for them to study? Are their closets organized so they can find outfits easily? Do they have a convenient place for their school materials, hobby supplies, play equipment, and dirty clothes? Ask students to make a list of changes they would like to make (even a drawing of their room if they want to rearrange furniture). After they get permission from their parents, have them make the changes they desire. Then, in one week, ask students to write about how the changes helped them and share their results in journal entries that can be displayed in the room to give classmates additional ideas for future improvements to their rooms. Blackline Master 19 in BLM section is a sample floor plan on which students can draw their newly organized rooms. Blackline Masters 20 and 21 in BLM section is a furniture and floor plan that they can use to simulate the layout of their room. (You could also use this activity and Blackline Master 21 in BLM section for students to rearrange the classroom.)

Organizing my locker. Complete the foregoing activity, only using students' lockers at school as the subject.

What organization means. Discuss one or more of the quotations, and ask the following questions:

- How and why is organization important?
- How many times have you misplaced your pencil or other school supplies?
- How much time have you wasted looking for things you needed or wanted?
- What does prioritizing do to increase organization of materials and to organize your things?
- How do people know exactly what they want to accomplish first and what is needed?

At the end of the discussion, ask students to meet in groups and write a quotation from the unit, a slogan, or an advertising campaign that depicts what they learned, and to share their work with the class at the end of the period.

(RRG) *What unorganized means.* Divide students into small groups, ask them to select from the following list, and have them make a short skit about the situation, to be performed in front of the class. Explain that each group must have an example of using some of the principles of organization they have learned from the quotes or books in this unit. The topics for the skits are as follows:

1. *Organizing a team at recess:* Your first person wants to play football and be captain, but you only have a kickball. You do not know who would be best for each position, and you have only fifteen minutes to organize the team and begin the game.

2. *A group project is not done:* Each student in the group didn't complete it because of lack of organization and the project has to be complete by the end of the day.

3. *Getting ready for school:* Each student assumes one of the following roles—getting ready for school, fixing breakfast for a younger child, taking other people to school. Each is unorganized.

After each group's presentation, list the strategies students demonstrated that could have increased the organization in each situation. Before you begin this activity, members of the class could read *Success Hero, Trouble at the Mines, Save the Earth,* or other books in this unit that describe strategies of organization.

Nature's organization. Plan nature walks and, at the beginning of each season, take the early morning walks along the same route. Take a box or bag for the children to pick up treasures along the way. Also take magnifying glasses so students may view small creatures and look for signs of the season—the clothing people wear, ice, smoke from chimneys, steam from the mouth, wet or dry windows, trees, flowers, insects, clothes hanging on the line. When you return to class, ask students to report their findings on how nature organizes herself.

(BLM) *Organizing a game.* Ask students to form small groups to invent a game and the rules and guidelines that govern it. Allow students to play each other's games. Gameboards on Blackline Masters 13 and 14 (in BLM section) can be used for this activity.

Our own class rules. Allow students to give ideas on rules that should govern the classroom. For each rule, discuss the pros and cons of implementing it in class. Then write the rules, consequences, and rewards the class has established on a chart, and allow students to write about what these rules will enable their class to attain. At the end of the period, have students share what they've written with the class.

(BLM) *My time is organized.* Ask students to list as many ways as they can that they have not wasted time. Tell them to write out a time schedule of how better not to waste their day, and how much money they would have saved if they had not wasted their time. Some students may enjoy it if you actually pass out play money and have them "put money in" if they wasted time and "take money out" if they didn't waste time on their assignments that day. Once students have listed ways that they have not wasted time for a week, have them write out a time schedule of how better not to waste time in their day. Blackline Masters 22 and 23 (in the BLM section) are designed to be used with this activity.

(JW) *Journal writing.* Near the end of this unit, ask students to apply strategies they have learned to a specific aspect of their life that is disorganized. Then, have them write a one-month plan in which they use as many specific actions and strategies as possible to overcome their disorganization, and to describe at least five actions they will take during the month. At the end of four weeks, ask students to return to this journal entry and evaluate their success.

Multicultural Emphasis on Following Directions: Rules and Guidelines Followed in Other Cultures

Native American. Native Americans know the rules and guidelines of their family. It is a disgrace for anyone not to obey them. A simple "I'm sorry" is rarely enough to regain lost respect.

Greece. The family is the center of Greek society. Both parents generally are lenient toward their children. Greek men try never to lose face in public. They try never to disgrace their family honor but always to defend it. Young boys receive special pampering.

Multicultural. Every culture has its own rules and guidelines that are made for the improvement of individual people and the group. When rules are not followed, stronger rules may be made in an attempt to protect the majority. To let children get a clear idea of the importance of rules and guidelines, compare the process to cooking. The following book can be used to introduce the variety of foods eaten in different ethnic groups while teaching the value of following cooking guidelines, rules, and directions carefully: *The Little Cooks: Recipes from Around the World for Boys and Girls,* adapted by Eve Tharlet.

Mexican American. Students from all cultures enjoy learning about the types of games and rules that were followed by older generations. *Juegos de Ayer y de Hoy* by Maria Claret describes such rules as they existed in Mexican-American culture. It is an interesting book comparing games that grandparents played in past times with those that children play today.

Germany. Let's Travel in West Germany, edited by Fran Dyre, illustrates the value Germans hold for organization. Characteristic German values are cleanliness and orderliness, and these are carried over to business and political dealings. Detailed reports or systems were typical of businesses in the former West Germany. Now, with the dismantling of the Berlin Wall that divided Germany, East Germany is displaying the same organizational skills as it attempts to rebuild.

Your Own Additions to the Unit

11 Getting Along with Others

Learning Objectives   In this unit, students need to acquire the ability to work and learn together. Many children learn to share in kindergarten and first and second grade. The quotations, activities, and books in this unit teach students that getting along with others involves bringing things together to benefit all. It can mean sharing objects, experiences, and pleasures. Students also learn how to maintain a supportive and productive group climate and how to strengthen their interpersonal relationships.

Resources   *Select a different quotation to discuss and write on the board each day of this unit's study.*

Sharing makes one happy.

None but a fool is always right.

Be gentle and you can be bold.
—Chinese philosopher

Isn't it fun to be you and share all that you can do?

If you can share, you can grow.

Take the trouble to serve people rather than to impress them.

A rejected opportunity to give is a lost opportunity to receive.

A better me will make a better you.

Am I not destroying my enemies when I make friends of them?
—Abraham Lincoln

Forgiveness is the attribute of the strong.
—Mahatma Gandhi

*Those who bring sunshine to the life of others
cannot keep it from themselves.*
—J. Barrie

*Of all the awkward people in your house, there is only
one whom you can improve very much.*
—C. S. Lewis

*Who is wise?
He that learns from everyone.*
—Ben Franklin

*One of us may do more than
Another of us, but none
Us can do more than
All of us together.*

Finding the Right Book Concerning Getting Along with Others to Meet Students' Needs

Difficulty code: I = Introductory; E = Easy; M = Medium

		Book
I	How we all share	*We All Share* by Dorothy Corey
I	Siblings	*Will There Be a Lap for Me?* by Dorothy Corey
I	Sharing with others	*Everybody Takes Turns* by Dorothy Corey
I	Sharing stories	*Aunt Flossie's Hat* by Elizabeth Howard
I	Sharing work	*Doing Things Together* by Carol and Elizabeth James Barkin
I	Rivalry	*Gus and Buster Work Things Out* by Andrew Bromin
I	The meaning of giving	*The Best Train Set Ever* by Patricia Hutchins
I	Verses about sharing	*What Does It Mean? Sharing* by Susan Riley
I	Sharing with others	*Mine, Yours, Ours* by Burton Albert
I	Show and tell	*What Mary Jo Shared* by Anne Tompret
I	Sharing as part of friendship	*Best Friends for Frances* by Russell Hoban
I	Poetry to share	*Taking Turns: Poetry to Share* collected by Bernice Wolman
I	Sharing and appreciating nature	*One Step, Two . . .* by Charlotte Zolotow
E	Sharing and understanding emotions (four stories)	*Stories from Snowing Meadows* by Carla Stevens
E	The meaning of giving	*Tim and the Red Indian Headdress* by Geraldine Kaye
E	Feelings between siblings	*Princess Pooh* by Kathleen M. Muldoon
E	Understanding and empathizing with elders' memory loss	*Wilfrid Gordon MacDonald Partridge* by Mem Fox
E	Lack of consideration for other's feelings	*Crow Boy: Sign of the Beaver* by Taro Yashima
E	How the youngest in a family gained confidence	*Adams Key* by Eleanor F. Lattimore
E	African American facing racial prejudice	*Song of the Trees* by Mildred Taylor
E	Getting along with friends	*Marinka, Katinka and Me (Susie)* by Winifred Madison

		Book
E	How a girl finds a need for her six-year-old brother	*Getting Rid of Roger* by Ellen Matthews
E–M	Family bonding	*Mom, the Wolfman, and Me* by Norma Klein
E–M	Multicultural bonding	*Black like Kyra, White like Me* by Judith Vigna
E–M	Seeing the good in others	*The Tenth Good Thing about Barney* by Judith Viorst
M	Patience	*All It Takes Is Practice* by Betty Miles
M	Human relations	*Tulla's Summer* by Rose Lagercrantz
M	Wanting everyone to like you	*Last Was Lloyd* by Doris Smith
M	The doctrine of nonviolence	*I Have a Dream: The Life and Words of Martin Luther King, Jr.* by Jim Haskins

Activities to Use with Quotes and Books

Opening the School Day Discussion

Remind students that most people they meet in life will be ordinary individuals who often do extraordinary things. This is why they should look inside others to find what is truly exceptional. Through sharing parts of yourself, you can see others more clearly.

(BLM) *Our advice book.* Teach students the following to help them get along with others in groups:

1. Do forced turn taking if necessary to set up equality. Forced turn taking requires that each person takes a turn to comment on an idea before anyone else can make a second comment. All members have the right to say, "I pass." If too much passing becomes a problem, go back and examine what you can do to make the climate safer.

2. When there is a dispute in a group, let one person go first and have a second person goes first the next time.

3. Do not be sidetracked by excuses.

4. At the end of each group session, they should implement one agreed-upon action immediately to maintain the group's enthusiasm.

5. Avoid conflicts by requiring both people in a dispute to generate two ways to resolve the issue. In this way, each person cannot commit to only one position, and this will make compromises easier.

6. Focus on only one issue at a time.

Then, ask students to give examples of times when they have witnessed the positive effects of some of these strategies for getting along with others in group situations. You may also wish to videotape students in one of their small-group meetings in a content area before and after this lesson to judge whether their skills of getting along well are greatly improved.

Last, ask students to make an Advice Book about what they have learned about group work. This book can be duplicated and placed in the school library and in classroom libraries of peers in other groups. Blackline Master 4, in the BLM section, is a book pattern to use for this activity.

(JW) *Journal writing.* Ask students to discuss the quotation and to think of how they have "brought sunshine to the lives of others." Then ask them to (1) think about people who have brought sunshine into their lives, (2) describe these people and incidents in a formal piece of writing which they edit, and (3) share final drafts in an Author's Chair at the end of the lesson.

Improving myself. Write the following quote on the board: "Of all the people in your house, there is only one whom you can improve very much." Then ask students to write one thing they could do to improve themselves. Next, divide students into groups of four to compare what they wrote. Ask them to identify commonalities, explain their findings to the class, tell their reasons for wanting to improve, and discuss how they plan to do it.

(RRG) *Making my day.* Have students read a book from this unit. Then divide them into small groups to share something they learned about getting along with others. After all have shared, have students write how they will apply points from their discussion to their lives.

(JW) *Journal writing.* Read *The Big Block of Chocolate* by Janet Slater Redhead or another book from this unit. Discuss: Who got to eat the chocolate? Why? What do you like to share? With whom? Then ask students to draw or write about something they like to share.

Sharing. Each child receives a paper shopping bag to take home and fill with things that are important to him or her. Next, have students describe the contents of the bag to the rest of the class and tell why each item is important to them.

Sharing poetry. Read *Taking Turns: Poetry to Share* by Bernice Wolman. On the first day, introduce the book and allow students to choose the poems they wish to learn. Explain that students will practice reading the poems in a learning center with you and/or a classmate. Then they will share their poems with classmates. On the second day, students answer: (1) How did sharing with your classmates help you to learn? (2) What did you learn about sharing that is important? Last, have students draw pictures and/or write what they liked about their poem and the sharing experience.

Group sharing. Have groups discuss and write five ways that their group will try to share more. Have younger students do this as a whole class discussion, with you writing items on the board.

A sharing station. Set up sharing stations with games all around the room. Have students visit different stations while sharing games and toys. Then ask one child to be in charge of each center to teach sharing, show others how to play the game, and model sharing. This will develop that student's leadership skills.

(BLM) *Letter swap.* Divide students into four groups and give each student a list of words to spell. Each student also receives the number of laminated letters that are contained in a few of these words, but no student receives all the letters needed to spell their words. Tell students they must share and swap letters until every member of the group has correctly spelled his or her word. Start by writing the words on the board. Blackline Master 18, in the BLM Section, has all the letters in these words: *as, at, on, joy, water, dog, apple, bird, drink, cake, milk, fog, exit, very, soup, chair, boy, quick, zoo.* There are 70 letters on the Blackline Master, with at least one of every letter of the alphabet. If this Blackline Master is laminated, the letters can also be used in other word games.

Sharing with others. During a holiday, have students make pictures, cards, poems, toys, colored Easter eggs, or something similar. Then they can go on a field trip to share what they have done with children who are in the hospital during that holiday.

We can share. Read the book *We All Share* by Dorothy Corey. Discuss the things the children in the book were sharing. Ask students to tell some things that they can share. Write the sentence, "I can share _____" on the chalkboard and read the sentence together. Then have each student write one sentence on a piece of paper and fill in the blank with whatever they would like to share—for example, "I can share my book." Then ask them to draw a picture to illustrate their sentence. Put all the papers together and make a class book entitled "We Can Share." Place the book in the reading center.

(RRG) *Working together.* Remind the students that they have been talking about sharing and getting along with others this week, and that today's lesson will require them to use their sharing skills. Have the students work in groups of four. Each group is given a posterboard, newspaper, two pairs of scissors, two bottles of glue, and other miscellaneous items. Have students decide on an object they want to make and then make it. The object should relate to one of the books you've read from this unit or to a science or social studies theme they are studying. When they are finished, each group presents its object to the class. After all the presentations are complete, have students discuss what they learned and the benefits of sharing and getting along with others as they worked together.

Multicultural Emphasis: Concepts about Getting Along with Others That Come from Many Cultures

China. Read the book *Chinatown Sunday, The Story of Lillia* by Carol Boles. The story is about a ten-year-old Chinese girl living in Chicago. In this book, students will learn ways they are like her and ways they are different. They discuss actions that they can take to help people from different cultures and backgrounds get along better and feel more comfortable in a new school.

Many Chinese fathers left their families in the late 1800s and early 1900s to come to America in order to find a better life for their families. The plan was to come ahead of their families, who would follow after the father had made enough money to send for them. How these fathers were treated and how they lived in America are well told in *Dragonwings* and *Child of the Devil,* both by Laurence Yep. Discuss the differences and similarities between the United States and China today.

Germany and Italy. In the era of the Roman Empire, Romans spread their power toward the Germanic tribes and a clash began. Then an alliance was made between them, and the wealthy Romans built several cities in Germanic land. Ask students to (1) research this period in history to identify how these two groups of people learned to work together, and (2) share their findings with the class.

Mexican American. Mexican culture began as a sharing of the Aztec Indian and Spanish ways. In the nineteenth century, English-speaking explorers added another element to the culture, but the Spanish-Aztec culture continued to dominate because these two groups had learned to coexist through sharing. The following books depict other ways Mexican Americans and other cultures share:

> Alberti/Wolfsgruber. *Simon y Los Animales.* Spain: Ediciones S.M., 1987. In this well-illustrated story, Simon finds that the noses on his snowmen are missing. When he discovers they were taken by hungry animals, he compassionately feeds the animals.
>
> Flores, Rosa. *Caracolitos: Me Siento Feliz al Ayudar.* Oklahoma: Economy Company, 1979. A young boy becomes aware of the importance of helping others.
>
> Larreula, Enrica. *Las dos Nubes Amigas.* Spain: Editorial Teide, 1984. Two friendly clouds spend their days together enjoying all the seasons of the year. They have a wonderful time until one day they are separated by a storm.
>
> Diaz, Oralia A. *Los Condijitos de Don Julio.* Guatemala: Editorial Santa Piedra, 1984. Generous Don Julio takes pride in sharing his rabbits with his nieces.
>
> D'Atri, Adriana. *Asi Son los Abuelos Que Viven Cerca.* Spain: Editorial Altea, 1977. Clara and Enrique share their experiences with an attentive grandpa and grandma who live nearby. After reading these books, students can understand the importance of sharing joys and responsibilities with family members. Have students bring photographs of family members and make a class family album. Students can also place their photographs on 8fi" ˜ 11" sheets of construction paper and may write descriptive captions. The following caption is used as well: "*Estale es mi* _____." ("This is my _____.")

If recording student-dictated captions, type them or use a yellow or light pink marking pen. Then have students trace their sentences and read them to you or to a partner.

During Mother's Day or another holiday period, discuss the concept of teamwork and the things for which students are appreciative of their parents. They can write these descriptions beginning in Spanish (*Un papa es . . . Un mama es . . .*) and send thank you cards to family members.

Your Own Additions to the Unit

12 Giving Kindness

Learning Objectives — Sometimes students demonstrate traits of selfishness and hoarding. The quotations, activities, and books in this unit enable students to become more sympathetic, friendly, and generous, and to learn the benefits of being kind to themselves and others.

Resources — *Select a different quotation to discuss and write on the board each day of this unit's study.*

Kindness is giving.

Kindness is the beginning and the end of the law.
—Hebrew proverb

Bring kindness into your heart.

*Kindness, when shown, radiates
like the warmth of the sun.*

Be kind and you'll be fine.

Kindness in giving creates love.
—Lao-Tzu (604–531 B.C.)

He who acts badly ends badly.

When you give, give of yourself.

*When I share, the remainder multiplies
and grows, but only what is done in love lasts.*
—A. J. Russell

*The best portion of a good life is the little,
nameless, unremembered acts of kindness we give away*
—William A. Ward

*I will not play at tug o'war,
I'd rather play at hug o'war.
Where everyone hugs instead of tugs,
Where everyone kisses and everyone grins,
And everyone cuddles, and everyone wins.*
—Shel Silverstein

Finding the Right Book Concerning Giving Kindness to Meet Students' Needs

Difficulty code: I = Introductory; E = Easy; M = Medium

		Book
I	Love for one's family	*Nana Upstairs and Nana Downstairs* by Tomie De Paola
I	Teasing	*Never Tease a Weasel* by Jean Soule
I	Envy and treating others with kindness	*I Wish I Were Sick Too* by Franz Brandenberg
I	Mother–son relationship	*I Love You Forever* by Robert N. Munsch
I	Kindness with friends (cassettes)	*Frog and Toad* by Arnold Lobel
I	Solving problems with kindness	*Feona's Bee* by Beverly Lou Keller
I	Consideration	*Be My Valentine* by Miriam Cohen
I	Respect	*Magic and the Night River* by Anne Evelyn Bunting
I	A toy bear friend	*The Winter Bear* by Ruth Craft
I	Pig finds kindness and love	*Perfect the Pig* by Susan Jeschke
I	How kindness brings out the best	*Rose Meets Mr. Wintergarden* by Bob Graham
I	Mother and daughter take a walk	*Say It!* by Charlotte Zolotow
I–E	Japanese fisherman shows kindness through birds	*Magic and the Night River* by Anne Evelyn Bunting
E	Indian legends about kindness	*Dream Wolf* by Paul Goble
E	Children help	*Another Mouse to Feed* by Robert Kraus
E	Kindness toward a grandmother	*Mandy's Grandmother* by Liesel Moak Skorpen
E	Kindness to dolphins	*Dolphin Adventure* by W. Grover
E	Kindness to animals	*Rabbit Hill* by Robert Lawson
E	Respect for wildlife (wordless picture book)	*The Hunter and the Animals* by Tomie de Paola
E	Emily Deckinson's poetry and kindness	*Emily* by Michael Bedard
E	Activities a child and grandmother do together	*Grandma According to Me* by Karen Beil
E–M	Family's response to a girl whose best friend deserts her	*Rainbow in the Twelfth Row* by Anne Marie Drew
E–M	Two youngsters examine their feelings about handicapped boy	*Stay Away from Simon* by Carol Carrick
M	Helping create a celebration	*Mr. McFadden's Halloween* by Rumer Godden

		Book
M	The value of families	*Circles* by Wilmer C. Jones
M	Putting personal danger aside to help others	*Flame-Colored Taffeta* by Rosemary Sutcliff
M	Risking punishment to help	*Summer of my German Soldier* by Bette Greene
M	Understanding a boy in a foster home who befriended a stray cat	*The Cat Was Left Behind* by Carole Schwerdtfeger
M	Helping friends	*Twenty and Ten* by Claire Huchet Bishop
M	African American girl trying to fit in at a private girl's school	*Maizon at Blue Hill* by Jacqueline Woodson
M	Kindness in a relationship brings conformity	*The Laser* by Elizabeth Allen
M	Looking at life from different perspectives	*M. E. and Morton* by Sylvia Cassedy

Activities to Use with Quotes and Books

Opening the School Day Discussion

Ask students to recall kind acts people did for them. Have a few students share their experiences each day. On the last day of the week, ask students why they think society is not as kind as it could be and what they want to do to make society kinder.

(RRG) *Giving kindness.* Define *kindness*. Then read *The Giving Tree* or another book from this unit. Discuss what the tree and the little boy in the story did that was kind. Next ask students how they think the tree and the boy felt throughout the book. Last, ask each student to write the message about giving kindness the author was trying to convey in the book and share students' interpretations with the class.

(JW) *Journal writing.* Have students describe times when they gave something to someone else without expecting anything in return, and how they felt.

(RRG) *Kindness is everywhere.* Have the entire class listen while you read a book from this unit or newspaper article about someone or a group of people doing something kind for others in a natural disaster such as a hurricane or flood, relief work, a heroic rescue, or a group getting together and repairing and repainting houses in a depressed neighborhood. Then ask students to bring articles from a magazine or newspapers about someone or a group who helped another person or group. Ask them to write a three- or four-sentence synopsis of their article. Last, display articles and synopses on a bulletin board depicting the theme of kindness.

Our kind project. In small groups, have students brainstorm about projects they could do to show kindness to others. Ask each group to select their best project, and have the class vote on one they all want to do. Then plan how to put it into action. After the project is complete, ask students to write their personal contribution to it, how they felt, and how the other person or persons felt when the kindness came. If you do not do the project, ask students to write about a time they were kind and a time when someone was kind to them, and how they and others felt.

Make someone feel better. Before you begin this activity, have students make a nonbaked candy—for example, combining M&M's, bridge mix, and coconut. Then, ask students to think of someone at home who had a bad day the day before. Have the student write this person a letter to help make him or her feel better, and then take the candy and the letter home to the person.

(BLM) *Kindness has many meanings.* Tape a piece of posterboard onto the chalkboard with the word *kindness* written on it. Explain that to gain a better understanding of the quotes, students will construct a semantic map using a strategy called *webbing*. Then ask them to say as many words as possible that relate to kindness. Write these words on the poster with a marker, stemming each one from the central word, *kindness*. Blackline Master 24, in the BLM section, can be enlarged for this activity (and other webbing lessons throughout the book) by writing out the word *kindness* and inserting it or another concept in the center of the web.

Kind actions. On an overhead projection sheet, list the kind actions students experienced or saw the day before. Tell them that they will take a few minutes at the opening of this unit's study each day to continue making this list. Explain that this will not only help them to see and do kind acts, but also make them more aware of acts of kindness around them. On the first day of this activity, ask students to predict how many items the class can list by the end of the unit. On the last day, compare the actual number to the predicted one.

(RRG) *Semantic webbing.* Read several unit quotes and books from this unit. Talk about the meaning of the quotes and books. Then, in groups of four to five, have the children read a book from this unit together about a family whose members comfort each other. Have them discuss in their groups their definition of *kindness* and how it can be expressed in a family.

The definition of kindness. Ask the class for their definition of *kindness*. Then read the dictionary definition. Write down all the new words that children used that they may not be able to read. Expand by explaining the *ness* suffice and how it can be added to other words. List words that end in *ness*.

Special person of the week. Each week, have the class select a new person on Friday to be featured on the bulletin board for the following week. Tell them the decision should be determined by actions of kindness and character displayed during the entire week. Create a special section on the bulletin board for this.

Multicultural Emphasis: Concepts That Depict Kindness in Many Cultures

Multicultural. The following books describe kindness as it is expressed in six different cultures. Students can select the book of greatest interest to them and report to classmates about their culture's definition of, value placed on, and examples of kindness.

M	*Meet the North American Indians* by Elizabeth Payne
E–M	*Let's Visit Thailand* by Francis Wilkens
E	*Africa* by D. V. Georges (A New True Book)
E–M	*Our Friends in Viet-Nam* by Inor Forney and E. H. Forney
M	*And It Is Still That Way: Legends told by Arizona Indian Children* by Byrd Baylor
E–M	*Kwanzaa: Origin, Concepts, and Practice.* by Dr. Maulana Karenga. Los Angeles: Kawaida Publications, 1977. Dr. Karenga is the founder of Kwanzaa.
E–M	Walter, Mildred Pitts. *Have a Happy . . . A Novel* An African-American youth prepares for Kwanzaa and the happiness it brings.
E–M	Alonso, Fernando. *El Arbol Que no Tenia Hojas.* Spain: Santillana, S.A., 1975. A leafless tree learns he is ugly and asks the elements for help. The elements cannot help, but through the kindness of thoughtful children, he becomes a beautiful tree.

Korea. In Korea, a day in spring is designated as Teachers' Day. On this day, students give their teachers a corsage of flowers together with another gift. They also write notes thanking teachers for their education. You could bring a special vase to class and tell students about this above custom. Ask them if they want this vase to mark a spot to place notes and questions they design for you. They can put their notes there throughout the year.

Your Own Additions to the Unit

---

13 Improving Myself

Learning Objectives The quotations, activities, and books in this unit help students improve so they become the best that they can be.

Resources *Select a different quotation to discuss and write on the board each day of this unit's study.*

Be able to laugh at yourself.

Be all you can be.

I can be a better me.

Just be me and I will be.

Your limitations are up to you.

Isn't it fun to just be you,
Being proud of all you can do!

Every day in every way I am getting better and better.

Aim for the top,
Allow for the drop.

When looking in the mirror, be proud of the view.

It won't slow down for me, so I'll have to catch up with it!

A person completely wrapped up
in himself makes a small package.

All improvement is founded on tolerance.
—George Bernard Shaw

Attempt the impossible in order to improve your work.
—Bette Davis

Our chief want in life is for someone to make us do what we can,
But the best thing is to make ourselves do it.

And so, my fellow Americans, ask not what your country
can do for you, ask what you can do for your country.
—John Kennedy

Finding the Right Book Concerning Improving Myself to Meet Students' Needs

Difficulty code: I = Introductory; E = Easy; M = Medium

		Book
I	Improving one's life against the odds	*Picture Book of Helen Keller* by David Adler
I	Emotions	*Something on My Mind* by Nikki Grimes
I	Conquering a feeling of invisibility	*How I Faded Away* by Janice May Udry
I	Children's emotions	*I Am Not a Crybaby* by Norma Simon
I	Children's emotions	*How Do I Feel?* by Norma Simon
I	The importance of being yourself	*Dandelion* by Don Freeman
I	Capturing every day for happiness	*Benjamin's 365 Birthdays* by Judi Barrett
I	Not giving up on yourself	*The Fastest Quitter in Town* by Phyllis Green
I	The dangers of pride	*Osa's Pride* by Ann Grifalconi
I	Logic and identity	*Duckat* by Gaelyn Gordon
I	Realizing the special talents he contributes to others	*Nick Joins In* by Joe Lasker
I	Trying to outdo one another almost ends in disaster	*Look What I Can Do* by Jose Aruego
I	Overcoming anxiety	*The School Mouse* by Dorothy Harris
I	Finding out if she really wants to do something, she can	*Will I Ever Be Good Enough?* by Judith Conaway
I–E	Improvements people want to make in other people	*I'll Fix Anthony* by Judith Viorst
E	Discovering that love means allowing independence	*Island Baby* by Holly Keller
E	Twenty fables of a trickster who becomes wiser with each adventure	*Doctor Coyote: A Native American Aesop's Fables* by John Bierhorst
E	On one's own	*George on His Own* Laurie Lawlor
E	Fear of making an oral presentation	*Donna Jean's Disaster* by Barbara William
E	Handling disappointment	*The Cardboard Clown* by Clyd Bulla
E	One method for self-improvement	*I'm Terrific* by Marjorie W. Sharmat
E–M	Results of using drugs and overcoming drug dependence	*Johnny Cash* by Paula Taylor
E–M	Learning things to appreciate about oneself	*I Like Me* by Nancy Carlson
E–M	Gaining self-confidence through loving a pet	*The Singing Hill* by Meindert De Jong

		Book
E–M	A strategy for improvement	*Tell Me Your Best Thing* by Anna Grossnickle Hines
E–M	Improving the self-image of a boy ashamed of his glasses	*The Fourth Grade Four* by Marily Levinson
E–M	A boy who hides his knitting from his friends	*Knitwits* by William Taylor
M	Discipline, fresh air, and hard work transform four spoiled sisters	*The Exiles* by Hilary McKay
M	Finding a new role in life	*D.J.'s Worst Enemy* by Emil Weiss
M	Historical figures who had a positive impact on others	*The Road to Damietta* by Scott O'Dell
M	Self-esteem	*The Cat Ate My Gymsuit* by Paula Danziger
M	Values and jealousy	*Connie* by Anne Alexander
M	Bigotry and patience with interracial parents	*All It Takes Is Practice* by Betty Miles
M	Determination gained through self-confidence	*Shape Up Burke* by Richard Shaw
M	Understanding the problems of growing up	*Wait for Me* by Susan Shreve
M	Positive role models for self-improvement (Native-American biographies)	*Daisy Hooee Nampeyo* by Carol Fowler
M	Finding importance	*Time Flies!* by Florence Heide

Activities to Use with Quotes and Books

Opening the School Day Discussion

(BLM) Have students set unit goals and check results at end of study. Discuss how goals not met could be accomplished. Discuss the importance of editing and how to do it. Then write the steps to revising on the board. Next, have students divide into groups and edit a one-page story they wrote previously. Ask students to exchange stories with others in their groups to assess each other's editing. When they have finished, have them complete the self-evaluation form on Blackline Master 25 in BLM section.

Self-discovery. Read *I'm Terrific* by Marjorie Weinman Sharmat or another book from this section. This book talks about the idea of self-discovery, as a child discovers who he is and what makes him special by becoming friends with children who are different from him. When you have finished reading the book, have students apply its strategies to their lives.

(JW) *Journal writing.* Read one of the quotations and books from this section that relate to ways people build their self-confidence by contributing to others. Then have students choose a talent they want to develop in art, music, communication, or a content discipline, and select a book about their area of study. For example, a student who selects "Indian art" will spend a day reading books about typical Indian designs and color combinations. On the second day, ask students to make a poster, report, or model about their topic to contribute to the class and place on display. On the third day, spend thirty minutes having students read and view classmates' work and twenty minutes describing in their journals the thoughts and emotions they experienced as they reviewed others' contributions. Last, ask students to answer the question: "How does contributing to others help people improve themselves?"

(RRG) *Appreciate every success I achieve.* Read one or more of the following books: *I Like Me, The Singing Hill, Tell Me Your Best Thing, The Fourth Grade Four.* You can allow students to select one book they want to read and divide them into response groups. After the book is finished, ask students to compare ways the main characters appreciated and congratulated themselves for improvements they made. After characters have been compared, ask students to describe (orally or in writing) how they can acknowledge their own successes and why it is important to do so.

Something I want to improve. Ask students to read the quote for the day and, on a separate sheet of paper, write one thing they could improve about the classroom and one thing they could improve about themselves. Have the students form groups of four and compare their suggested improvements for the classroom. Next, ask each group to write a proposal for one classroom improvement. Explain that the proposal should contain (1) four steps or actions that could be taken to implement the improvement, (2) three reasons that the improvement would be of value to the class, and (3) reference to one quote and book from the unit that contributed to or relates to the group's proposal. After all the proposals have been shared, ask students to select and implement as many as you and they desire. After the class has implemented the improvements for one week, (1) ask students to discuss how improving their surroundings makes it easier for them to improve, (2) have them return to the self-improving proposals they wrote at the beginning of this activity and assess whether the classroom change aided in their self-improvement, and (3) have them write one change they could make at home to continue to improve in the areas they identified.

I don't want to be wrapped up in a small package. Discuss the quotation "A person completely wrapped up in himself makes a small package," and read either *Noah's Castle* or *The Lottery Rose.* Conclude the activity by discussing ways in which students can avoid becoming self-absorbed by sharing stories about changes they made in their life to become better, or by inviting a guest speaker to share activities they can do to avoid self-absorption.

Teaching students a strategy for self-improvement. Share with students that working to improve oneself is one of the best means of reaching one's potential. Tell them that Dan Zadra, author of *Unlock Your Potential,* published by Creative Education Publishers, defines potential as:

One part natural talent

Two parts knowledge or training

Three parts inner motivation or desire

Ask students to think creatively about using this definition as a method of improving themselves. Prompt their thinking, if necessary, by offering the following example: Each time you recognize a natural talent, commit to read two books or become involved in a training program to advance that talent, and state three actions you will do to improve your talent. Afterwards, describe several plans of action, ask students to commit to one, initiate it, and evaluate it after a time period they have specified.

(BLM) *Liking myself.* Explain to students a time you laughed at yourself. Have students write or tell their meaning of the quote, "Be able to laugh at yourself," and ask why they need to be able to do this. Then, have them write or describe something they can laugh at about themselves. Afterwards, read *Amanda and the Witch Switch* or another book from this section. Last, have each child make his or her own semantic map about the feelings and meanings they gained from the stories. You may use Blackline Master 24 (in BLM section) with this activity.

Each day is important to me. Say, "If you wake up each morning and think of everything you need to do, and of the people that need you, then you will realize each day is important because you are in it." Have the students draw sequenced pictures of what they do each morning.

I can improve. Present different stories written on paper for each small group. These stories concern academic situations in which your students feel they cannot catch up. Have one member of each group read the situation the group created to fellow group members. Then, have each group come up with a way that students could catch up to where they want to be by using the message they learned through the quotations and other activities in this unit.

Multicultural Emphasis: Concepts about Self-Improvement That Come from Other Cultures

African American. Nia (NEE-ah) is a word of Swahili origin that means to have a reason or purpose for doing what you do. It also means making African-American people as great as they can be by making their collective vocation the building and developing of their community.

Korea. In Korea, the turtle is an important symbol of self-improvement. For Koreans, the turtle represents a healthy way of life because it is never in a hurry and it always thinks things through.

Mexican American. The following books teach different strategies to improve oneself. Although students from all cultures will enjoy and profit from learning these strategies, Mexican-American students will receive extra benefits. These stories occur in settings with which they are familiar, making transfer to their lives easier.

Larreula, Eric. *La mona saltarina.* Spain: Editorial Teide, 1984. When an active little monkey bravely and skillfully rescues his friends, they learn that it pays to keep physically fit.

Kraus, Robert. *José el Gran Ayudante.* New York: Windmill Books, 1977. José loves to help. He helps his family, his friends, his entire community, and, most important, himself.

Your Own Additions to the Unit

14 Learning to Listen Better

Learning Objectives In this unit, students strengthen their ability to pay attention and listen actively in group settings. The quotations, activities, and books increase students' conscious effort to attend to information and opinions that are presented orally.

Resources *Select a different quotation to discuss and write on the board each day of this unit's study.*

*Listen carefully and you will know
What to do or what to show.*

You can see without your eyes.

I can listen.

We must listen well so words are understood.

Speak for a reason and you'll be heard.

Did you understand what was said?

*A mind is boundless
As it listens.*

Listen or thy tongue will keep thee deaf.
—Native American Proverb

*It is good for you to talk, but at
the right time; when it's your turn.*

Learn to listen and understanding will come.

Use your senses well and discover knowledge.

*Our class would be like a big dunce
If everyone talked all at once.*

*Learn to listen,
Listen and learn.*

Finding the Right Book Concerning Listening to Meet Students' Needs

Difficulty code: I = Introductory; E = Easy; M = Medium

		Book
I	What fox has to do to get his tail back	*One Fine Day* by Nonny Hogragian
I	Listening	*Fantastic Mr. Fox* by Roald Dahl
I	Animal sounds	*Polar Bear, Polar Bear, What Do You Hear?* by Bill Martin
I	Attention to listening: nursery rhymes and poetry	*If Wishes Were Horses* Illust by Susan Jefferson
I	Book of rhymes	*Alphabears* by Kathleen Hague
I	The use of music to communicate meaning (video)	*Peter and the Wolf* by Sergie Prokofiev
I	Listening to detect sequence	*The Very Hungry Caterpillar* by Eric Carle
I	An opportunity for students to listen so they can retell events from beginning to end	*Nothing Much Happened Today* by Mary Christian
I	A child who gets the wrong idea from the teacher	*Ramona the Pest* by Beverly Cleary
I	Misunderstanding	*Amifika* by Lucille Clifton
I	48 rhymes set to music	*Jane Yolen's Mother Goose Songbook* by Jane Yolen
I	Comfort through parents' communication	*The Leaving Morning* by Angela Johnson
I	Communication—more than just words (game at end)	*Face Talk, Hand Talk, Body Talk* by Sue Castle
I–E	Learning a special way to listen hard inside yourself	*If You Listen* by Charlotte Zolotow
I–E	A common experience for all children	*Shhh!* by Suzy Kline
I–E	Gaining mother's attention	*My Mother Never Listens to Me* by Marjorie Sharmat
E	Asking the right questions	*Well! Why Didn't You Say So?* by Joanne Wold
E	An altered message	*The Surprise Party* by Pat Hutchins
E	Listening and predicting	*The Red Box with Wheels* by Maud and Miska Petersham
E	Easy-to-follow hand games	*Hand Rhymes* by Marie Brown
E	Understanding messages	*Faces* by Barbara Brenner

		Book
E	Being noisy	*Noisy Nora* by Rosemary Wells
E	Listening to images	*Listen, Children, Listen* by Myra C. Livingston
E	Searching for an unidentifiable noise	*What's That Noise?* by Frank Aech
E	Having your attention elsewhere while talking	*Good News* by Eloise Greenfield
E	Poetry with notes on listening	*Dogs and Dragons, Trees and Dreams* by Karla Kuskin
E	When to talk and when to listen	*Periwinkle* by Roger Anloine
E–M	Good stories for reading aloud	*The Candlemaker and Other Tales* by Victoria Forrester
E–M	The listening and talking skills necessary for good discussions	*How to Carry on a Discussion* by Diane Stanley
E–M	Easy-to-follow steps to Japanese art of paper folding	*Easy Origami* by Dakuihtel Nakano
M	A teen learns to listen and helps older people	*The Rocking Chair Rebellion* by Ethel R. Clifford

Activities to Use with Quotes and Books

Opening the School Day Discussion

Put a quote on the board and discuss the importance of listening well. Discuss how most of the information students will receive in life will come from effective listening.

Listening to my favorite thing. Each student brings a favorite song, poem, or story to school. Before they start a section of it, they tell why they like it.

Communicating with hands. Have students put their hands over their ears. Then ask how it feels not to be able to hear or get through to someone who cannot hear. Use gestures or sign language to communicate, and discuss what it would be like to be deaf.

(BLM) *Telephone listening.* Each child makes a telephone using a construction paper and a pattern to trace. After the telephones are finished, have students practice telephoning their friends to practice listening. You may use Blackline Master 26 in the BLM section and use yarn as the telephone cord.

Show and tell: A modern version. Students describe an object they brought to school or would like to bring, *but* they do not show it. Listeners guess what the object is.

Making rhymes. Read *Alphabears,* by Kathleen Hague or another book of rhymes. Have children follow the print as you point to the words you are reading aloud. Pause before the last word that is covered. Students figure out the last word of each rhyme.

Music talks. Watch a video of *Peter and the Wolf* by Sergei Prokofiev or another video, TV show, or movie where music is used to convey information. Children listen carefully to the different types of music for each character in the story. Show pictures of the types of instruments used for each character.

The good listener. Read *Periwinkle* by R. A. Duvoisin or another book from this section. Discuss the giraffe's problems and why it is important to listen when someone is talking.

Putting in order. Read *The Very Hungry Caterpillar* or another book from the list. Listen to learn the order (sequencing) in the story. What happened first? Next? Last? (e.g., First Caterpillar was small, ate lots of food, and then became a butterfly).

What's next? Read *The Box with Red Wheels* by Maud and Miska Petersham. Read the first page and have students predict what is in the box. List their predictions on the chalkboard. Then have students listen for new clues in the story and change their predictions if they wish. Discuss whether the original predictions were correct. Ask, "What did you hear in the story to change your predictions?"

Barriers to listening. Ask students to think of reasons they can't learn from listening (e.g., another person is making too much noise, they are not paying attention, they are thinking of something else). Describe how they can overcome these obstacles when they listen. Then ask students to try to overcome these obstacles as they listen to the following poem. When the poem is complete, discuss what students did to improve their listening abilities and allow students to write their own poem.

Listening

Listen. Listen.
To the birds that sing
And all the bells go ding-a-ling.

To the music so soft and sweet
Always makes you tap your feet.

To hear the noises when you play
It's important, wouldn't you say?

It's such a joy just to hear
All the sounds that reach the ear.

Listen. Listen.
And you'll be free
To learn so much of what you see.

*And always remember the gateway will glisten
All you have to do is choose to listen.*

Communication has many forms. Discuss and show pictures of early types of communication—pictures of cave dwellers communicating, for example. Discuss the meaning of communication and research its meaning in an almanac (e.g., "two moons" means two months in traditional Native American cultures) Next, ask how you communicate with the class without talking. Finally, review the topics in books in this section and discuss the ways the books made students more aware of the importance of good communication.

Helping students who dominate discussions. Students who dominate discussions either have an unmet need for attention or are simply unaware of their distracting speech habits. If students ramble because they need attention, you can help by detecting and acknowledging the feelings they express in recitations. For example, suppose you are discussing a book from this unit, and a student interjects that his uncle is a very good writer, and that his uncle is coming to visit soon, and drives a red truck, and likes dogs, and so on. Detect this student's feelings about his uncle's visit, whether they are apprehension or of longing, and acknowledge those feelings by asking a yes-or-no question about the feeling: "I think you're fond of your uncle. Am I correct?" These actions address the student's need to be understood and enable him to listen more completely, without causing embarrassment for the student's extraneous statements.

If students' problems stem from distracting speech habits, teach them to state their main idea first and then stop talking. If classmates ask no questions, it means that their statements probably were effectively made and communicated so completely that further comment was unnecessary.

Listening attentively. Before you read one of the books in this unit, teach the following strategies that students can use to improve their listening. Then ask students to use the strategies as you read. After you have read the book, ask students to write what they did to use the strategies. *Directions:* In the blanks below, write examples of times when you used a strategy to help you listen better.

1. *When a word is unknown to me:* Ask myself if it could be similar to another word that was said: _____

_____

2. *When my mind wanders and I'm confused:* Ask myself if the idea the speaker is saying is a detail or the main point: _____

_____

3. *When I'm confused because I expected the speaker to say something different from what was said:* Ask myself if I did not hear the word *not*, *but*, or *yet*:_____

_____

4. *When I'm hearing so many new points that I'm forgetting some of them:* Ask myself what are three main points I do remember: _____

5. *When I can't remember what the speaker said:* Tell myself to remember the most important thing I want to tell others from the speech: _____

(BLM) *Listening better.* Distribute Blackline Master 27 (in BLM section). Ask pairs of students to use the six steps as one student reads a book for ten minutes. Then have the listener retell the story with as many details as possible. Next, emphasize the importance of listening and ask students to reverse roles in order to give both students the opportunity to improve their listening. Finally, ask the pair to discuss the strategies they used to improve their listening and to turn in a written list at the end of their discussion.

Listening carefully. Discuss the quotation, "You can see without your eyes." Then have students form pairs. Explain that one person should tell a partner what to draw by giving directions *only* but not giving any clues or names of the objects being drawn (e.g., "Move your pen to the right and make a straight line"). In the end, students will realize that they can see without their eyes by listening and using their other senses. Then have students reverse roles. Last, ask them to share their drawings. Those who drew the best will describe what they did to increase their listening abilities.

Take a walk. Either on the way to school, at recess, or just as a class experiment, ask students to take a walk and listen for sounds while they are walking. Record these sounds in a chart like the one below, and share them with the class:

Take a Walk

Describe sound:	What was it?	How did you know?

Multicultural Emphasis: Facts about Listening That Come from Other Cultures

Indochina. Indochinese children are not accustomed to speaking in front of a class, but they have learned to listen carefully. If any students from this culture are in your class, ask them to share strategies they use to focus their mind while they listen.

Africa. Listening is an important skill in many nations of Africa, where people often live far from towns and have not had the advantage of going to school. People who do not know how to read or write listen to the radio to keep in touch with their culture and their country.

Native American. Traditional Native Americans were good listeners. Through listening, they could tell where game animals were grazing, what type of animal was moving behind trees, or if danger was heading their way, long before it was sighted.

Mexican American. The following books demonstrate the value of listening in Mexican-American culture.

> *Colleccion Piñata: Ritmos y Sonidos.* Mexico: Editorial Piñata, 1985. This book explores the wonders of sound.
>
> Parramon, J. M., & Puig, J. J. *El oido.* Illustrated by Maria Rius. New York: Barron's Educational Series, 1985. This book illustrates the most enjoyable sounds in the world.
>
> de Podendorf, Illa. (1979). *Sonidos.* National Textbook. This is an interesting presentation of sounds and how they are a part of our daily lives.
>
> Smith, Kathie Billingslea, & Crenson, Victoria. (1988). *Coleccion mil Preguntas: Oyendo.* Buenos Aires: Editorial Sigmar. The sense of hearing is explored through questions and answers, with interesting explanations and illustrations.
>
> Wolf, Bernard. (1979). *Ana y su Mundo de Silencio.* New York: J. B. Lippincott. This is a true story of Ana's daily life experiences as a deaf child.

Japan. It is difficult for Japanese-speaking children to pronounce the sounds of the letters *L, Q, V,* and *X,* as these are not included in their language.

When Japanese words are translated into English, the vowels are always pronounced the same: *a* is pronounced "ah," as in *father*; *e* is pronounced "eh," as in *pet*; *i* is pronounced "ee," as in *see*; *o* is pronounced "o," as in *bone*; *u* is pronounced "oo," as in *stool*. When students are taught this, they find it easier to understand and listen to Japanese classmates. See *Chocho Is for Butterfly: A Japanese–English Primer* by Jeannie Sasaki and F. Oyeda.

Your Own Additions to the Unit

15 Making Decisions and Taking Responsibility

Learning Objectives

Making decisions and taking responsibility are difficult for some students. The quotations, activities, and books in this unit demonstrate the importance of reflection, time, positive goals, and avoiding easy ways out in reaching effective decisions. In addition, this unit presents the following perspectives about assuming responsibility. It illustrates how responsibility is intertwined with accountability, the ability to distinguish right from wrong, the ability to think and act rationally, and an understanding of the close relationship between personal and collective freedom, on the one hand, and individual and group responsibility on the other.

Resources

Select a different quotation to discuss and write on the board each day of this unit's study.

You can count on others when they can count on you.

*Make sure that whatever you do today is important,
for it will cost you a day in your life.*

*I have pencils, colors, and clay
That I must care for every day.*

When I'm bad, it makes others sad.

*I can choose shows on TV
That are just right for me.*

When one gets under a good tree, a good shade covers him.
—Rosemary Holman

*Freedom is the power to do what you
Know you have to do and ought to do.*

Never buy what you do not want because it is cheap.
—Thomas Jefferson

*Is it right or wrong?
The answer is in your heart and head.*

*When I'm good and get things done,
I can work harder and have more fun.*

*To be blind is bad, but it is worse to
have eyes and not see.*
—Helen Keller

Let others grow with you.

15 MAKING DECISIONS AND TAKING RESPONSIBILITY

Be the best you can be.

I am responsible for my day, and I can make my day great by the responsibilities I take.

It's nice to know when you're right, but better to admit when you're wrong.

Making effective decisions often means selecting from competing and attractive alternatives, or inventing a better option.

Finding the Right Book Concerning Making Decisions to Meet Students' Needs

Difficulty code: I = Introductory; E = Easy; M = Medium

		Book
I	Keeping a secret	*The Two o'Clock Secret* by Bethany Roberts
I	Accepting responsibility	*Awful Alexander* by Judith Choate
I	Helping at home	*What Did Mommy Do Before You?* by Abby Levine
I	Realizing one's responsibilities	*Who Will Pick Me Up When I Fall?* by Dorothy Molnar and Stephan H. Fenton
I	Comparing responsibilities of parent and child	*Meredith's Mother Takes the Train* by Deborah Lee Rose
I	Avoiding responsibility	*My Friend, Jasper Jones* by Rosamond Dauer
I	Responsibility in friendship	*I'll Tell on You* by Joan Lexau
I	Changing bad actions to good ones	*Bee My Valentine* by Miriam Cohen
I	How responsibility brings love	*I Love You, Mouse* by John Graham
I	Not being responsible	*Oh, Kojo! How Could You!* by Verna Aardema
I	Accepting new responsibilities	*Pig, Pig Grows Up* by David McPhail
I–E	Jobs that need doing	*Everyone Has a Job to Do* by Bill Hohman
I–E	Making decisions about how to use your talents	*Walter the Wolf* by Marjorie Weinman Sharmat
I–E	Finding ways to help	*I Am a Big Help* by Marian Parry
E	Not understanding what is really yours	*If He's My Brother* by Barbara Williams

		Book
E	Taking responsibility when changes happen at home	*When Mama Retires* by Karen Ackerman
E	Having responsibilities	*Joel: Growing Up a Farm Boy* by Patricia Demath
E	Making decisions under group pressure	*The Wave* by Margaret Hodges
E	Assuming responsibility and doing what has to be done	*A Day No Pigs Would Die* by Robert N. Peck
E	Feeling invisible at school but finding a way to be seen and appreciated	*How I Faded Away* by Janice Mayudry
E	A wrong decision made right	*Mr. Tamarin's Trees* by Kathryn Ernst
E	Family problems with a summer company	*Addie's Long Summer* by Laurie Lawlor
E–M	Making a commitment	*Martin Luther King, Jr.: Free at Last* by David Adler
E–M	Biography of someone who took on great responsibility	*Thomas Jefferson: Father of Our Democracy* by David Adler
E–M	Torn between playing games and caring for ill parent	*Hurry Home* by Donald Honig
E–M	Taking responsibility	*Magic Johnson: Hero On and Off Court* by Bill Gutman
E–M	Children working to save the planet	*Save the Earth: An Action Handbook for Kids* by Betty Miles
E–M	Different teen messages—stay in school, stay away from drinking, drugs, gangs, and crime	*I Am a Jesse White Tumblers* by Deane Schmidt
E–M	Befriending an old cat and making many decisions	*Old Cat and the Kitten* by Mary E. Little
M	Making decisions	*From the Mixed-Up Files of Mrs. Basil E. Frankenweiler* by E. L. Konigsburg
M	Learning what responsibility really is	*Emma's Dilemma* by Gen Le Roy
M	Decisions made by a homeless father and daughter	*The Journal of Jenny September* by Isaacsen-Bright
M	Choosing between her dream and helping someone	*Becky's Horse* by Winifred Madison
M	Giving and receiving	*Hot and Cold Summer* by Johanna Hurwitz
M	Following the lead of another person without deciding for yourself what is right	*Breaking the Fall* by Michael Cadnum

			Book
	M	Watching TV	*The Day the TV Blew Up* by Dan West
	M	Adventures of two children left alone during World War II	*The Wind Is Not a River* by Arnold Griese
	M	Deciding on your own goal	*Seven Feet Four and Growing* by H. Alton Lee
	M	An adventure with a need for decision making	*The Far Side of Fear* by Bill Leigh
	M	Taking responsibility in the family	*Little House in the Big Woods* by Laura Ingalls Wilder
	M	The struggle to make amends	*One-Eyed Cat* by Paula Fox
	M	Hawaiian legend of the relationship between people and the environment	*Backbone of the King: The Story of Paka's and His Son Ku* by Marcia Brown
	M	Life problems for two who play basketball	*Get Those Rebounds!* by Leo Etter
	M	Facing decisions about how to conduct your life	*Wrestling with Honor* by David Klass
	M	A big decision for a football star	*Soccer Duel* by Thomas Dygard

Activities to Use with Quotes and Books

Opening the School Day Discussion

Ask students to reflect on a recent decision they made, what the quote means, and how it could be applied to that and future decisions.

Using fables. Have students participate in self-selected reading of *Aesop's Fables* and other fables with morals at the end. Explain to the class how these stories teach a principle or judgment they can use in decision making. At the end of the period, ask students to share what they have learned about making decisions from their fables.

(JW) *Journal writing.* Read *Hurry Home* by Donald Honig or a comparable book from this unit. In this book, a young boy has to make a decision between staying with an ill parent and going to a baseball game. Have children write their own endings, and/or role-play them before you read the author's ending. Then talk or write about similar decisions they have to make and how they made them.

(BLM) *Difficult decisions in our lives.* Ask students to meet in small groups and discuss effective decisions the main character in their selection from children literature made (see the books listed in this unit). Allow students to discuss their favorite books. Then have them make a chart listing qualities of effective decision making that were common to most of the processes their characters used. Once the lists are complete, have each group decide on a difficult decision they have to make in their lives, and apply the principles of decision making to that situation by writing a positive scenario and outcome. Last, ask groups to share their charts and decisions. You can use Blackline Master 29, in the BLM section, as a sample to begin student's thinking.

Why facts are needed. Ask the entire class to participate in a discussion about when and where they might need facts to support their decisions, and why it is good to have them. Then have students read a peer's creative writing story from earlier in the year. Ask students to work in pairs to write three facts that could be added to increase the validity and value of their own and their peer's writing.

Teaching students to improve their decision making ability and the value they place on it. Share the following fact with students: Save $2.00 a day, every day, and you will have as much money as 25 percent of the largest savings accounts in the United States. Then ask students to decide, individually and realistically, how much money they could save each day. Even if the answer is only a penny a day, encourage them to start saving that amount. They must decide where to keep it safe and how to keep a record. At the end of the school year, ask students to share how much this decision earned for them and the positive effects of other decisions they made during the year.

I can spell. When you give spelling tests, present an alternative to the usual one-shot approach to receiving a grade. After the initial test has been given and graded, have students study their misspellings and concentrate on only those words. Then give students one week in which to reschedule a second spelling test. Provide a signup sheet with times that you will be available to give the test again. The object of the spelling test is to have the student remember correctly, so a second chance to improve retention gives students the responsibility for shaping their spelling skills. Last, have students describe how they benefited from assuming responsibility over their own spelling ability.

Friends' responsibility. Say: "Suppose you told one of your best friends a secret and he or she told it to some other people. How would you feel? Should you tell your friend? What would you tell him or her? Write it down on your paper. Have you ever been the person who told a secret when you were asked not to do so? What other responsibilities does a friend have? What other responsibilities have you assumed that caused others to trust you? How can you know when people trust you?" Students may respond individually or in small groups, either in writing or orally.

Definition of responsibility. At the end of the unit, ask students to write a personal definition of *taking responsibility* and examples of how they have learned to assume responsibilities more successfully.

Teaching students to improve their ability to assume responsibility. Share the following fact with students: "If you devote just twenty minutes a day, consistently, to your physical fitness program, then you will be in the top 15 percent of the young adult population in terms of fitness" (from *The Secret of the Slight Edge* by Dan Zadra, page 14).

Next, ask students if they feel they have already assumed responsibility for taking care of themselves physically. If they haven't, ask if they are willing to take the responsibility to use this strategy to improve themselves physically or if they want to use this strategy to build their responsibility in improving another aspect of their lives, or to help someone else. Last, have them make a contract with themselves to take responsibility for this area of their life.

(JW) *Journal writing.* Read a book from this unit. Discuss how the main character made good decisions and assumed responsibility. Have the children write or draw a story to tell about a good decision they want to make and to share their ideas.

Taking care of pets. Have a show and tell in which each student explains how he or she takes care of a pet, a little brother or sister, plants, and so on. They can bring photographs or drawings to class. Those who don't have a pet or sibling can describe a job that they might have at home or school and how they are responsible for it. Last, have students list what they want to be responsible for in school. In small groups, have them figure out what they would need to do to take that responsibility, and then give them control over it. Before they begin, read *Everyone Has a Job to Do* by Bill Hohman.

Multicultural Emphasis: Facts about Making Decisions and Taking Responsibility That Come from Many Cultures

Share the following information about decision making in different cultures and discuss the differences between the way decisions are made by different groups of people.

Native American. Decision making for Native Americans often was done by the wise elders of the tribe. Traditionally, Native Americans would gather around the fire and discuss a situation; then the elders would decide what was needed to benefit the tribe as a whole. Chiefs of each tribe were selected because of their wisdom, courage, and ability to make wise decisions. Ask students to practice making decisions in this way by dividing into groups. Have each group elect a chief, and pretend that their village has no food, no bricks or lumber for building houses, no department stores, and no wheels for travel. All they have is the wilderness in which to live. What decisions would they make to survive?"

Japan. In Japan, the emperors were the main decision makers. From the beginning of that culture until 1946, the emperor was regarded as the divine descendant of the sun goddess. All decisions were believed to be made by gods and therefore could not be questioned. A new constitution was adopted in 1947 to change this belief. Since then, Japanese leaders have become constitutional monarchs, and more people have become involved in the decision-making process.

Thailand. The Thai proverb, "If you love your buffalo, tie him up," means: If you love your child, protect him. Ask students what this proverb demonstrates about the value the Thai people place on responsibility.

African American. Introduce the following information about the African-American flag, Bendera. It has three sections. The middle is a black bar that represents the value of African-American people banding together. The red bar at the top is for their long struggle for fairness and freedom. The bottom bar is green and stands for hope. Then ask students to draw the flag they picture.

(BLM) *Africa.* In the early history of Africa, people lived much as Native Americans did. They survived by using their ingenuity against the environment. European and Asian countries had the advantage of being able to exchange ideas among themselves and thus became more advanced and powerful. European and Asian explorers and settlers often took advantages of Africa's riches, claimed leadership, and ruled over African peoples and their countries. Not until the 1950s were decisions made to grant the African states their independence. Now, Africa consists chiefly of independent nations, as depicted on Blackline Master 30 (in BLM section). Ask students to suggest how this history influences the events that are occurring in Africa today.

Mexican American. The following books are written in Spanish. Students from all cultures, can benefit from reading them or having a guest read them in Spanish. After the reading, have students discuss what they have learned about Mexican-American culture and the value this culture places on accepting responsibility and making effective decisions.

>Ruille, Bertrand. *Historia de la Nube Que Era Amiga de Una Niña.* Madrid: Editorial Minon, S.A., 1973. This is a story of friendship between a cloud and a girl. The cloud generously gives water to all the creatures until one day it begins to dissipate. The girl and all the animals devise a plan to save it.
>
>Steadman, Ralph. *El Puente.* Spain: Editorial Minon, S.A., 1972. Teo and Dimitri are two boys separated not only by a wide river but also by the prejudice of the adults in both their hometowns. Despite the differences among their elders, they remain good friends.

Your Own Additions to the Unit

16 Overcoming Fears

Learning Objectives Although students experience many rational and irrational fears, most do not understand what causes these fears or how to overcome the negative influence of fear on learning. Students benefit from knowing that timidity, fright, terror, and apprehension can arise from facing a test or in the presence of danger, evil, pain, concern, dread, or doubt. The quotations, activities, and books in this unit discuss strategies for understanding the source of fear and methods for turning fears into positive motivations and goals.

Resources *Select a different quotation to discuss and write on the board each day of this unit's study.*

It is O.K. to be afraid.

Sometimes it's hard to be brave.

Fear is imagining the worst.

When it is dark at night, why should I feel a fright?

When I talk about my fear, it helps to make it disappear.

I will use what I have learned to be braver whenever I am afraid.

It's no fun to be afraid. I want to learn how to be brave.

I have a fear I want you to hear.

Fear of failure can keep you from trying,
Failing to try is the only real failure.

Left to themselves, things can go from bad to worse.

I have known a great many troubles,
but most of them never happened.
—Mark Twain

A ship in harbor is safe, but
That is not what ships are for.
—Jay Blue

Ability is often inability that has lost its doubts and fears.
—Wm. A. Ward

Worry about what tomorrow may bring and today might pass you by.

A mistake is only unfortunate and
unbeneficial when you don't learn from it.

> *We pay a heavy price for our fear of failure.*
> *It is a powerful obstacle to growth.*
> *It assures the progressive narrowing of*
> *the personality and prevents exploration*
> *and experimentation.*
> —John Gardner, *Self-Renewal*

Finding the Right Book Concerning Overcoming Fears to Meet Students' Needs

Difficulty code: I = Introductory; E = Easy; M = Medium

		Book
I	Parents going out at night	*The Good-Bye Book* by Judith Viorst
I	Going to the doctor	*My Doctor* by Harlow Rockwall
I	Fear of the doctor	*A Shot for Baby Bear* by Doug Creshman
I	Fear of independence	*Arthur Goes to Camp* by Marc Brown
I	Nightmares	*The Bad Dream* by Jim Aglesworth
I	The courage to overcome your fears	*That Big Bruno* by Sylvia Tester
I	Fears of many things	*Will It Be Okay?* by Crescent Dragonwagon
I	A solution to fear	*What Does It Mean? Afraid* by Susan Riley
I	Chicken's fear scares others	*Chicken Little* by Aesop
I	Needing to prove yourself and face your fears	*The Cellar* by Ellen Howard
I	Standing up to fears	*Jim Chimp's Story* by Muriel Blaustein
I	Using curiosity and courage to overcome fears and follow your dreams	*Eeny, Meeny, Miney Mole* by Jane Yolen
I	Fear of the dark	*In a Dark, Dark Room, and Other Scary Stories* by Alvin Schwartz
I	Bedtime fears	*The Things at the Foot of the Bed* by Maria Leach
I	Fear of unexpected events	*When the Lights Go Out* by Margaret Mac Donald
I	Fear of moving	*We Are Best Friends* by Aliki
I	Accepting death of a father	*Everett Anderson's Goodbye* by Lucille Clifton
I	A different kind of funeral	*The Happy Funeral* by Eve Buntings
E	How friends help you overcome fear	*I'll Protect You from the Jungle Beasts* by Martha Alexander

16 OVERCOMING FEARS

		Book
E	Different types of fears	*Robbers, Bones, Mean Dogs* by Barry and Velmal Berkey
E	Dealing with childhood fears	*Anna Banana and Me* by Lenore Blegvad
E	Fear of wearing a hearing aid	*A Button in Her Ear* by Ada Litchfield
E	Facing fears	*There's a Nightmare in My Closet* by Mercer Mayer
E	Overcoming fears	*Lester's Overnight* by Kay Choras
E	Fear of rejection	*Aaron's Door* by Miska Miles
E–M	A riotous spoof of Timothy's fears and his mastery of them	*Timothy Twinge* by Florence Heide and Roxanne Pierce
E–M	A straightforward way to present death	*When People Die* by Joanne E. Bernstein and Stephen V. Gullo
E–M	Finding a solution to fear of a bully	*Bootsie Barker Bites* by Barbara Bottner
E–M	Fear of storms	*Storms in the Night* by Mary Stolz
E–M	Avoiding talking about fears	*Ramona the Brave* by Beverly Cleary
M	Fear as the cause of prejudices	*The Diary of Anne Frank* by Frances Goodrich
M	Unwarranted fear of someone with a learning disability	*Stay Away from Simon* by Carol Carrick
M	Fear of dogs	*A Dog Called Kitty* by Bill Wallace
M	Desperation	*Nothing to Fear* by Jackie French Koller
M	Help in solving fears	*Cracker Jackson* by Belsy Cromer Byars
M	Fear of adventure	*If You Seek Adventure* by Fulvio Testa
M	Shyness and anxiety	*The Faraway Island* by Barbara Corcoran
M	Superstition and fear	*Julia and the Third Bad Thing* by Barbara Wallace
M	Learns to admit to her fears instead of lying	*Otherwise Known as Sheila the Great* by Judy S. Blume
M	Jewish immigrants' experience on their voyage to America	*Letters from Rifka* by Karen Hesse
M	Nine short stories of fears and longings on the island of Jamaica	*A Thief in the Village and Other Stories* by James Berry
M	Fears when performing	*Come Sing, Jimmy Jo* by Katherine Paterson

Activities to Use with Quotes and Books

Opening the School Day Discussion

Have the students give examples of rational fears, then irrational fears. Make a list of their comments. At end of the unit, go over that list again to determine their understanding.

Differences on fears. Read *Anna Banana and Me* by Lenore Blegvad or another book from this unit and talk about the fears most people share, even those we experience in friendships.

Family member fears. Have students ask family members about fears they had when they were young and how they overcame it. On the following day, divide students into small groups to share the results of their interviews, and make a poster listing some methods for overcoming fears. After the posters have been shared, ask students individually to diagram or describe a plan they will follow to overcome a personal fear.

How fear makes me feel. Have students list physical changes that often occur when they become fearful—"butterflies in the stomach," sweaty hands, a headache, a flushed face. Then discuss how students can use these signals in positive ways. Last, ask them to draw a picture that conveys how they feel when they are afraid and to write how they will overcome this fear in the future. When they have finished, post the pictures and writings for all to read.

(BLM) *Spinner game (fear quotes).* This game can be used to study any unit in this book. Using Blackline Master 14 (see BLM section), place the quotes from "Overcoming Fears" (or any unit) in separate sections of the circle. Then, divide the class into four or five groups and spin the arrow. The quote it lands on will be the one used by all groups. Explain to students that they are to list as many justifications as possible to prove the quote is valid and correct, and impose a five-minute time limit. When the time has elapsed, have the first group read their list. Each item mentioned is tentatively worth 2 points. When the next group reads their list, any item mentioned that was also on previous lists will count as 1 point for each group (including the first group to mention the item). Any reasons that do not apply to the quote do not score any points. Continue until all groups have had a turn and the total points per group have been awarded. Then spin the spinner again and follow the same procedure, except that the second group goes first in reporting their reasonings this time. Continue this rotation until all groups have had an opportunity to read their reasons first. The group with the most points wins. All groups can receive a prize, with the prizes being as simple as allowing first- and second-place winners to leave first and second (and so on) for lunch or recess.

Talking fears away. Read a book from this unit, like *There's a Nightmare in My Closet* by Mercer Mayer, and ask questions about the sequence of events and characters. Then discuss the story, students' responses to it, and their own "nightmares in the closet." Next, have students suggest ways they can overcome negative effects of their fears.

Describing my fears to overcome them. Explain to students that they can overcome their fears if they describe their feelings to others. Add that occasionally everyone has a feeling that is difficult to explain, and in such situations it is also helpful to discuss or write about the confusion they feel. Next, ask students to think of how they feel and complete the sentence that is most applicable for them:

I feel _____ because . . . ; or

I'm feeling _____ and I don't really know how

to describe it but it feels similar to the time I was _____

_____.

When all students have written their sentences, ask them to select a quotation from this unit that could help them to describe their feelings. Last, have students write about the way they can recall the quotation in the future and how its message can improve their abilities to describe their feelings and overcome their fears.

Rap your fears away. Write the first line for a rap song that students can create, which includes suggestions for overcoming fears. An effective opening line is, "Whenever I fear . . ." Next, divide students into groups of three to five and ask them to write their own rap song, or keep the class together as one large group and compose one class song. Begin composing the song by providing the first line and asking volunteers to suggest subsequent lines. You can offer rhyming words whenever students are having difficulty.

Looking at your fears. Have students draw the thing that scares them the most. Then, when students have finished, ask volunteers to describe their pictures and ask classmates to discuss what students can do to overcome similar fears the next time they experience them.

Multicultural Emphasis: Facts about Fears That Come from Other Cultures

Multicultures. Students may enjoy knowing that all cultures use the arts to express their fears. In some cultures, objects are also used to fight fears—for example, using noise to chase away evil spirits. Most anthropologists believe that people used such objects to overcome their fears when no other strategies were available to them. Their children learned to use the same items to express their own fears, and in this way traditional objects and artistic items for "fighting evil spirits" were handed down from generation to generation. In each new generation people added their own imaginative ideas to these items.

As cultures became more sophisticated, new types of arts and art objects were created to chase away fearsome things—for example, war paint to scare off evil spirits. Ask students to think of ways that arts and crafts are used in the United States to chase away our fears. For example, teenager girls may wear makeup and color their hair to overcome the fear of rejection or of not being pretty enough. Ask students to research fears that were common in a former civilization that is of interest to them in order to identify ways people in these cultures fought their fears.

Japan. After Japan bombed Pearl Harbor in December 1941, many people feared that Japanese-American citizens living on the West Coast would side with Japan. A nonfiction account of the U.S. government's internment of these U.S. citizens can be read in *Behind Barbed Wire* by Daniel S. Davis. Other stories on this subject are *Journey to Topez: A Story of the Japanese-American Evacuation* by Yoshiks Uchida and Uchida's sequel, *Journey Home*. To compare the treatment of Japanese Americans with that of Japanese Canadians, students can read *The Eternal Spring of Mr. Ito* by Sheila Garrique and Joy Kogarva's *Naomi's Road*. After these books have been read, ask students to cite examples of how fear can lead to mistreatment of others.

Here is another interesting fact about the fears that arise in wartime. During World War II, zookeepers at the Ueno Zoo in Tokyo killed the animals because they feared that a bomb falling on the zoo would cause the animals to run loose. This event was described in a book published in Japan in 1951 and translated into English in 1988: *Faithful Elephant: A True Story of Animals, People and War* by Yukio Tsuchiza. Two other books about peace and war are *Rain of Fire* by Marion Dane Bauer and Toshi Maruki's *Hiroshima No Pika*.

Wars between countries and cultures always cause a fear of losing one's land, culture, and way of life. Many Laotian, Vietnamese, and Cambodian families have been forced to leave their homeland in the late twentieth century, because of the conditions in their war-torn lands. Thailand set up camps for these refugees, the United States and other countries sponsored many of them to immigrate and start a new life. Can you imagine the fear of going to a different country with a unfamiliar culture and customs and a language strange to you?

Your Own Additions to the Unit

17 Persevering, Trying, and Working Hard

Learning Objectives Most people in our society value perseverance. The quotations, activities, and books in this unit help students develop perseverance even when obstacles emerge. They encourage students not to give up but to look for new ways to approach difficulties, even though some require sacrifice or compromise.

Resources *Select a different quotation to discuss and write on the board each day of this unit's study.*

I can try.

*See what I can do
when I try.*

*If at first I don't succeed,
I'll try, try, and try again!*

Triumph is try *followed by* umph.

*When I just try,
I can do it by and by.*

*If you do your fair day's work,
you are certain to get your fair day's wage—
in praise or pudding,
whichever happens to suit your taste.*
—Alexander Smith

*Trouble usually is produced by those
who don't produce anything else.*

*The best preparation for tomorrow
is to do today's work very well.*

*When homework becomes a habit,
you have it made.*

*Don't stand for lower standards.
Be willing to bring others up to your higher standards,
and both you and they can rise to even better standards.*

*Do not let what you cannot do interfere
with what you can do.*
—Coach John Wooden, UCLA

*Sixty seconds make a minute—
How much good can I do in it?
Sixty minutes make an hour—
All the good that's in my power.*
—Traditional

*Attempt the impossible
in order to improve your work*

*There comes a time
when both sides fear that they have lost,
and the winner is the one who never gives up.*

Invalidation only gives strength to non-production.
—Ellen Hall

*A change in circumstance can make
the strong weak and the weak strong.*
—The Lion and the Mouse

*He who is determined
is going to get somewhere.*
—Pat Gobel

Perseverance is a great element of success.
—Longfellow

Finding the Right Book Concerning Persevering, Trying, and Working Hard to Meet Students' Needs

Difficulty code: I = Introductory; E = Easy; M = Medium

		Book
I	Working hard	*Hired Help for Rabbit* by Judy Delton
I	A chimpanzee who tries hard not to be a wimp	*Willy the Wimp* by Anthony Browne
I	Trying to be nice to someone who wasn't nice to you	*Anyhow, I'm Glad I Tried* by Judith Vigna
I	Searching for something special	*Where Is It?* by Tana Hoban
I	Skills to try	*I Can! Can You?* by Carol Adorjan
I	Trying hard in sports	*Pig and the Blue Flag* by Carla Stevens
I	How curiosity can help us try new things	*The Curious Cow* by Esther K. Meeks
I	Cassette and video available	*The Little Engine That Could* by Watty Piper
I	Beginning to read text that leads to independent work	*I Did It* by Harlow Rockwell
I	Keeping right on trying	*Try It Again, Sam* by Judith Viorst
E	Perseverance	*How to Dig a Hole to the Other Side of the World* by F. M. Nulty

17 PERSEVERING, TRYING, AND WORKING HARD

Book

E	Success from work, not luck	*Where the Good Luck Was* by Osmond Molarsky
E	A spider whose work is never done	*The Very Busy Spider* by Eric Carle
E	Overcoming many failures	*The Beetle Bush* by Beverly Lou Keller
E	Siblings working together to handle the new baby	*New Life New Room* by June Jordan
E–M	Pioneer aviator trying to fly over the Atlantic	*The Return of Freddy Le Grand* by Jon Agee
E–M	Cooperation at work and home	*Doing Things Together* by Carl and Elizabeth James
E–M	Helping children appreciate Eskimo culture	*The Seal Oil Lamp* by Dale De Armond
E–M	African American influence over the Old West	*Black People Who Made the Old West* by William Katz
E–M	Maturing through trying	*Edward Troy and the Witch Cat* by Sarah Sargent
E–M	An amusing object lesson	*Treehorn's Wish* by Florence Heide
E–M	Birds adapting to city life	*Urban Roosts: Where Birds Nest in the City* by Barbara Bash
E–M	Conquering the unknown	*On Top of the World: The Conquest of Mount Everest* by Mary Ann Fraser
E–M	A day working in the cotton field—migrant farm workers	*Working Cotton* by Sherley Williams
M	Dealing with curiosity about marijuana	*The Grass Pipe* by Robert Coles
M	Trying to prove to his father that he is a competent shepherd	*And Now, Miguel* by Joseph Krumgold
M	Working to achieve success	*Jockey—or Else!* by Fern G. Brown
M	Overcoming opposition to do what he loves—dancing	*A Special Gift* by Marcia Simon
M	An African American overcomes prejudice to complete his dream (a biography)	*Arthur Mitchell* by Tobi Tobias
M	Living alone	*Two That Were Tough* by Robert J. Burch
M	Overcoming obstacles to get a horse	*Hard Luck Horse* by Fern G. Brown
M	A documentary of the courage and strength of this proud family	*In This Proud Land: The Story of a Mexican American Family* by Bernard Wolf

		Book
M	How King Midas finally rids himself of his curse	*The Adventures of King Midas* by Lynne Banks
M	A never-give-up attitude	*Maudie in the Middle* by Phyllis Naylor
M	Working hard to succeed	*The Fourth Grade Wizards* by Barthe De Clements
M	Men and women working to succeed	*Blue Trees, Red Sky* by Norma Klein
M	Adjusting to a new country	*In the Year of the Boar and Jackie Robinson* by B. B. Lord
M	The struggle of slaves	*The People Could Fly* by Virginia Hamilton
M	A girl's determination to get father well	*Red-Dirt Jessie* by Anna Myers
M	A Wild West spoof—adventures of an unlucky champion of justice	*The Righteous Revenge of Artemis Bonner* by Walter D. Myers
M	Great aunt has to persevere to fit in baseball and fishing	*Stealing Home* by Mary Stolz
M	Overcoming a physical handicap	*Steinmetz: Wizard of Light* by Anne W. Guz
M	The courage to overcome peer pressure	*The Way of Our People* by Arnold Griese
M	Survival	*Island of the Blue Dolphins* by Scott O'Dell
M	Two children who go back in time to the Erie Canal	*The Erie Canal* by Jack Reber
M	The curiosity and hard work involved in proving and developing ideas	*Benjamin Franklin: Printer, Inventor, Stateman* by David Adler
M	Girl with cerebral palsy—and with "true grit"	*On Being Sarah* by Elizabeth Helfman
M	Overcoming racism by excelling in his work	*Arthur Mitchell* by Tobi Tobias
M	A Thai peasant who works hard to get an education	*Sing to the Dawn* by Minfong Ho
M	An amputee's determination	*Pete Gray: One-Armed Major Leaguer* by William Nicholson
M	Survival	*Julie of the Wolves* by Jean Craighead George
M	Working hard for a dream	*The Man Behind the Magic: The Story of Walt Disney* by Katherine and Richard Greene

		Book
M	Doing today's work well	*Making the Most of Time* by Christopher Garrioh
M	How much you can accomplish in an allocated time	*The Riddle of Time* by Thelma Bell

Activities to Use with Quotes and Books

Opening the School Day Discussion

Discuss the unit objectives and write a new quotation each day. Ask students how its meaning relates to their lives.

How can I try? Ask the class, "How many of you have tried something and couldn't do it?" "How did you feel?" "What were some of the ways you tried?" "What new ideas have you learned in this unit that they can try in the future to perserve."

Trying is common. Read any two or three books from this unit. Then ask students what the main characters in these books have in common, and what the students learned from reading these books.

If at first I don't succeed. Write on the board, "If at first I don't succeed, I'll try, try, and try again." Ask students to select one thing to try to do better at school by Friday of this week. Students write or tell you their goals and you approve them. Each student writes the goal in his or her learning log. They try to accomplish their goal each day. At the end of each day, the class return to their learning log and write what they tried that day and what they learned about trying (or they can meet as a class and discuss these questions). At the end of the week, students write what they learned about trying.

The children decide on something they want to learn to draw. They draw their first attempt on the space marked "Monday." The next day they draw the same thing and compare it with the last drawing. They continue to draw it on Wednesday and Thursday. On Friday, the children can share their drawings with the whole class or in small groups, depending on time. Last, discuss how trying can make it easier.

Newspaper creating. Read to the class *Blue Trees, Red Sky,* which illustrates cover stories in newspapers and introduces students to newspaper clippings about people who achieved in history. Then have students write two cover stories for a newspaper about events that occurred in class or that happened to a famous person. Next, distribute examples from sports stories, comics, and front-page stories. Have students choose one of these types of writing to do. (If they select comics, have them make at least four, with at least four screens each.) Explain that when each student has written two selections, they are to trade their work with another student, who will edit and critiques both selections and decide which piece should be placed in the class newspaper. Simultaneously, some students work on the layout for the newspaper. When the newspaper is completed, each student will receive a copy to take home. At the end of the activity, ask students to describe aspects of the project that helped them persevere until completion, and discuss other strategies students can use to increase their perseverance in times of difficulty.

Teaching students to try. Have students conduct the following research activity and list specific actions famous persons took to try harder. Then have the class compile a poster of the strategies they identified for the class's future reference. Students can pick one of the following to research: Mozart, who wrote a symphony at age 6; Shane Gould, who won an Olympic medal at age 12; Annie Oakley, who traveled in Wild Bill Hickok's Wild West Show as a markshooter at age 16; and Joan of Arc, who, at age 17, led an entire army to defend Europe. They can also choose someone who became famous much later in life: Ray Kroc, who founded McDonald's at age 57; Grandma Moses, who didn't start painting until age 78; or Cal Evans, who wrote a book about American cowboys at age 104.

People who persevere. Have students check out a biography they would enjoy reading from the library or a book from this unit. Ask students to write a report on the book listing how the person worked through obstacles to achieve success, including at least one way they would have handled each situation in a similar way or differently from the person in the book. After this activity is complete, ask the class to compile a master list of strategies, which is placed in the room for future reference.

(BLM) *I have persevered.* Have students think of a tough school assignment they completed. Then ask, "What were some of the things you thought and the actions you took to work with more effort then usual? If you had to complete a similar activity in the future, could you improve on what you accomplished to obtain better results? How? What obstacles did you encounter, and do you know a better strategy to overcome them now?" Blackline Master 31 (see BLM section) can be used with this activity.

Situations where perseverance is needed. Help students understand that perseverance is often needed when circumstances that are out of their control emerge. List such circumstances on the board and then ask students to suggest some that they have experienced—for example, working very hard to learn a concept but still not understanding it; learning that someone dislikes them for no apparent reason; wanting to purchase an item but not having the money. Next, read a book from this unit that relates to one of the situations students listed, or invite an adult to class for students to interview who may share insights on how perseverance could be exercised in that situation. On the next day, have students make a chart listing strategies for persevering. Then ask, "Do you think that successful people—star athletes, business professionals, teachers—use perseverance to reach their goals? What do you think when you try to do something difficult? Does the person you most admire think the same thing, in your opinion? Why or why not?" You could also conclude this activity by asking students to read a biography of the person they admire to verify their answer.

Increasing my own perseverance. Ask: "Do you remember the book *The Little Engine That Could?* This is a book about positive thinking. The train was able to do a task that was difficult by thinking positively. Think of something that might be difficult for you to do. What will you think to yourself to accomplish it?" Then have students respond orally or in private by writing a sample story of an incident in which they will use thinking positively to increase their own perseverance.

Teaching students to persevere. Share the following information with students and ask them to identify the strategy it describes that increases perseverance: "Since there has never been another you, it is almost pointless to measure your worth by comparing yourself to others. The only meaningful evaluation comes in how you measure up to your best. Compete with yourself, not with others. You are one of a kind, and you are important" (from *There Will Never Be Another You* by Dan Zadra, Creative Education Publishers).

(JW) *Journal writing.* Have students write in their journal about a personal success they achieved from working hard from any of the activities they completed on the previous day. Then ask them to describe what they learned about working harder, and to tell how they can work harder outside of school to achieve their goals.

Teaching students to increase how hard they work and their value for working hard. Share with students that working hard will help them reach their goals and become more successful. Tell them that recalling one or more of the following stories, taken from *Unlocking Your Potential* by Dan Zadra, can help them increase their ability to work hard on tasks they value.

Throughout the world, it was believed that it was physically impossible for any human to run a mile in less than four minutes. Yet Roger Bannister, on May 6, 1954, did just that. Here is his comment: "You see, the barrier is all in your mind. You've merely hypnotized yourself into believing that you can't run any faster. The truth is, you can—if you just will."

Does the power of thinking you can do something seem unrelated to helping you be able to do it? If so, consider this: Jo Beth Ravellette won top honors in cursive writing in fourth-grade. She also became an accomplished typist, pianist, and painter. She did all this through her belief that she could—and by using her toes. She was born without arms!

Also, consider this: Tommy Sullivan was born blind. He runs marathons by listening to other runners' footsteps. He also plays golf in the low eighties. A reporter asked him why he devoted the time and determination needed to learn and play golf. "Quite frankly," Tommy replied, "I found that I can play golf better than I can play tennis."

Multicultural Emphasis: Concepts about Persevering, Trying, and Working Hard That Come from Other Cultures

Mexican American. Folk drama is very important in the Mexican-American culture. It helped people to persevere. Folk drama began in Spain and was used to recreate the victories won in battles with Moors and Christians, and to sustain folk beliefs (e.g., it is commonly believed that Saint Francis of Assisi started the Nativity drama tradition in 1223). Although most Mexican-American plays were never printed, they have been replicated virtually intact for centuries. 'Los Pastores ("The Shepherds") is the most famous Mexican folk drama. It is common to the entire U.S. Southwest from California to the Texas–Mexico border. Folk drama in Mexico is also used to register social protests—for example, *El Teatro Campesino* ("The Farmworker's Theater") deals with the repression and exploitation of *los de abajo* (the underdogs) and leaves impressions of "If we survived this, we can persevere." Ask students to discuss dramas they have seen and to hypothesize about values and purposes that each represents in American culture.

According to Brian Sutton-Smith in *The Folk-Games of Children* (Austin: University of Texas Press, 1972), the basic reason children play games is to create a world where they, not adults, are in control. Then they can vary situations with "wild invention, hilarity, and sometimes complete nonsense" (p. xiv). Engage students from different ethnic backgrounds in a discussion of the games they play. They should note that although names of games differ, children from all cultures play similar games. For example, the Mexican-American game "El Chicotito" is a variant of the Anglo game "Crack the Whip"; "Las Escondidas" is "Hide and Seek"; "La Patada del Bote" is "Kick the Can." Then discuss how children use games to develop their determination and perseverance.

Egyptians. Egypt is almost entirely a desert, but around 5000 B.C. the Egyptians built canals on the Nile River to irrigate their fields so more food could grow. They were great engineers and architects who the pyramids, which are among the great wonders of the world. Their accomplishments have endured for seven thousand years.

Germany. After devastating defeats in two World Wars, the German people have persevered and made their country a world power again. The hard work of the German people resulted in a tremendous recovery after World War II. The nation was in shambles, with no federal government. Many of its cities were unrecognizable, with over two million buildings destroyed by bombing and other attacks. Food was in very short supply, and there was almost complete destruction of shipping and rail lines. Through the perseverance and labor of all its people, the democratic nation of Germany was reborn.

France. The French have had many invaders through their history. Even when their villages were destroyed, the French have persevered to become even stronger than before.

African American. Many African-Americans know the Swahili name *kujichagulia* (koo-ji-cha-goo-LEE-ah), which means acting and speaking for yourself. It communicates a special type of trying: trying to define ourselves, name ourselves, create for ourselves, and speak for ourselves, instead of being defined, named, created for, and spoken for by others.

African Americans also value the concept of trying and sustaining effort in their Kwanzaa celebration. An African-American professor, Dr. Maulana Karenga wanted to teach his people about their history, so he created Kwanzaa in 1966. Kwanzaa has now become an African-American holiday that lasts seven days from December 26 to January 1. Karenga describes Kwanzaa as a time for gathering of African and African-American peoples to celebrate their achievements and to rededicate themselves for the hard work ahead. *Black People Who Made the Old West* by William Katz, discusses African Americans' effect on the Old West.

About 200,000 African Americans fought in the Civil War against the South. A good work of historical fiction is *Which Way Freedom?* by Joyce Hansen. Other good books about slaves and their fight for freedom are *Freedom Train: The Story of Harriet Tubman* by Dorothy Sterling; Virginia Hamilton's *Anthony Burns: The Defeat and Triumph of a Fugitive Slave;* and *Lion and the Ostrich Chicks and Other African Folk Tales* by Bryan Ashley, which includes folktales demonstrating triumph over a powerful figure.

Imani (ee-MAH-nee) means a special type of sustained effort: to believe with all our hearts in our people, our parents, our teachers, our leaders, and the righteousness and victory of our struggle. Martin Luther King, Jr., did much to bring equality to his people. Michael Jordan is one of the most famous basketball players in history and does more than his share of charity work with children. Both worked hard to achieve their goals.

Native American. Through their hard work, Native Americans have survived more changes in society than any other race. They began as a race at least 15,000 to 20,000 years ago. Students may enjoy learning the personal strategies some well-known Native Americans used to work toward their goals.

Jim Thorpe (Native American name: Bright Path) is thought to be among the greatest athletes who ever lived. He won two gold metals in the Stockholm Olympics (1912): the pentathlon (an athletic competition in which each athlete must compete in five events) and the decathlon, in which each athlete takes part in ten events. Students can read many books about him and other famous Native Americans.

Chief Joseph is an example of a famous tribal chief. He achieved much for his people through his quiet strength. He is believed to have best understood the ways of whites. His tribe was named Nez Perce and was located in Idaho, southeastern Washington State, and northeastern Oregon.

Indochina. Indochinese children are taught to be modest about their achievements. It may be difficult for them to accept praise for hard work.

Multicultures. Plan a social event for Indochinese and American parents to share their cultures. Have students establish a school library for Indochinese parents and parents from other cultures represented in your school, with books, brochures, recordings, and short information sheets.

Your Own Additions to the Unit

18 Quarreling Less

Learning Objectives Few school years pass without two or more students engaging in a quarrel. The quotations, books, and activities in this unit teach students how to mend their disagreements. The unit also helps students to refrain from finding fault with others.

Resources *Select a different quotation to discuss and write on the board each day of this unit's study.*

*Playing is more fun
When my work is done.*

*Make it a joy
To share your toy.*

*There are lots of ways you play
that build your body and mind each day.*

*Isn't it fun to say
Let's all go outside and play.*

*Fun is fun when
It is fun for all.*

*It is misunderstanding that causes quarrels;
Gaining new knowledge and understanding
is the antidote to quarrels.*

*Every story has three sides to it—
yours, mine, and the facts.*
—Foster M. Russell

*If you truly believe each person has a right
to his or her own opinion,
how could there be cause to argue?*

*Weakness on both sides is the motto
of all quarrels.*
—Voltaire

*When we quarrel, how we wish
we had been blameless.*
—La Rochefoucauld

*If you think you are right,
back it with facts, not opinions.*

Force can only subdue, not win.

Peacemakers are those who help to manage thoughts and actions.

Nonviolence is the first article of faith.
—Mahatma Gandhi

You cannot shake hands with a clenched fist.
—Golda Meir

Finding the Right Book Concerning Quarreling Less to Meet Students' Needs

Difficulty code: I = Introductory; E = Easy; M = Medium

		Book
I	Playful poems	*Monster Soup and Other Spooky Poems* by Dilys Evans
I	Cooperation in play	*That's Mine* by Elizabeth Winthrop
I	Arguing when playing	*The Snowman* by Jim Erskine
I	Rain and play	*Rainy Day Magic* by Marie Louise Gay
I	Three pigs playing from morning until night	*You Push, I Ride* by Abby Levine
I	Simple approaches to problems that arise when playing games	*Everybody Takes Turns* by Dorothy Corey
E	A quarrel in friendship	*Are We Still Friends?* by Carol Barkin & Elizabeth James
E	Friends who quarrel and the outcome	*Marinka, Katinka, and Me (Susie)* by Winifred Madison
E–M	Children as well as parents quarreling	*Tulla's Summer* by Rose Lagercrantz
E–M	Adopted and birth son who quarrel but finally realize both are loved	*Seven Years from Home* by Rose Blue
M	Nonviolent ways of solving disagreements	*Peace on the Playground* by Eileen Lucas
M	Fighting between siblings	*Tales of a Fourth Grade Nothing* by Judy Blume
M	Two boys who don't get along	*Echo Summer* by Jean Blackie
M	A modern outlook about quarreling with family, friends, and gangs	*The Outsiders* by S. E. Hinton
M	A rivalry	*Best Enemies Again* by Kathleen Leverich
M	Two stepsisters who quarrel and solve their problem	*Gardine vs. Hanover* by Joan L. Oppenheimer

			Book
M		How to turn a quarrel into a positive outcome	*One of the Boys* by Scott Johnson
M		Violence leading to violence	*The Game on Thatcher Island* by T. Degens
M		How quarrels begin wars, particularly the Civil War	*Across Five Aprils* by Irene Hunt

Activities to Use with Quotes and Books

Opening the School Day Discussion

Write a new quote on the board each day. Discuss how that quote could prevent a quarrel.

My rainy day list. Have students list activities they can do at home when it is raining. Then read *Rainy Day Magic* by Marie Louise Ray and add new activities to their list.

(BLM) *Quarreling depicted in literature.* Ask students to recall incidents in literature where main characters quarreled, and list features of these quarrels on the board. Then have students list the outcomes of each and describe how the quarrels contributed to the plot and why the author wrote about them. Last, have students compare these features with incidents in their lives. Blackline Master 32 (see BLM section) is designed for this activity.

(RRG) *Is quarreling good?* Read one or more reference books of this unit, and ask students if the author implies that quarreling is positive or negative. Then ask students to divide into debate teams and use the quotations and books in this unit, interviews, and their own life experiences to debate this question.

Gaining composure. Have students lie comfortably on the floor. Explain that this is an ancient relaxation practice. They can use this activity whenever they are stressed or angry and want to act calmly. Play soft, mellow music in the background. Walk your students through their body, from head to foot, having them tense their muscles tightly and then completely release them before moving on. Bring them back gently. Ask students how this made them feel. Did they think it would help them control their actions when upset? Have them write their answers to hand in to you.

Being a "peacemaker." Before starting this activity, teach the strategies for negotiation described here. Negotiation involves a number of steps:

1. Define the issues; have all persons involved in the confrontations state their goal for the discussion as clearly as possible.

2. Listen to both sides of the issue (immediately following the goal statement, have each person add a description of the benefits everyone could expect if his or her goal were attained).

3. Use the "all-around" strategy, each person has the opportunity to speak before any person is allowed to speak a second time.

4. Don't get sidetracked, avoid discussions about things that cannot be changed, and focus on one issue at a time.

5. When stuck, generate three alternatives.

6. Put the agreement into action as soon as possible after the conflict is resolved.

After teaching these negotiation strategies, divide the class into groups of three and have each group select a moderator. Next, give the two remaining students a slip of paper on which a suggested conflict is written and have the pair develop an enactment of this confrontation situation (e.g., an opinion, whose turn it is in a game, etc.), or ask each pair to reenact an actual event in their lives, subject to your advance approval.

While the pair are creating the scripts for their enactments, meet with all moderators to develop strategies by which they can implement the negotiation strategies they have been taught. Next, let the enactments go on for a few minutes. Then have the mediator intervene, trying to keep the fight "fair." Conclude the activity by discussing and asking students to write about the following questions:

1. How did it feel to be a peacemaker?

2. What was hard about it?

3. What did you do to be effective?

4. What are three situations you will face in the future where you will use the negotiation strategies you learned in this activity, and which ones will you use?

Overcoming my tendency to quarrel. Duplicate the booklist in this unit for students or project it onto the overhead. Then have students select a book they would like to read. At the end of the unit, have students choose one or two quotes (or write their own) that best depicts the author's message in the book and have them write about ways they can overcome their tendencies to quarrel.

How to stop quarreling. Explain that quarreling often occurs when two people view the same situation differently and that quarrels end when both people try to understand each other's point of view. Unresolved disagreements often cause people to feel frustrated and angry and to take their hostilities out on others not involved. This is called scapegoating. Share with students that psychologists have discovered that people who resolve quarrels most rapidly have the following beliefs:

1. It's O.K. to disagree with other people

2. People who disagree with someone else are not strange or bad.

3. When people disagree with another person's idea, it doesn't mean that that person's idea is stupid or unimportant.

4. When two people disagree, it doesn't mean one person is right and the other is wrong. It's possible both could be right or both wrong.

5. Not all disagreements have to end with both people agreeing. Disagreement doesn't mean the parties are angry with one another or dislike each other.

Ask students if they hold these beliefs and teach the following steps for overcoming quarrels effectively.

Step 1: First find out exactly what the disagreement is about; for example, you want to play football, but he wants to go to the show.

Step 2: Listen to the other person and find out why each thinks the way he or she does. Do not interrupt or make judgments about what the person is saying before he or she finishes, and don't be thinking about anything else while he or she talks—just listen. Put yourself in the other person's place and try to understand why that person is thinking as he or she is.

Step 3: Tell the other person honestly why you think as you do. Be sure he or she understands your point of view.

Step 4: Research both opinions together and decide on the best option for both people.

You can always agree to disagree and agree on something entirely different. If you have a problem following these steps, get someone you trust and respect to help resolve the disagreement.

Multicultural Emphasis: Concepts about Preventing Quarrels That Come from Other Cultures

Mexican American. Mexican culture arose from the sharing of values and customs between the Aztec Indians and European Spanish settlers. In the nineteenth century, other English-speaking explorers added new elements to the culture but the combined Spanish-Aztec culture continued to dominate because people from these two cultures had learned to avoid quarrels by sharing. The following books depict ways in which Mexicans and Mexican Americans overcome quarrels:

Flores, Rosa. *Caracolitos: Me Siento Feliz al Ayudar.* Oklahoma: Economy Company, 1979. A young boy becomes aware of the importance of helping others.

Diaz, Oralia A. *Los Condjitos de Don Julio.* Guatemala: Editorial Santa Piedra, 1984. Generous Don Julio takes pride in sharing his rabbits with his nieces.

D'Atri, Adriana. *Asi Son los Abuelos Que Viven Cerca.* Spain: Editorial Altea, 1977. Clara and Enrique share their experiences with an attentive Grandpa and Grandma who live nearby.

After reading these books, ask students to discuss the importance of sharing joys and responsibilities with family members to avoid quarrels, and how these behaviors are important in the Mexican and Mexican-American cultures. Then, during Mother's Day or another holiday period, discuss the concept of teamwork and the things for which students are appreciative from their parents. Next, have them write these descriptions beginning in Spanish (*Un papa es . . . Un Mama es . . .*) and send thank-you cards to family members.

Switzerland. The Swiss decided long ago to become a nation that advocated peace, justice, and international cooperation. As a result, the Swiss are the oldest democracy in the world. They remained neutral during both world wars and have profited by their decision. Many countries' diplomats meet in Geneva for summit conferences because Switzerland is a neutral country. These summit meetings have allowed nations to settle quarrels by meeting in a neutral environment where they can present their countries' views on the problem and find a solution that is agreeable to all. Many of these decisions have helped to make the world safer for all. Ask students to research qualities of Swiss culture that have contributed to their peace-loving values. On the basis of this history, ask students to hypothesize about the value the Swiss place on, and the methods they use to avoid, conflict and quarrels.

Thailand. Read *A Family in Thailand* by Ruth and Neil Thompson. Many games in this book demonstrate that the games Thai play are very similar to those played in the United States. Similarities between Thai schools and U.S. schools are also noted in this book.

Egypt. Several games from Egypt are designed for two players only. The book *Tic Tac Toe: and Other Three in a Row Games from Ancient Egypt to the Modern Computer* by Claudia Zaslowsky traces these games back to similar games played in Egypt many centuries ago.

Your Own Additions to the Unit

19 Reading Better

Learning Objectives The purpose of this unit is to increase students' value for self-selected reading and to teach that reading is an important pursuit for gaining information, pleasure, escape, and alternative points of view. The quotations, activities, and books in this unit increase students' affective response to reading.

Resources *Select a different quotation to discuss and write on the board each day of this unit's study.*

Learn to read; read to learn.

*Learn the sounds and you will see
That you can read as well as me.*

*When I learn to read,
I'll have much of what I need.*

A dictionary is your friend.

A new book is like a new friend.

Words are your fortune.

Read and you can experience many things.

*We need not burn books to kill our civilization;
we need only leave them unread for a generation.*
—Robert M. Hutchins

*Reading makes possible the living of a thousand
lives instead of only one.*
—G. Robert Carlson

*Every reader reads himself.
The writer's work is merely a kind of optical instrument
that makes it possible for the reader to discern
what, without the book, he would perhaps
never have seen in himself.*
—Marcel Proust

*What is a great love of books?
It is something like a personal introduction
to the great and good men of all past time.*
—John Bright

*A Word
A word is dead when it is said, some say.
I say it just begins to live that day.*
—Emily Dickinson

Finding the Right Book Concerning Reading Better to Meet Students' Needs

Difficulty code: I = Introductory; E = Easy; M = Medium

		Book
I	Easy to read	*My Parents Think I'm Sleeping* by Jack Prelutsky
I	Easy to read	*Oh, How Waffle! Riddles You Can Eat* by Judith Matthews and Fay Robinson
I	Reading skills	*Story Hour—Starring Megan* by Julie Brillhart
I	Importance of learning to read	*Louis James Hates School* by Bill Morrison
I	Things to read while walking down the street	*I Walk and Read* by Tana Hoban
I	Beginning readers	*I Read* by Susan Green and Sharon Somon
I	Necessity of reading	*The Little Old Man Who Could Not Read* by Irma Black
I	Having a book does not make you smart	*Petunia* by Roga Duvoisin
I	A book for beginning readers	*Spencer Is Small* by Christer Chevalier
I	Learning beginning sounds	*ABC Book* by Dr. Seuss
I	Encourages beginning readers by its predictability and use of pantomiming	*Busy Monday Morning* by Janine Domanska
I	Illustrations that entice children to note the details	*The Funny Little Woman* by Arlene Mosel
I–E	A boy who wants to learn to read	*When Will I Read?* by Miriam Cohen
E	Refusing to read	*The Tale of Thomas Mead* by Pat Hutchins
E	Sounds	*Dogs and Dragons, Trees and Dreams* by Karla Kuskins
E	Just for the joy of it	*The Kooken* by Julia Lebentritt
E	Eight short stories done to reinterest students in nursery rhymes	*Past Eight O'Clock* by Joan Aiken
E	Old West rodeo	*Rodeo* by Murray Tinkelman
E–M	A city boy in Africa reads about his "wild" Africa	*Somewhere in Africa* by Ingrid Menner

		Book
E–M	The ins and outs of Indy car racing	*Racing Indy Cars* by George Sullivan
E–M	Historical facts in 1826	*The Giraffe That Walked to Paris* by Nancy Milton
E–M	A book for someone afraid of going into the hospital	*It Can't Hurt Forever* by Marilyn Singer
E–M	A must for car buffs	*The A to Z Book of Cars* by Angela Royston
E–M	Nine of the famous storyteller's most popular tales	*Fairy Tales from Hans Christian Anderson* by Russel Ash and Bernard Higtion
M	Waterbirds in full color	*Wings Along the Waterway* by Mary Barret Brown
M	American folktales about America's first folk heroes	*American Tall Tales* by Mary Osborn
M	Suspenseful story that will entertain even reluctant readers	*Man from the Sky* by Avi
M	Fascinating information about a great playwright	*Bard of Avon: The Story of William Shakespeare* by Diane and Peter Vennema
M	Adventure and drama	*Treasure Island* by Robert Louis Stevenson
M	Understanding life long ago	*Sarah, Plain and Tall* by Patricia MacLachlan
M	Life in early Wisconsin	*Little House in the Big Woods* by Laura Ingalls Wilder
M	Senselessness of war; Japanese culture	*Sadako and the Thousand Paper Cranes* by Eleanor Coerr
M	Adventures of a pioneer family life	*Caddie Woodlawn* by Carol Ryrie Brink

Activities to Use with Quotes and Books

Opening the School Day Discussion

Write a new quote on the board each day. Ask students what it means. Discuss some good books they've read recently. Ask them to explain why they liked these books and to describe ways in which reading enriches their lives.

Five-finger method. Ask students to go to the library and pick a book they have never read before by using the "five-finger method." Explain that the five-finger method is a strategy to help students select books that are at the appropriate reading level. Then demonstrate the method. Students open a book to any page and hold up one hand as they read that page. Every time they come to a word they do not know, they put one finger down. If all five of their fingers are down before they reach the end of the page, the book will likely contain too many difficult words for them to read and enjoy it independently. (This strategy is based on a page averaging about 100 words.) When students have selected books, ask them to read silently for fifteen minutes and then discuss whether the five-finger method enabled them to enjoy reading more than in the past.

(RRG) *Award-winning books.* Ask each student to select a book from a selection of Caldecott and Newbery award winners. After reading the book, they should write down what they liked best about it, the author's name, the main character(s), and a brief summary of the plot. Then they should give the book a rating of one to five stars. Form groups of four or five students and ask them to talk within their groups about the books they read and to identify the book that received the highest overall rating.

(BLM) *All kinds of books!* Have the whole class discuss the kinds of information and ideas they can get from books, and the kinds of books that give them these different kinds of information, including encyclopedias, biographies, and resource books. A trip to the library will give them a chance to find examples of each category. Then, form groups of four or five, give each group a general topic, and have each group member identify (and read) a different type of book about that topic. After all have read and summarized their books, ask them to describe the values they identified that each genre holds in gaining and enjoying new information. Have students share the types of books they preferred and the information they received. Last, have the whole class discuss different kinds of books and why it is important to read more than just one kind. Then distribute Blackline Master 33 (see BLM section), a form on which students can record the titles and genres of books read during a period of time designated by you or the students.

Author's Chair. The Author's Chair is an excellent way for students to share their work and receive recognition. To implement the Author's Chair, set aside a time each week (or each day) for one student to have a turn reading a book or their writings aloud to the class. Afterward, conduct an open forum in which students question or comment about the work. Explain to students that respect is a vital part of the forum and that sharing provides an objective method of viewing one's work.

How our reading lessons can be improved. Share the following list of ideas from fifth-grade students for improving their reading lessons. Then ask your students if they agree with the list or if they have additional items to add. Finally, ask for their suggestions as to ways they can put the most significant ideas into effect in their class. The ideas given by fifth graders were:

- Teacher should help sound out words.
- Teacher reads to the class.
- Let us read more.

- Have a top group and a need help group.
- Let us read aloud more.
- Repeat instructions over and over so they are understood.
- Make reading fun.
- Reduce the difficulty of having to go back and answer questions after book is read.
- Put ideas on the board.
- Let us divide in small groups to read to each other.
- Make a play.
- Go over one skill more than once.
- Give examples or write on the board.

(BLM) *Story map and writing.* Have children pick a story to read and complete a story map for the main characters, main ideas, and problem. Alternatively or in addition, ask students to make a story map of a story they would like to write themselves. You may use Blackline Master 34 (see BLM section) with this activity.

Teaching students to value reading. Share the following fact with students and have them complete the following book card as they implement the strategy it describes:

Name _____ Date _____

Book Read _____ Author _____

What I Gained by Reading It _____

_____

_____

_____

Fact: Reading one book every month will place a student in the top 2 percent of the world's literary elite (from *The Secret of the Slight Edge* by Dan Zadra, Creative Education Publishers, page 14).

(JW) *Journal writing.* Have students use the first letter in their names and write five other words that begin with the same letter and sound. They then record these words in their journals. Younger children can use a children's dictionary to come up with a word they recognize that begins with the same letter.

Reading our alphabet. Groups of five students make a chart with all the letters of the alphabet and one word that starts with each letter (e.g., A—*apple*, B—*ball*). Each group then presents its chart to another class. All charts are hung on the wall as a representation of the words and sounds that can be formed by our alphabet.

Learning beginning sounds. Read aloud Dr. Seuss's *ABC Book* or another book from this unit. Put words from the book on cards. Next, ask students to read over the words together. Then have students group the words according to their beginning sound. For example, *ball* and *bed* would be grouped together because they are both *b* words.

Where I read. Small groups of students comes up with five different places they go to read (for example, they have to read the menu at a restaurant.) Read the book *The Little Old Man Who Could Not Read*. Add to each list other places where they need to be able to read.

What's the ending. Read a wordless book like *Clifford*. Have the students work together as a class to predict how the story will end from the pictures, and then read the book. Stop about half way through and have each group dictates one sentence for an ending they create. In the end, read the story again with the new ending.

Word parts. Discuss structural analysis. Then have students look at the word *ball*, which has the word "all" in it. Let students come up with other words with "all" in it and write them on the board. ex. call, fall, hall, mall, tall. Students look at a familiar book and attempt this strategy with other words in pairs.

My teddy bear. Write each of the sentences in the poem that follows on sentence strips. From each sentence, omit one word with which you want the class to become familiar, or use the words that have been encircled in a box. Then read the poem leaving out the word you chose or the ones indicated below if you prefer to teach word parts or rhyming words. Have students tell you which word belongs at the end of the sentence. Then place that word in the pocket chart or tape it to the end of the proper sentence written on a chart pad. You can use students' exact word choice as long as it make sense, even if it is not the one originally used by the author. When all sentences are complete, ask the class to read the entire poem together and then to draw or write about things of which the poem reminded them.

My Teddy Bear

My teddy bear is nice to hold.
The one I have is getting old.
His paws are almost wearing out
And so's his funny furry snout
From rubbing on my nose of skin,
And all his fur is pretty thin.
A ribbon and a piece of string
Make a sort of necktie thing.
His eyes came out and now instead
He has some new ones made of thread.
I take him everywhere I go
And tell him all the things I know.
I like the way he feels at night,
All snuggled up against me tight.

by Margaret Hillert

Pet project. Begin this activity by making a list of pets that students have or would like to have. Number the pets as they are listed on the board or chart. Then, on each subsequent day of the week, review the names of pets and increase students' abilities to read the names of the animals by asking, "What pet is number 1?" (etc.). When the correct word has been read, ask students to write the word on their papers. In addition, if class pets are allowed, use this list to determine the pet the class would like to have. You can repeat this activity on subsequent days by identifying a different category of words you want students to learn.

Multicultural Emphasis: Concepts about Reading That Come from Other Cultures

Share the following information with students and ask for their comments about differences between literature from each of the cultures represented.

Asia. The literature of southeastern Asian countries is based on religion, the writings of Confucius', and the Jakarta tales from India.

Asian-American literature. Chinese and Japanese Americans are the main Asian cultures represented in children's literature in the United States. The reason is probably that these two cultures have lived here longer than other Asian cultures. Themes in their literature concern oppression in their homeland, prejudice in a new land, and learning to appreciate their heritage while adjusting to their new life in the United States.

It would be interesting to compare the character of Little Red Riding Hood and/or Cinderella with their Asian counterparts in *Lan PoPo: A Red-Riding Hood Story from China,* translated by Ed Young, and *Yeh Shen: A Cinderella Story from China* by Ae-Long Louie, illustrated by Ed Young.

Switzerland. Famous children's books from Swiss authors are *Heidi,* written in 1880 by Johanna Spyri; *The Swiss Family Robinson,* written in 1813 by Johann David Wyss; and *William Tell,* a folktale dating back to the fourteenth century.

Vietnam. The Land I Lost: Adventures of a Boy in Vietnam by Quang Nhuony Huynk is an autobiographical account of a boy's childhood in the central highlands of Vietnam. Two other interesting books about Vietnamese culture are *The Beggar in the Blanket and Other Vietnamese Tales* by Gail B. Graham and Chi Ngayen's *Cooking in the Vietnamese Way.*

Native-American literature. Native American folktales and history are told and retold in picture books, historical fiction, and informational books. Some well-known authors are Paul Goble (*Her Seven Brothers*), Scott O'Dell, and James Houston. Famous nonfiction authors include Ann Nolan Clark, Russell Freedman, Milton Meltzer, and Alex Bealer. Virginia Drivinghawk is known for her poetry and novels including *When Thunders Spoke,* and Shonto Begay for his illustrations, as in *The Mud Pony. Her Seven Brothers* by Paul Goble and *Cheyenne: Legend of the Creation of the Big Dipper.*

African-American literature. The Dark-Thirty: Southern Tales of the Supernatural by Patricia C. McKissack. African-American history and tradition from slavery to the civil rights era. *Mop, Moondance, and the Nagaski Knights* by Walter Dean Myers is a funny book that also explores serious issues.

African-American culture in the United States has produced a large and rapidly growing body of children's literature. Every genre is well represented, but none better than poetry, which portrays a culture with all its personal emotion. Poets like Arnold Adoff, Gwendolyn Brooks, Nikki Giovanni, Eloise Greenfield, and Langston Hughes make this evident in their powerful but sensitive works. Favorite U.S. folklore characters came from African Americans' rich oral tradition—*Anansi the Spider, Br'er Rabbit, High John the Conqueror,* and *John Henry the Steel Drivin' Man* to name a few.

China. Show students the difference between stories in the United States and China by reading *Lon PoPo: A Red-Riding Hood Story from China* or *Yeh Shen: A Cinderella Story from China,* both translated by Ed Young. Then compare them to our versions of the tales.

Japan. Read *The Gift of the Willows* by Helena Clare Pittman. A willow plays a significant role in the lives of a Japanese family. *Japanese Children's Favorite Stories* by Florence Sakade and *Japanese Fairy Tales* by Lafcadio Hearn will give the students a sense of the stories Japanese children read and enjoy.

Hawaii. If your children are interested in Hawaiian culture, *A is for Aloha* by Stephanie Feeney will provide information and photographs for your class.

Germany. Show and read the following German tales in picture books, and then compare them to ours: *Hansel and Gretel,* retold by Rika Lesser; *The Bremen-Town Musicians,* retold by Ilse Plume; and *The Pied Piper of Hamelin,* retold by Barbara Bartos-Hoppner.

Your Own Additions to the Unit

20 Setting Goals

Learning Objectives Many children have difficulty completing tasks. In this unit, students learn strategies for attaining their goals. The quotations, activities, and books focus students' aims and increase their ability to start tasks on time and work steadily to complete their objectives.

Resources *Select a different quotation to discuss and write on the board each day of this unit's study.*

*It is easy to begin a plan
When you first find out all that you can.*

*I can, I can,
I know I can.*

Be proud of what you can do.

*If you always do what you've always done,
you'll always get what you've always gotten.*

*If you have a worthy dream, nurse it,
nourish it, and nurture it into reality.*

*To live only for some future goal is shallow.
It's the sides of the mountain which sustain
life, not the top.*
—Zen Proverb

*To achieve a purpose or a goal
a person must have the courage
to attempt it, and the faith
that he can accomplish it.*

I have promises to myself to keep.

*A goal is not something you need to
accomplish but something you want to accomplish.*

Finding the Right Book Concerning Setting Goals to Meet Students' Needs

Difficulty code: I = Introductory; E = Easy; M = Medium

		Book
I	Learning to whistle	*Whistle for Willie* by Ezra Jack Keats
I	Portrait of the first president of the United States	*George Washington: A Picture Book Biography* by James Cross Giblin
I	Overcoming the habit of losing things	*Molly's Moe* by Kay Chorao
I	How a handicapped student helps himself	*Howie Helps Himself* by Joan Fassler
I	Main character achieves organization	*A Very Messy Room* by Muriel Stanek
I	Boy helps bear get rid of a toothache	*The Bear's Toothache* by Frank Asch
I	A rabbit rescues his friend	*Dance Away* by George Shannon
I	Achieving courage	*Eugene the Brave* by Ellen Conford
I	Even something simple can be an achievement	*The Visit* by Diane Wolkstein
I	What you accomplish each day is important	*Someday, Said Mitchell* by Barbara Williams
I	Chicken achieves acceptance	*Super Cluck* by Jane and Robert O'Conner
I	Leads to independent work by young children	*I Did It* by Harlow Rockwell
I	Excellent model for children to tell their own stories	*Cherries and Cherry Pits* by Vera B. Williams
E	About setting goals	*Arthur's Pet Business* by Marc Tolon Brown
E	African boy's dream needs faith to achieve	*Brother to the Wind* by Mildred Pitts Walter
E	Boy realizes the way he went about accomplishing his goals was wrong	*Hawk, I'm Your Brother* by Byrd Baylor
E	A girl who is teased by peers teaches them a lesson	*The Hundred Dresses* by Eleanor Estes
E	Owl smiles and changes a boy's bad day to a good one and a frown to a smile	*Bad Day* by Jeni Couzyn
E	Building a sand castle	*Castillos de Arena* by Sara Gerson
E	An imaginary fish	*Un Cuento de Un Pez Grande* by Joanne and David Wylie

		Book
E	Impossible to read without a smile	*Voyage to the Bunny Planet* by Rosemary Wells
E–M	Wanting to be a reporter in the late nineteenth century	*Nellie Bly: Reporter for the World* by Martha Kendall
E–M	Becoming enthusiastic about setting goals.	*The Secrets of Goal Setting* by Dan Zadra
E–M	The importance of a slight edge	*The Secret of the Slight Edge* by Dan Zadra
M	A pro pitcher with only one arm	*Jim Abbott: Star Pitcher* by Bill Gutman
M	Girl learns about achieving goals	*Coast to Coast* by Betsy Byar
M	Dreaming and imagining with self-understanding and inner strength	*Zeely* by Virginia Hamilton
M	Native American sets goal on preserving her ways	*Daisy Hooee Nampeyo* by Carol Fowler
M	How to set life goals	*The Outsiders* by S. E. Hinton

Activities to Use with Quotes and Books

Opening the School Day Discussion

Write a new quote on the board each day. In their journals or through discussion, have students answer for each quote: "What does this quotation suggest that I must do in order to achieve my goals?" At the end of a week, ask students to read all their journal entries or recall discussions and rank the things that are most essential to them in achieving their goals.

(JW) *Journal writing.* Tell students that an organization known as the Power of Positive Students Program conducted a research study and found that 87 percent of the people in the world do not set daily and weekly goals. This organization also found that of the 13 percent who do set goals, only 3 percent write them down. This 3 percent of our population accomplishes 50 to 125 times more than the other 97 percent. Then, read one of the books listed for this unit and discuss the types of goals that the main character set. Next, ask students to select a goal for themselves. It can be as simple as learning ten new words or learning more about a desired career or dream they have by reading three library books. Next, tell the class that they will have twenty minutes to work toward their goal each day for five days, and that they are to divide their goal into steps that can be taken each of the five days during that twenty-minute period. At the end of each day's twenty-minute period, ask students to refer to their plan, assess how much they accomplished, and set a goal for the next day. Last, ask students to write what they learned in this activity that will help them achieve more of the New Year's goals that they establish for themselves each year. At the end of the week, discuss whether or not students have achieved their goals and what they have learned about the most difficult and most rewarding aspects of goal setting. Before they set a second goal for the next week, ask them to describe what they learned about this first experience with goal setting and what they will add to their second week's attempt to increase their likelihood of success.

If you would like you can use Blackline Master 31, in the BLM section, ("I Have Persevered") with this activity. If you do, ask students to write their plan for reaching their goals on the steps leading to the dome. The first step of the plan would be written on the bottom step. Then have students fill in the next five steps for their daily goal that will reach their ultimate goal.

Promises to myself to keep. Discuss the quote relative to this activity and ask students what kind of promises they want to keep for themselves. Suggest things such as good moral values, honesty, dedication, and learning. Then ask the students how they would keep these promises and why they would want to keep them. Have students write a list of ten promises to themselves that would help them succeed in life. You may also want to tally all responses to determine the group's most important, personal goals/promises.

(RRG) *Explorers who achieved their goals.* Have students select books about explorers (or the unit's books) to read in their literature groups. Then have each group dramatize the lives and achievements of the people about whom they have read. Last, have the class create pictures and replicas they make for a bulletin board on courage and achievements and on the goals their explorers achieved.

Goals for the future. Ask each student to write about things they would do if:

1. They had all the money in the world.
2. They were the most powerful person (in muscles, brains, creativity, business sense, etc.) in the world.
3. They could do anything they ever wanted to do.

Students can also write about what they already have (personality, ability) that can help them achieve some of their dreams.

(JW) *Journal writing.* At end of the day, ask students to write or draw in their journals, or a paper to take home, about what they achieved today.

Words I already know. Have each student bring one or more items that they can read in things that they have seen outside of school or, for older students, a new word they have learned to read. Younger students can bring in labels found in their environment—on milk cartons, bread sacks, fast food and candy wrappers, cereal boxes, and so on. Then, ask students in turn to read their words to the class while you place each word on the bulletin board. At the end of the sharing period, have the entire class read the entire bulletin board and have older students write a story that includes as many words as possible from the bulletin board.

Multicultural Emphasis: Facts about Setting Goals That Come from Many Cultures

Discuss with students the following examples of ways people in other cultures achieve goals.

Mexican American. Begin a unit to compare the symbolism of apples in stories from different cultures. Discuss how apples are viewed as symbols of strength in several cultures. Ask students to identify other symbols common to several cultures and discuss why such commonalities are likely to exist. Then have students identify the role apples played in helping the main characters achieve goals in the following Spanish books. Ask students to compare the qualities apples posses in the Mexican-American folktales to the qualities apples represent in Anglo-American folktales—for example, the apple in *William Tell* or *Snow White*.

> Heuck, Sigrid. *El Poni, el Oso y el Manzano.* Spain: Editorial Juventud, 1986. A beautifully illustrated story about a horse and a bear who search for some lost apples.
>
> Pecanins, Ana Maria. *Manzanita.* Mexico: Editorial Trillas, S.A., 1986. The adventures of a talking apple.

Related titles in English for second language acquisition are as follows:

> Gibbons, Gail. *The Seasons of Arnold's Apple Tree.* San Diego: Harcourt Brace Jovanovich, 1984.
>
> *Magic Seed*: Have the students write about a magic seed. Use the following as a title: *Si Yo Tuviera una Semilla Magica . . .* ("If I Had a Magic Seed . . .").

Multicultural. Students bring in several beans that are unique to their native culture. They place the bean seeds between sheets of paper toweling and cover the towels with plastic wrap to keep the moisture in. Have them place the seeds in areas varying from dark to very sunny. Children may keep a record of the seed growth in their science logs. Children tell classmates the name of their bean and how it is cooked in their countries. Students set goals about the amount of time needed and the amount of light needed for beans to sprout, based on the size of their beans.

Seeds also may be placed on a bulletin board or chart along with a picture of the fruit the seed produces. Children may also place seeds in envelopes with pictures of fruit on the outside along with pertinent information on planting. These seeds and fruits should be those that are native to their homelands. The culture that is being represented is also included on the front with the picture so it can easily be associated with the country.

Your Own Additions to the Unit

21 Smiling

Learning Objectives The quotations, activities, and books in this unit will demonstrate the power of a smile, pleasure, amusement, affection, and friendliness in changing situations to become more positive for themselves and others.

Resources *Select a different quotation to discuss and write on the board each day of this unit's study.*

*It makes more muscles to frown
than to smile.*

Happiness comes with a smile.

Smiling causes a ripple effect.

Share your smile.

*If you see someone without a smile,
Give them yours.*

A smile is magic.

*The world seems a better place
when you smile.*

*Smile and the world smiles with you,
frown and you frown alone.*

*What's in a smile?
Try it for a while and see.*

*Someone observed that smiles are difficult to
give away because they're always coming back to you.*
—Bill Ward

I can make my day happy with a smile.

Happiness is being a part of things.

*There is no duty we underrate as much
As the duty of being happy.*
—Robert L. Stevenson

*You can be happy,
You can be sad,
The feeling is yours to be had.*

Happiness is a by-product of your actions.

Greet every challenge with a smile.

Finding the Right Book Concerning Smiling to Meet Students' Needs

Difficulty code: I = Introductory; E = Easy; M = Medium

		Book
I	Humorous bear	*Bearhead: A Russian Folktale* by Eric A. Kimmel
I	Typical action of the group	*Anna's Goodbye Apron* by Julie Briblhart
I	Brings a smile to the reader	*Second Grade Dog* by Laurie Lawlor
I	Letter to fairytale characters	*The Jolly Postman and Other People's Letters* by Janet Ahlberg
I	A happy song to cheer up a dog	*Clifford, We Love You* by Norman Bridwell
I	Learning to laugh at oneself	*I Hate Red Rover* by Joan M. Lexau
I	Feelings of laughter, fear, and joy	*Gilberto and the Wind* by Marie Ets
I	The value of smiling	*The King Who Learned to Smile* by Seymour Reit
I	Family memories bring smiles	*Grandmama's Joy* by Eloise Greenfield
I	Happy memories from the penny box	*The Hundred Penny Box* by Sharon Bell Mothis
I	Rhythm, rhyme, and fun	*By the Light of the Halloween Moon* by Caroline Stutson
I	Tons of smiles	*George and Martha, Tons of Fun* by James Marshall
I–E	Rhyming tale of a lost teddy bear found in a real bear	*Where's My Teddy?* by Jez Alborough
I–E	Friendships that bring happiness	*Little Bear's Friend* by E. H. Minarik
E	Scary stories that are more fun than scary	*Skeleton Crew* by Allan Ahlberg
E	Aunt takes girl out for a thrilling evening	*Aunt Elaine Does the Dance from Spain* by Leah Komaiko
E	Learning to be happy when things change	*New Life: New Room* by June Jordan
E	Excitement of a traditional Mexican birthday celebration	*A Birthday Basket for Tia* by Pat Mora
E	Girl finds clues that lead to her birthday party	*The Thirteenth Clue* by Ann Jonas
E	Happiness in one's own home	*The Town Mouse and the Country Mouse* by Helen Craig

		Book
E	Happiness on the farm in the summertime	*Thimble Summer* by Elizabeth Enright
E	Fishing with grandfather	*In the Morning Mist* by Eleanor J. Lapp
E–M	Celebrating the holidays in verse	*Ring Out, Wild Bells* by Lee Bennett Hopkins
E–M	Humorous poems	*For Laughing Out Loud: Poems to Tickle Your Funnybone* by Jack Prelutsky
E–M	Poems	*A Very Nice Joke Book* by Karen Gorenaud
E–M	A light-hearted mystery filled with puns	*Nighty-Nightmare* by James Howe
E–M	The best laughs in children's literature	*The Random House Book of Humor*, compiled by Pamela Pollack
E–M	A boy who loses his parents finds a new friend	*Uncle Mike's Boy* by Jerome Brooks
E–M	Family happiness	*Christmas with Ida* by Robert Burch
E–M	Creating with everyday materials	*Shopping Cart* by James Seidelman and Grace Mintonge
E–M	Having fun with reflections	*Reflections* by Ann Jones
E–M	Using your imagination to have adventures	*Round Trip* by Ann Jones
E–M	Adventures of two mice and a friendly cat	*Tales at the Mousehole* by Mary Stolz
E–M	A fence lizard learns he needs more than a fence to be happy	*Tooky and Wood* by Mary Elise Monsell
M	Family happiness	*All-of-a-Kind Family* by Sydney Taylor
M	Two children become friends, then suffer a loss	*Bridge to Terabithia* by Katherine Paterson
M	The meaning of loving and being loved	*Three Dog Winter* by Elizabeth Van Steenayk
M	Desert dwellers' happiness	*I'm in Charge of Celebrations* by Byrd Baylor
M	Two lonely people who learn happiness	*Mildred Murphy, How Does Your Garden Grow* by Phyllis Green
M	A blind and deaf person, treated with respect, learns to live independently	*The Helen Keller Story* by Catherine O. Peace

		Book
M	A father who loses his social position gains respect from his children	*To Kill a Mockingbird* by Harper Lee
M	Happiness through working together	*Fast Sam, Cool Clyde, and Stuff* by Walter Dean Myers

Activities to Use with Quotes and Books

Opening the School Day Discussion

Write a quote on the board and discuss it each day. Ask students to think of a person they know who smiles a lot. Ask them why they think that person smiles and what they like about that person.

Ghost writers. Have students explore the characters in a book by taking on the personality of one character through letter writing. Have them choose their favorite characters and then, either with partners or in small groups, write letters back and forth while in character—for example:

> Dear Heidi,
> How are you? Have the goats grown much? I would like to come and visit you and your grandfather in the mountains. I am having trouble with that terrible wolf again. He keeps frightening my grandmother and he follows me through the woods. What can I do about it? Please write back soon with your answer.
> Your Friend,
> Little Red Riding Hood

Encourage students to make inferences about their characters' thoughts and feelings and to create sequels in which their characters report incidents in which they were happy.

Warm fuzzies. Have the class sit in small circles of six to eight students each. Then have students write their names on an envelope. Next, give each student enough slips of paper to write a positive, uplifting comment about each classmate in the circle. Explain that students are to rotate the envelopes around the circle until everyone has written a comment to all their classmate and placed it in their envelopes. These comments should be anonymous. When all comments have been inserted in the envelopes, have students return to their desks, read the comments, and write a response about the importance of being happy and sharing positive comments with others. If students finish early, they can write a note to one of their classmates to express their appreciation for a comment they made in their envelopes.

(BLM) *If you see someone without a smile, give them yours.* Begin the lesson by asking the students to name places in which they could find people who need a smile. Make a semantic map of these places. (Blackline Master 24 (in BLM section) can be used with this activity.) Next, have students read a book from this unit about people who found a way to overcome adversity and smile. Last, have students describe ways they can help someone in their lives to become happier or a way they can increase their own happiness.

(JW) *Journal writing.* Stand very quietly before students. Secretly, note what time you began standing before them. Do not smile until someone smiles at you. As soon as a student smiles, return the smile and note the time on the clock. Then tell the class how long it took before they felt compelled to turn the dreariness in the classroom, created by your frown, into a positive climate with a smile. Next, ask them to discuss what it is about people that attracts them to smiles. Why do smiles have a "ripple effect"? Have students recall a time when they caused someone else to smile and how it made them feel. Have them describe what this discussion and reflection has caused them to think.

Happiness is... Have every student complete the sentence, "Happiness is ..., because ..." Then have each student illustrate and sign the page. Next, post all pages as a mural around the room so students can learn more about their classmates.

Extending your happiness. Have students visit a children's hospital or a nursing home and interview a patient or resident to identify what has helped these people to be happy. You can bring speakers into the classroom who help people every day—a firefighter, police officer, doctor, nurse, or someone who volunteers in the community—to describe events and actions that make them happy in their professions.

Pet happiness. Have students discuss their pets and how a particular pet makes them happy. List the different things a pet does to make them happy. Now, ask students to take each item on the list and see how they could make someone else happy by doing things similar to the things pets do that make other people happy.

(RRG) *Learning about happiness from books.* Read three of the selections from this unit and discuss commonalities and differences between the ways that the authors describe happiness.

How smiling feels. Ask the class to smile, frown, laugh, stare, and smile again. Discuss how they felt doing these things. Then have them draw the face that felt the best and write or tell why it felt best.

Multicultural Emphasis: Concepts about Smiling That Come from Other Cultures

Vietnam. In Vietnam, birthdays bring special happiness. Vietnamese people have two birthdays: the actual date of their birth and a second birthday that is celebrated at the lunar New Year. Thai people especially enjoy poetry as a celebration of happiness. Cradle songs, frequently sung to make babies happier, are some of the first poems Thai children learn.

Native Americans. Native Americans have traditionally celebrated happiness through verse, similar to the Navajo verse in William Sleator's *Whale in the*

Sky (translated by Ann Siberell). Students can learn these verses easily, and motions may be added to the farewell. After students have learned and performed the verse, ask them to explain the value Native Americans hold for developing happiness in others.

> Hogooneh ("So be it").
>
> There shall be happiness before us.
>
> (Arms stretched out in front.)
>
> There shall be happiness behind us.
>
> (Arms stretched behind body.)
>
> There shall be happiness above us.
>
> (Arms stretched over head.)
>
> There shall be happiness below us.
>
> (Bend and touch the floor.)
>
> There shall be happiness all around us.
>
> (Turn around with arms spread out.)
>
> Words of happiness shall extend from our mouths.
>
> (Touch lips with both hands and stretch arms outward.)

Descriptions of Native-American celebrations can be found in *Powwow: Festivals and Holidays* by June Behrens. Even today, all tribes in a region come together to celebrate the specific holidays described in this book.

Southeast Asia. Southeast Asian people may smile in both happy and sad situations. They may smile when they don't understand, cannot answer a question, or are being reprimanded. In Indonesian culture, smiling is a polite, respectful behavior, used to express more than joy and happiness.

China. Read and discuss June Behrens's book *Gung Hay Fat Choy,* which presents ideas for celebrating Chinese New Year, one of the happiest festivals in Chinese life. The book depicts this holiday through colorful photographs and informative text.

Japan. The Japanese celebrate Children's Day (also called Boys' Day, *Kodomo-no-huh*) on May 5. Children's specific wishes for when they grow up, as well as how they want to find happiness, are expressed on this day. Children also express appreciation to their mothers. Discuss which holidays we have in which these same values are communicated.

Mexican American. On December 28, many Mexican Americans celebrate a Mexican version of April Fool's Day. On this day some South Texas ranchers play tricks on one another. If the trick works and a friend smiles, realizing he has been fooled, the trickster recites the following verse to the person who was fooled:

Innocent little dove,
That let yourself be fooled
Knowing that on this day
Nothing should be lent.

Bahamas. Under the Sunday Tree by Eloise Greenfield introduces children to the Bahamas. The subtropical climate has made the islands a favorite resort. This book, in bright-colored paintings and poetry, brings the Bahamas to life through descriptions of fishing, sailboat racing, weddings, and family togetherness. One of these islands, probably San Salvador, was where Columbus first made landfall in 1492.

Your Own Additions to the Unit

22 Solving Problems

Learning Objectives The quotations, activities, and books in this unit build students' problem-solving skills. Through this unit, students learn new approaches to solving difficult and perplexing situations.

Resources *Select a different quotation to discuss and write on the board each day of this unit's study.*

>When we have a doubt,
>We don't just pout—
>We work until we figure it out.

>A problem is always
>worth solving.

>Solve each problem
>as you meet it.

>Problems not solved
>just don't dissolve.

>There are ways, but these ways are uncharted.
>—Taoism

>You don't have to plan to fail.
>All you have to do is to fail to plan.

>It's when things seem worse
>that you mustn't quit.

>If there is something to change,
>where do you start to rearrange?

>Never let a difficulty stop you.
>It may be only sand on your track
>to prevent your skidding.

>Don't find fault,
>find a remedy.
>—Henry Ford

>Every noble work is at first impossible.
>—Carlyle

>What the mind can conceive and
>perceive the mind can achieve.

>The greatest thing in the world is not so
>much where we stand, as in what
>direction we are moving.

>There is always an opportunity and a way offered to you.

Finding the Right Book Concerning Solving Problems to Meet Students' Needs

Difficulty code: I = Introductory; E = Easy; M = Medium

		Book
I	Solving a childhood problem	*Ira Sleeps Over* by Bernard Waber
I	Deaf girl learns to use other senses	*Mandy* by Barbara Booth
I	Outsmarting a fox	*Rosie's Walk* by Pat Hutchins
I	Exploring dolls and wooden blocks	*Changes, Changes* by Pat Hutchins
I	Gaining independence by solving her problem	*Sara and the Door* by Virginia Allen Jensen
I	Bear's solution	*Theodore* by Edward Ormondory
I	Example of problem solving	*Frog Goes to Dinner* by Mercer Mayer
I	Figuring out the next page	*Look Again* by Tana Hoban
I–E	Not getting on parents' nerves	*Rainy Day Magic* by Morie-Louise Gay
I–E	Questions with preposterous results	*Would You Rather . . .* by John Burningham
I–E	Solving the problem of a bully	*King of the Playground* by Phyllis Naylor
E	Changing places	*Mary Alice: Operator #9* by Jeffrey Allen
E	Deciding which activity is best	*Another Day* by Marie Hall Ets
E	Solving how to say a name	*Tell Them My Name Is Amanda* by JoAnne Wold
E	Ingenious solutions	*Amy Belligera and the Fireflies* by Paul Buckley
E	Electricity goes out of Electric House	*Lazy Tommy Pumpkinhead* by William Pene DuBois
E	Putting problems in perspective	*It Could Always Be Worse* by Margot Zemach
E	Sending a cat away	*The Cat Came Back* by Bill Slavin
E	A schoolchild solves a mystery	*The Case of the Stolen Bagels* by Dela Crayder Colman
E–M	Escaping from witches	*Hansel and Gretel* by Jacob Wilhelm
E–M	A rabbi comes up with a fair solution that also teaches a miser a lesson	*In the Month of Kislev: A Story of Hanukkah* by Nina Jaffe
E–M	Deciding whom to trust and how to use one's powers	*Secret Life of Dilly McBean* by Dorothy Haas
E–M	Being objective in a disagreement	*No Roses for Harry* by Gene Zion

		Book
E–M	Mysteries from many countries	*Stories to Solve: Folktales from Around the World* by George Shannon
M	Learning about oneself and overcoming parents' divorce	*Dear Mr. Henshaw* by Beverly Cleary
M	Studying the Vietnam War to	*Charlie Pippin* by Candy D. Boyd
M	Solving a problem to benefit three friends	*The Big Deal* by Alison C. Herzig
M	Winning a princess (Norwegian folklore)	*Boots and the Glass Mountain* by Claire Martin
M	Bringing order to chaos	*Matilda* by Roald Dahl
M	Solving a problem of possible clubhouse destruction	*Who Goes There, Lincoln?* by Dale Fife
M	Delight and pitfalls of making money	*Kid Power* by Susan Pfeiffer
M	Solving a 147-year-old mystery	*Buried in Ice: The Mystery of a Lost Arctic Expedition* by Owen Beattie and John Geiger
M	New means of problem solving for a 4H problem solver	*Chicken Bucks* by Susan Sharpe
M	A scheme to conquer injustice written entirely in dialogue	*Who Was That Masked Man, Anyway?* by Avi
M	Inventing the airplane	*The Wright Brothers: How They Invented the Airplane* by Russell Freedman
M	Elderly people solving problems	*The Rocking Chair Rebellion* by Ethel Rosenburg Clifford
M	Mystery involving problem solving	*Dear Napoleon, I Know You're Dead, But . . .* by Elvira Woodruff
M	Problem-solving strategies to save a business	*The Pushcart War* by Jean Merrill
M	Outwitting the rainmaker	*Dr. Dridd's Wagon of Wonders* by Bill Brittain
M	Adventure story where boy solves many problems	*The Great Rat Island Adventure* by Charlene Talbota
M	Not passing judgment until you know the facts	*The Witch of Blackbird Pond* by Elizabeth Speare

Activities to Use with Quotes and Books

Opening the School Day Discussion

Write a quote on the board and discuss it. Address the deficits of pouting and expecting others to solve problems. Help students learn that they need to think things through for themselves and that pouting wastes time. Students can also discuss why it is helpful to think about their problems before asking a teacher or neighbor for help. They may realize that some advice is not valid for them and that if someone else solves their problems for them they will receive one solution, but if they learn to solve their own problems, they will learn how to find solutions throughout life.

Deck the halls. State the following problem to students: "The back wall of our classroom is too bare. It needs decorations." Then have students divide into small groups to solve the problem. Allow them to put their plan into action and give them supplies.

(JW) *Journal writing.* Spend the week reading this unit's books that describe solutions to problems students have. At the end of the week, ask students to describe or draw an action they have learned from one of the main characters in the book that they will use if they ever face a similar situation.

Creative problem solving. Explain that the "creative problem-solving process" was created by two researchers, Alex Osborn and Sidney Parnes. In comparative studies of students who had and had not learned the "creative problem-solving process" (CPS), students with the knowledge showed a statistically superior ability to produce good ideas. Add that CPS helps students devise solutions to challenges. Then teach the process as described here:

Step 1: **Mess-finding** involves considering your goals, concerns, and personal orientation to determine your starting point for problem solving. Find facts, write, say, and think about the fuzzy statements that need to be explored before you can find the true problem.

Step 2: **Fact-finding** is turning facts into a problem-finding statement. State as many problems and subproblems as possible.

Step 3: **Problem-finding** is selecting the best problem statement.

Step 4: **Idea-finding** is brainstorming alternative solutions and ideas. In step 4, apply all the decision-making tools and problem-solving strategies described previously in this chapter.

Step 5: **Solution-finding** is selecting criteria that will demonstrate a problem has been solved, not yet thinking about possible solutions. Solution-finding is writing feelings and values relative to the problem before selecting a solution.

Step 6: **Acceptance-finding** is using the criteria in step 5 to accept a best solution. Consider everything that will or won't work and stretch beyond first ideas.

Step 7: **Plan-of-action** is checking progress in implementing the solution.

(JW) Now ask students to think of a problem they have at school or outside of school that needs solving. Ask them to use the process to solve the problem by writing the steps in their journal. Last, ask students to describe how they can use the creative problem-solving process at home, play, and school.

(RRG) *Main characters model problem solving.* Read one of the books from the unit and have students discuss the successful and unsuccessful actions these people took to solve their problems. Next, in small groups, have students write a sequel to that book by posing to this character a problem they face as adolescents, as a class, or as a school. Keeping the literary figure in character, have students propose actions that that person would take to solve the problem and share their sequels with the class.

What we've learned. Near the end of this unit, ask small groups of students to write their own summary of what they've learned to do to improve their problem-solving abilities. The best message from each small group is then read to the class.

Fable writing. At the end of the unit, duplicate all quotes for students and have them select two favorites. Form groups of those students who selected the same quotes and have each group discuss why each quotation was important to them. Then have each group create a fable to teach the meaning to another class of students at a lower grade level or to another group of classmates who selected different quotations. Explain that the quote is to become the last sentence (moral) of the story. Last, ask students to revise, edit, compile, and share their fables.

Multicultural Emphasis: Facts about Problem Solving That Come from Different Cultures

Brazilian. Share *The Rain Dance,* a Brazilian legend. Ask students what it taught them about problem solving.

> Once the sun, the moon, and the water lived on earth just as people do. The sun kept the people warm, the moon lit the nights, and the water quenched their thirst.
> But the people grew spoiled with this good life and chased them away—the sun because it was too hot, the moon because it was too bright and kept them awake at night, and the water because it drenched their homes.
> The earth became cold and cheerless. The plants and animals began to die for lack of water.
> Then the people turned to the Wise One, old Na-ma-ka-ra-ne, for help.
> "What can we do? We have no warmth, no water, and our children are dying!"
> He told them, "Drum without pause until the old man Rain hears you and sends you water for your thirst."
> So the people drummed and danced for days and days in their first rain dance until drops of rain fell to moisten the earth again. This was how the rain dance first came into existence.

22 SOLVING PROBLEMS

African American. The Swahili word *ujima* (oo-jee-mah) means "working together and helping each other." To build and maintain a community, African Americans and African people believe in solving problems by calling on their sisters and brothers. In this way, their problems became everyone's concern and all assist in solving them.

Mexican American. Read or have a guest read the following books in Spanish. They will teach students many things about the role language plays in a culture, about Spanish, and about the ways Mexican Americans solve problems:

> Grimm, The Brothers. Adapted by Rossana Guarnieri. *Los Musicos de Brema.* Mexico: Fernandez Editores, S.A., 1983. This is an adaptation of the classic folktale about four animals who work together to solve a problem.
>
> Pecanins, Ana Maria. *La Cometa.* Mexico: Editorial Trillas, S.A., 1986. A girl and a flock of birds rescue a trapped kite. They become friends and have a wonderful summer together.
>
> La Fleur, Tom, and Gale Brennan. *Lucho el Aquilucho.* Mexico: Editorial Trillas, S.A., 1984. A fable about a nearsighted eagle and a fly who become good friends and together make a perfect flying team.

(BLM) *Multicultural.* Divide students into groups based on the countries of the world students select to study from Blackline Master 35 (see BLM section). Then have each group choose some of its members to research problems that people in that country overcame in the past and how they overcame them. Instruct other members of the groups to use current event literature to identify problems their country faces now. After two days of research, have group members present the problems and solutions they found. Next, have each group prepare a posterboard depicting the problems, solutions, and patterns that were evident in that culture's approach to problem solving. Instruct students to select the quotation from the unit that most accurately portrays the values for problem solving in their country. Last, all posters are shared with the class and differences between problem-solving strategies are discussed.

Your Own Additions to the Unit

23 Standing Up for Myself

Learning Objectives Some students are ridiculed by peers because they do not know how to stand up for themselves. Books, quotations, and activities in this unit teach students strategies for presenting themselves in more effective ways.

Resources *Select a different quotation to discuss and write on the board each day of this unit's study.*

*Speak for a reason and
you'll be heard.*

*When things go wrong—
don't go with them.*
—Anonymous

*It never gets easier
but you can get stronger.*

*Begin somewhere; you cannot build
A reputation on what you intend to do.*
—Liz Smith

Give your attention to the right direction.

There is always a way offered to you.

*If I am not for myself, who will be for me?
and if I am only for myself, what am I?*
—The Talmud

*If you don't stand for something,
you're likely to fall for anything.*
—Don Zadra

*Always hold your head up
but be careful to keep your
nose at a friendly level.*
—Max L. Forman

Your character is your fate.

*I can do what I can do
And sometimes what you do too*

I feel good about myself.

Finding the Right Book Concerning Standing Up for Myself to Meet Students' Needs

Difficulty code: I = Introductory; E = Easy; M = Medium

		Book
I	Outgrowing actions	*Someone New* by Charlotte Zolotow
I	Being happy with yourself	*The Sneetches* by Dr. Seuss
I	Applying yourself	*Annabelle Swift, Kindergarten* by Amy Schwartz
I	Being yourself adapted from an old German folktale (filmstrip)	*The Little Pine Tree* by Ina E. Lindsby
I	Being happy with yourself	*Biggest House in the World* by Leo Lionni
I	Realizing one's own beauty	*I Wish I Were a Butterfly* by James Howe
E	Developing slowly	*Leo the Late Bloomer* by Robert Kraus
E	A nose that makes him special	*Arthur's Nose* by Marc Tolon Brown
E	Being yourself	*Everyone Goes as a Pumpkin* by Judith Vigna
E–M	Becoming brave	*Cowardly Clyde* by Bill Peet
E–M	A disabled boy learns to stand up for himself and meet his parents' and friends' high expectations	*Kelly's Creek* by Doris Buchanan Smith
E–M	Learning about your potential	*Unlocking Your Potential* by Dan Zadra
E–M	Girl shows father her sport is best for her	*Jenny and the Tennis Nut* by Janet Schulman
M	Shyness because of height	*Seven Feet Four and Growing* by H. Alton Lee
M	A Jewish boy learns to stand up for himself	*The Difference of Ari Stein* by Charlotte Herman
M	A boy learns to stand up for himself in the face of recovering from major surgery	*A Boy Called Hopeless* by David Melton
M	Not being taken advantage of	*Brighty of the Grand Canyon* by Marguerite Henry
M	Thought-provoking story	*Koya DeLancy and the Good Girl Blues* by Eloise Greenfield
M	Prejudice shown a boy who loves to dance	*A Special Gift* by Marcia Simon
M	Courage and values	*Ryan White: My Own Story* by Ryan White and Ann Marie Cunningham

		Book
M	Taking an unpopular stand	*The Preacher's Kid* by Rose Blue
M	A sixth grader reads a book to first graders and finds she has to defend it	*Maudie and Me and the Dirty Book* by Betty Miles
M	Bicultural Chinese-American identity	*Child of the Owl* by Lawrence Michael Yep
M	Different men taking a stand on issues of importance	*Profiles in Courage* by John F. Kennedy

Activities to Use with Quotes and Books:

Opening the School Day Discussion

Write a quote on the board each day and ask students to list situations in which they had to stand up for themselves. Keep this list on the board all week. As each new quote is written, ask students to relate its message to ways it can be used in each situation on the list.

Mobiles. Have students make a mobile. Ask them to put what they want to become at the top of the mobile and to hang important characteristics of themselves below that description or drawing. Then display each child's mobile above his or her desk. Explain that one section on each mobile must present, in pictures, graphics, or words, a way they will present themselves effectively in a previously difficult situation. In this section of the mobile, have students also include their favorite quote from the unit.

(RRG) *Role models.* Have students, alone or in pairs, select and read a book from this unit. When four students have completed the book, ask them to divide into an interest group and plan how they can report to the group the message of the book and strategies the book illustrated for standing up for oneself.

Teaching students to stand up for themselves effectively. Share this advice from United Technologies which appeared in the *Wall Street Journal*:

> Submit to pressure from peers and you move down to their level. Speak up for your own beliefs and you invite them up to your level. If you move with the crowd, you'll get no further than the crowd. When 40 million people believe in a dumb idea, it's still a dumb idea.

And simply swimming with the tide leaves you nowhere. So if you believe in something that's good, honest, and bright—stand up for it.
Maybe your peers will get smart and drift your way (Dan Zandra, *The Secret of the Slight Edge,* Creative Education Publishers, pp. 42–43).
After discussing this advice, ask students to list three actions they can take to stand up for themselves effectively. They can share their lists in small groups and add to their ideas if desired. At the end of the week, have students

return to their list and describe how they implemented their actions during the week, how they felt, and what they want to do next to improve their ability to stand up for their beliefs and for themselves in the coming week. Continue this cycle as long as necessary until students become self-reliant.

I do well. Start students thinking by mentioning things you do well. Get responses from the class about things they do well. Examples can be as simple as picking up their toys, brushing their teeth, or doing classwork. Have each child write or draw three things they do well or want to do better.

My idea matters. Read *Annabelle Swift, Kindergartener* or another unit book. Explain how students can relate themselves to the characters in the story to gain a better understanding of themselves and the story. Discuss their interpretations of the book and talk about how people understand things differently, but stress that everyone's interpretation matters.

(RRG) *Being myself.* Read *The Sneetches* by Dr. Seuss, *The Dirty Boy* by Robert Kavet, *The Biggest House in the World* by Leo Lionni, and/or *Everyone Goes as a Pumpkin* by Judith Vigna. Discuss "being yourself" and being happy with yourself. Talk about strategies that the children learned from the book(s).

Meeting individual students' needs. Review the list of specific topics on self-esteem represented in the books of this unit. Select the topic about which your students need most instruction. Then have students read a book of choice and discuss ways they can use what they learned in their own lives.

Multicultural Emphasis: Standing Up for Myself

Multicultural. Have students research any culture's major holiday and write a report about it, or get permission for the class to attend a celebration in your area. Some suggestions are: Japanese Culture Day—November 3 (celebration of love and freedom, equality, and Japanese culture); the African-American celebration of Kwanzaa; or any culture's New Year's Day celebrations. Explain that the United Nations General Assembly adopted the Universal Declaration of Human Rights in 1948. The principal author of this document was Eleanor Roosevelt, the widow of Franklin Delano Roosevelt, who was president of the United States from 1933 to 1945. In 1979 the United Nations adopted the Declaration of the Rights of the Child in honor of the International Year of the Child. Encourage students to decorate a copy of this declaration and take it home for their parents.

UN Declaration of the Rights of the Child

The right

- to affection, love, and understanding.
- to adequate nutrition and medical care.
- to free education.
- to full opportunity for play and recreation.
- to a name and nationality.

- to special care, if handicapped.
- to be among the first to receive relief in times of disaster.
- to learn to be a useful member of society and to develop individual abilities.
- to be brought up in a spirit of peace and universal brotherhood.
- to enjoy these rights, regardless of race, color, sex, religion, national or social origin.

Students can express how these rights are important to them and ways they would like to ensure that all students have them.

Mexican American. In Mexican-American culture a high value is placed on family life. Many Mexican-American children develop a healthy sense of self-esteem from positive interactions with family members, but conflict within the family can be exceptionally detrimental to self-esteem in this culture. For this reason, Mexican-American students will especially benefit from reading the following books:

> Berenstain, Stan and Jan. *El Bebe de los Osos Berenstain.* New York: Scholastic, 1982. The family is preparing for the arrival of a new baby. When the baby arrives, Brother Bear helps but is worried about his place in the family.
>
> Carruth, Jane. *La Hermanita.* Argentina: Editorial Sigmar, 1978. Tili is a little mouse who feels left out when his new baby sister arrives.

Once these books have been completed, discuss other ways to overcome difficulties that can arise in a family or between friends at school.

Your Own Additions to the Unit

24 Succeeding

Learning Objectives One of the most common desires of all people is to achieve success. The quotations, activities, and books in this unit present strategies that increase students' abilities to achieve success, knowledge, prestige, and self-satisfaction.

Resources *Select a different quotation to discuss and write on the board each day of this unit's study.*

Isn't it great to be able to say "I did it!"?

*To complete your goal
is like winning the Super Bowl.*

*Excellence is to do a common thing
in an uncommon way.*
—Booker T. Washington

Success is failure turned inside out.

Success comes one step at a time.

*The journey of a thousand miles begins
with a single step.*
—Lao Tze

Success is achieved by those who try.

*Those who know what to do will succeed once,
those who know why they do as they do
will succeed again and again.*

What you are to be, you are now becoming.

*We must first succeed alone that we
may enjoy our success together.*
— Walden

*He has achieved success who has
lived well, and laughed often.*

*Success is not something to wait for
it's something to work for.*

*The talent of success is nothing
more than doing what you can do well
and doing well whatever you do.*

*In the wide arena of the world,
failure and success are not accidents,
as we frequently suppose,
but the strictest justice.*
—Alexander Smith

Finding the Right Book Concerning Succeeding to Meet Students' Needs

Difficulty code: I = Introductory; E = Easy; M = Medium

		Book
I	Making money	*Lemonade Parade* by Ben Brooks
I	Planting a seed	*The Carrot Seed* by Ruth Krauss
I	Values, honesty, and courage lead to success	*The Empty Pot* by Demi
I	Overcoming a feeling of failure	*The Beetle Bush* by Beverly Keller
I	A baker's oven breaks but he still wins	*The Man Who Entered a Contest* by Phyllis Krasilovsky
I	Flossie outsmarts the fox to complete her errand	*Flossie and the Fox* by Patricia McKissack
I	A shy boy stands up and faces the fear of being first to tell his story	*Jim Chimp's Story* by Muriel Bloustein
I–E	Self-confidence from success	*Will I Ever Be Good Enough* by Judith Conaway
I–E	Testimonial given by a young boy	*What Does It Mean, Success?* by Susan Riley
E	A boy who wants to succeed	*Gypsies Magic Box* by Christopher Neal
E	Success for a Hong Kong girl	*I Hate English* by Ellen Levine
E	Ideas for performing	*The Talent Show* by Nancy Carlson
E	Gaining praise after being momentarily defeated	*Daniel's Duck* by Robert Clyde Bulla
E	A lonely prince forms satisfying but dangerous friendships	*My Friend the Monster* by Robert Clyde Bulla
E	What makes birds successful	*Feathers* by Dorothy Henshaw Patent
E	Success, one step at a time	*Amelia Bedelia* by Peggy Parish
E–M	A real pro	*Michael Jordan: Basketball Champ* by Bill Gutman
E–M	First African American in professional baseball	*Jackie Robinson: He Was the First* by David Adler
E–M	Women who have succeeded in science	*Women Pioneers in Science* by Louis Haber
E–M	Success through hard work, not luck	*Where the Good Luck Was* by Osmond Malarsky
M	A fictionalized biography of a heroic Puerto Rican baseball player	*Pride of Puerto Rico: The Life of Roberto Clemente* by Paul R. Walker

		Book
M	Fable about the nature of wisdom and success	*Alberic the Wise* by Norton Juster
M	Three children left on their own draw on their resources	*A Lion to Guard Us* by Robert Clyde Bulla
M	Biography of the Mongol leader	*Chingis Khan* by Demi
M	Successes that changed history	*Great Lives: Invention and Technology* by Milton Lomask
M	Successes that started out as mistakes	*Mistakes That Worked* by Charlotte Jones
M	Achievement of women	*Twentieth Century Women of Achievement* by Samuel Kastman
M	Boy learns his own actions will lead to success	*Farm Boy* by Douglas W. Gorsline
M	Fables of traditional African culture	*The Crest and the Hide and Other African Stories of Heroes, Chiefs, Birds, Hunters, Sorcerers, and Common People* by Harold Courlander

Activities to Use with Quotes and Books

Opening the School Day Discussion

Put a new quote on the board each day. Discuss the understanding students have from each saying. Explain to students that to be successful, they may have to experience failures along the way, and that this is natural as people learn from their mistakes. Then have each student write about a personal experience where they first failed but tried again and became successful.

How others achieve success. Have students discuss someone they judge to be the best at what they do—a parent, friend, or famous person. Then ask them to write a letter or interview that person asking how they became the best. As an alternative, students can select a book from this unit and read it in pairs, and write what factors contributed to the main character's success.

Your mind can help you achieve success. Say: "Close your eyes and concentrate for one minute on something you would like to do that is very important to you. What steps would you take to achieve it?" Then explain to the students that their minds will enact the quotation: "If we can conceive it and believe it, we can achieve it." Tell students this is a very important concept to remember when faced with a difficult situation. If they keep an open mind, many things are possible. Next, ask students to think about what they have learned, look for a situation that is either difficult or seems impossible throughout the day, and return to school the next day with an action they will describe in writing that will address this situation.

Teaching students a strategy to be successful. Tell students that you are going to share a strategy Albert Einstein used to be successful. He said his success came partly because he set aside time each day to challenge others' opinions—and to think for himself. Ask students why this strategy would lead to success, and have them write what they will do to implement it in their lives.

(JW) *Past successes.* Think about a problem you solved that you thought could not be solved. Share it with the class. Then ask students to write or draw something that once was hard for them but isn't anymore. Then ask: "Has there ever been something you wanted to quit but you kept on trying and finally got it?" Share answers and journals with the class.

Subject success. Give each group an event that occurred in the story *I Hate English!* or events in another book. They briefly act it out and tell the class how they thought Mei Mei (or another character) felt during that situation in the story and what made her feel that way.

Learning about success through reading. Read *My Grammy*. Discuss something that is very hard for you to live with or understand. Students do the same and then retell the story *My Grammy* to each other in pairs. Ask the class how Amy's behavior changed toward her grandmother during the story and why they think it did. Then ask: "Can they think of anything that happened to them that is similar to Amy's situation?" Have them pretend they were Amy and write how they think they would have felt and reacted in her situation.

Multicultural Emphasis: Concepts about Success That Come from Other Cultures

Southeast Asia. Explain that some people in the Indochinese culture desire special recognition only through a smile, a soft thank you, or a similar small gesture of gratitude. They do not feel they deserve praise and will usually respond to a more demonstrative recognition of their success by reciting their faults. Then ask students how *they* most like to receive recognition, and why.

Mexican American. The following story describes several values and strategies used in Spanish-speaking nations to overcome difficulties.

> Stevenson, James. *Howard.* Spain: Ediciones Generales Anaya, 1982. Howard, the duck, is left behind in a cold northern city when his family flies south. He meets a frog and a mouse who teach him how to survive.

If this book is not available, describe the plot to students and ask them to create specific things that the frog and the mouse could have taught the duck. Students can research the habits of mice and frogs before making this list. Also, they can write their own version of *Howard,* either in small groups or individually.

Asia. Many Southeast Asians have been very successful in the United States. Some have won college scholarships and prizes. Some have been high school valedictorians and soccer champions. A high percentage finish high school and graduate from college. One factor to which this cultural group attributes success is that, in their early school years, Southeast Asian children are taught the value of school and learn that they should achieve success throughout their lives.

(BLM) *France.* The origin of modern science in France really goes back to the Renaissance. By reading the scientific writings of the Romans and Greeks, the French of the Renaissance learned many things about their world and started to question medieval superstitions. Many successes came from France. Antoine-Laurent Lavoisier is known as the father of modern chemistry; Marie and Pierre Curie discovered the chemical element radium; and Andr\ae Ampere's researched electricity and found and named the science of electrodynamics, known now as electromagnetism. The ampere (amp) is named after him; this is the unit of measurement of electrical current. Have students identify a country of their choice and name three accomplishments people made in that country that we use today. If time allows, have small groups working on different countries, make posterboard displays of the accomplishments. You may use Blackline Master 35 in the BLM section, with this activity.

Multicultural. The following nonfiction books give students a chance to read about successful people from different cultural groups: *El Chino* by Allen Say portrays the life of a Chinese American who became a matador. *The Last Princess* by Fay Stanley is the story of Princess Ka'uilani of Hawaii. *Now Is Your Time: The African American Struggle for Freedom* by Dean Myer chronicles individual and family histories in the African-American culture; and *Pueblo Storyteller* by Diane Hoyt-Goldsmith is a photo essay of Cochiti customs and traditions. These books can be read aloud as a class, read in small groups, or completed by individual students who may present special reports to the class for extra credit.

Spain. Think of Christopher Columbus and his success. Persisting after rejections from several countries, Columbus finally persuaded the queen of Spain to finance his trip to a new world. His success launched an exciting era of trade with a new land. What's more, Columbus, his crew, and his passengers were the first multicultural people to arrive in America.

Your Own Additions to the Unit

25 Thinking and Learning

Learning Objectives Developing students' critical thinking abilities is important. As our world becomes increasingly complex and competitive, students' success in life will depend on their abilities to resolve dilemmas and create new ideas. Quotations, activities, and books in this unit cultivate students' critical and creative thinking abilities.

Resources *Select a different quotation to discuss and write on the board each day of this unit's study.*

How can I know what I think till I see what I say?
—Graham Wallas, 1926/1979

Learn and grow.

Think you can and you will.

Learn something new every day.

I'm willing to learn, because I study to grow.

Perception is where cognition and reality meet.

*You can learn from a sister or brother
Just like you do from a friend or mother.*

Learn to seek; seek to learn.

Work your brain and your brain will work for you.

Strive to know and learn all you can.

Many problems result from action without thought.

*When I just pause and think,
many times I find the answer in a wink.*

Need is the gap between desired and current status.
—James Popham

*Give your attention in the right direction
and you will gain knowledge.*

Give every man thine ear, but few thy voice.
—Polonius in *Hamlet*

The important thing is not to stop questioning.
—Albert Einstein

Wonder rather than doubt is the root of knowledge.
—Abraham J. Heachel

*If people cannot write well,
they cannot think well, and
if they cannot think well, others
will do their thinking for them.*

Finding the Right Book Concerning Thinking and Learning to Meet Students' Needs

Difficulty code: I = Introductory; E = Easy; M = Medium

		Book
I	Curiosity	*Little Black Bear Goes for a Walk* by Berneice Freschet
I	Developing concepts and sequencing ideas	*Where's Mother?* by Elizabeth Thorn
I	Shapes	*Circles, Triangles and Squares* by Tana Hoban
I	Recognizing the difference	*Children Do, Grownups Don't* by Norma Simon
I	Ingenious counting book	*One More Thing, Dad* by Muriel Stanek
I	Numbers, groups, and sets	*Anno's Counting Book* by Mitsumasa Anno
I	Rhythmic verse	*Ten, Nine, Eight* by Molly Bank
I	About frogs, homework, and life	*Frog Medicine* by Mark Teague
I	Pennsylvania Dutch using alphabetic framework	*The Folks in the Valley* by Jim Aylesworth
I	What it was like to be a baby	*Why Is Baby Crying?* by Ryerson Johnson
I	Learning left from right	*Beach Ball—Left, Right* by Bruce McMillan
I	Distressed by test that fails to measure true aptitude	*First Grade Takes a Test* by Miriam Cohen
I–E	Learning money	*The Monster Money Book* by Loreen Leedy
I–E	Adding and subtracting	*How the Second Grade Got $8,205.50 to Visit the Statue of Liberty* by Nathan Zimelman
I–E	Earth view by aliens	*Blast Off to Earth! A Look at Geography* by Loreen Leedy

		Book
E	Tricks and games based on counting, simple computations, and logic	*Math-a Magic: Numbers Tricks for Magicians* by Ray Brockel and Laurence B. White
E	Sensitive explanation of how nature includes both life and death	*Annie and the Old One* by Miska Miles
E	Boots outsmarts his brothers (Norwegian tale)	*Boots and His Brothers* by Eric Kimmel
E–M	Children's thoughts	*Something on My Mind* by Nikki Grimes
M	Superstition	*Volleyball Jinx* by Bobbi Katz
M	Reconciliation of fact and fantasy	*The Enchanted Castle* by E. Nesbit
M	Comanche Indian legend	*The Legend of the Bluebonnet* by Tomie de Paola
M	A broad view of everyday events	*Where the Sidewalk Ends* and *A Light in the Attic* by Shel Silverstein
M	A challenge for young detectives	*Who Burned the Hartley House?* by Carole Smith
M	How some foreigners view Americans	*The Bicycle Man* by Allen Say
M	Things are not always as they seem	*Slave Dancer* by Paula Fox
M	Different interpretations of causes	*Junior Great Books Story—The Stone Faced Boy* by Paula Fox
M	Biography of a Hawaiian princess	*The Last Princess: The Story of Princess Ka'iulani of Hawaii* by Fay Stanley
M	Accomplishments of a brilliant thinker	*Galileo* by Leonard Everett Fisher
M	Different viewpoints about peace and conflict	*The Big Book for Peace* edited by Ann Durrell and Marilyn Sachs

Activities to Use with Quotes and Books

Opening the School Day Discussion

Discuss the definition of the words learning and thinking. Is one more important than the other? Why? At the close of this unit, see if students have any more to add to above question.

Challenge the critics. Assign a story or book from this unit to be read by the class. Tell the children that you agree with the author and that you think the antagonist is an evil person. Then have your students contradict you and write a character report in which the character's good qualities are identified. This activity teaches students that they can identify their points of view by defending them when they come into conflict with others. In this activity, students also learn to challenge their way of thinking and to avoid stereotypical thinking.

One of the most important thinking skills is predicting. Select a book and have students stop on the designated page before the ending is revealed. Then take a poll to identify their ideas for the conclusion. Group students with similar ideas and ask them to write their predictions, share the clues that led them to their opinion, read the ending they wrote to the class after sharing students' endings, and compare the author's version with theirs.

(JW) *Journal writing.* Show the students that if they wonder, it will help to generate more thinking, whereas "doubt stops the thinking process." Explain that wonder is the root of knowledge because it brings curiosity and excitement to learning. Then ask students to write about a time when their doubts stopped their actions, and to think about how they could have responded instead. Before they begin this journal-writing activity, read a description you wrote of a time in your own life when doubts limited your success and of how you overcame them. Next, instruct students to write or draw about something that sparks their curiosity. They should also describe how they would like to learn about it. Review the journals and plan activities based on the students' desires.

(BLM) *Think-alouds.* Divide the class into pairs and distribute "Puzzle Me," Blackline Master 36 (in BLM section). Ask students to describe their thinking as they complete the boxes in each square. Model the first one for them by describing your own thoughts as you try to identify four-letter words in which the *s* can appear in all four locations:

```
Correct answer:  D U E S
                 D E S U
                 U S E D
                 S U E D
```

After all six squares are complete, ask students to write the most important thinking strategies they learned from their partners.

Susan the seeker. The class invents a story titled "Susan the Seeker" that describes new ways Susan learns. The class publishes each student's story as a classroom book.

Guest speaker. Have the principal come to class and tell the students his or her experience in learning, how he or she has continued to learn throughout his or her life, and why lifelong learning is important.

Rhyming cards matching game. Divide students into small groups. Give each group 10 index cards. Then ask students to write one word on a card so that each card has a word with a different rhyming pattern. Students in Group 1 hold up one of their cards and say the word. Students in other groups hold up the card from their set of 10 that rhymes with that word and say their words. Older children can make a rhyme from the words given and use all the words in one or more sentences.

Identifying letters. Give each student a sheet of paper with several sentences on it. Ask them to circle every *R* that they see, then underline every *T,* and draw a square around every *I.* Check these over to make sure they understood the concept. Alternatively, give each student a bingo card with letters on it. Let students take turns drawing a letter from the box. Have the class give them hints on the letter if they do not know it. If the student has the letter he or she draws, then he can cover the letter. The first person whose card is full wins.

Multicultural Emphasis: Concepts about Thinking and Learning That Come from Other Cultures

Share the following examples of advanced thinking from other cultures and discuss students' responses to these incidents.

Native American. Share the following legend and ask students to imagine the story and tell what it explains about Native-American culture:

Hanuman, the Monkey God

Hanuman, the Monkey God, once had a craving for hot, spicy food. He became so hungry for it that he turned to the sun and swallowed the sun whole. With the sun inside him, Hanuman grew hotter and hotter, while the people on earth became colder and colder. The flowers died and the trees lost their leaves. Snow fell during the dark days and the dark nights. The birds went away, for there was no sun to warm them, and the animals hid in their caves. The people grew sad and wondered what they could do to bring back the sun.

Then a child suggested, "Let's make Hanuman laugh! He will laugh until he spits out the sun. Then we will be warm again."

The people thought about this and said, "Yes, that is a good idea! But how can we do this?"

They thought. Someone suggested telling Hanuman a funny story, but they knew he was too hot to listen. Someone else suggested painting a funny picture, but they knew he wouldn't look. Then a child said, "I know. We can paint one another!"

"What?" said the people. "That is a silly idea." Then they began to laugh. Someone picked up some red dirt and put it on a neighbor's head. Someone else threw blue powder over all the adults. Oh, how funny they looked. The colors flew and mixed, and the people laughed and laughed so loudly that Hanuman looked down.

"What is this?" he bellowed. Then he saw the blue, orange, purple, and green people and he smiled. He giggled. One huge laugh fell out and another, until Hanuman was rolling with laughter. He laughed so hard that tears came to his eyes. At last, out popped the sun.

"Hurrah!" said the people. "The plan worked." Then they, too, started to laugh as they felt the world become warm and sunny. Every year on Holi they remember Hanuman and throw colored powders over one another to make the Monkey God laugh again!

Ask students which of the quotations this legend best describes. Also, share that Native Americans used different signs of nature to calculate when and where to plant crops and to plant; when, where, and what to hunt; and when storms were coming—things they needed to know for the survival of the tribe.

France. Probably the greatest single advance in modern medicine was Louis Pasteur's discovery of bacteria. This French chemist's research led to the germ theory of disease. Pasteur understood that bacteria made people sick and that antiseptics that killed bacteria should be used to protect patients. He also developed a vaccine against rabies, a dreaded disease in his time.

China. Confucius (c. 551–479 B.C.) lived in many different parts of China. He considered education very important. Because of his great knowledge, he was an advisor to China's rulers on many issues. He felt that you must truly understand information if you want to use it in your own thinking and to create new ideas. Just memorizing something did not mean you could use this information in life. Confucius left the world with many wise philosophical sayings, which were collected after his death in *The Analects of Confucius*. These sayings and the Chinese classics, which he edited, form the content of traditional Chinese education.

Asian culture. Part of the Confucian philosophy is to value education. Families who follow Confucianism help their children to love learning. They know it holds a promise of a better life. Teachers are shown much respect.

Germany. In 1945, near the end of World War II, Germany had perfected the jet fighter plane but did not have pilots to fly the planes. If Germany had had the personnel to fly these planes, the Germans might have won the war. After World War II ended, the Soviet Union took many of German professors of aeronautical engineering who had been developing fuel for spaceships as prisoners of war. Their work helped enable the Soviet Union to be the first in space.

Thailand. Thai proverbs are used to teach children to do good and to be useful to society.

Mexican American: Comparing families. Using picture books and books from the list in this unit, present illustrations depicting all types of families in different situations. Guide students in a discussion by asking, "*¿En que se parecen estas familias?*" ("How are these families the same?") "*¿Cuales dibujos les recuerdan a sus familias? ¿Por qué?*" ("Which pictures remind you of your families? Why?")

(JW) In personal journals, have students write about the illustrations or story or draw what they learned to do at home.

(BLM) Finger puppets are used in many ways in Mexican-American schools. Show students the following clown and princess, Blackline Master 37 (in BLM section). Ask them to draw two characters with arms in air and two holes for legs, or use the two in the Blackline. Show how they can cut out the holes and place their fingers through them. By holding the puppets on an index card, students can put on a finger puppet show like those done in Mexican-American cities.

Greece. Greece is noted for its philosophers and teachers, such as Aristotle (384–322 B.C.) and Socrates (c. 470–399 B.C.). Euclid was the founder of modern geometry, and he died in 300 B.C. Moreover, Greek poetry is considered among the best of the twentieth century. Homer (c. 850–775 B.C.) was the author of the Iliad and the Odyssey, the oldest written poems of Greece and Western civilization.

Denmark. The *Denmark, My Country* series by Bernice and Cliff Moon provides good information to interest students in Denmark. It is about 28 people, of all life-styles, who describe their life in Denmark.

(BLM) *Also Turkey . . . in Pictures* is a visual geography series prepared by Stephen C. Feinstein. To help students understand the size of some of these countries, show Blackline Master 35 (in BLM section). Give examples of size comparisons—for example, Laos is a little smaller than Oregon; Yugoslavia is a little larger than Wyoming.

African culture. Africa Dream by Eloise Greenfield is a good book to introduce what Africa was like long ago. *I Am Eyes* by Leila Ward will assist students' understanding of the beauty of Kenya. Then you may challenge students with Claudia Zaslavsky's book, *Count on Your Fingers African Style.*

Your Own Additions to the Unit

26 Understanding Ecology and Nature

Learning Objectives *Ecology* is defined as the branch of biology that deals with the relationship between living organisms and their environment. In this unit, special attention is given to the relationship between humans' cultural and social patterns and their natural resources. The quotations, activities, and books increase students' ecological awareness and understanding of their personal responsibilities to nature. Moreover, students will learn about human nature by studying and caring for animals, will be introduced to the beauty and order of nature and natural phenomena.

Resources *Select a different quotation to discuss and write on the board each day of this unit's study.*

Nature is the World's art.

*Nature is so nice to show
Many things that we should know.*

*Love your pets
As you do your friends.*

*I have a pet
That is the very best yet!*

*Going to the zoo can't be beat,
To watch all the animals is so neat.*

*I like to sing about McDonald's farm,
It would be so much fun holding an animal in my arm.*

The earth is the home of the world.

*It is important for us all
to "clean up" our acts.*

*The world could have a problem
and it could be us.*

*Recycling is our plot,
When everyone helps
it means a lot.*

Be [the name of state or school you are in] proud.

Finding the Right Book Concerning Ecology and Nature to Meet Students' Needs

Difficulty code: I = Introductory; E = Easy; M = Medium

		Book
I	Animal friendship	*The Nervous Little Hare* (old folktale from India)
I	Animal friendship	*Squeaky Door* by Laura Simms
I	Animal determination	*The Turtle Who Wants to Fly South* by Michael Caduto
I	Animal self-esteem	*Nothing at All* by Wanda Gag
I	Story about animals	*Frog Went-a-Courtin'* by John Langstaff
I	Vet talks about health problems of dogs	*Taking My Dog to the Vet* by Susan Ruklin
I	Farm and zoo animals	*Big Ones, Little Ones* by Tana Hoban
I	Natural environments, months, and animals	*A Year of Beasts* by Ashley Wolff
I	Animals follow the sun to see where it goes	*Where Does the Sun Go at Night?* by Mirra Ginsburg
I	How the world works for us all	*On the Day You Were Born* by Debra Frasier
I	Classifying animals	*Benny's Animals, and How He Put Them in Order* by Millicent Selsam
I	A poetic metaphor about how nature cares for us	*Mother Earth* by Nancy Luenn
I	Flowers and their parts	*Flower* by M. Butterfield
I	From seeds to plants	*From Seed to Plant* by G. Gibbons
I	Trees	*Hello, Tree!* by J. Ryder
I	Dinosaurs	*Let's Go Dinosaur Tracking* by M. Schlein
I	Recycling	*Here Comes the Recycling Truck* by M. Seltzer
I	Plant kingdom	*My First Green Book* by A. Wilkes
I	A fairytale about preserving the forest (film, video)	*Fern Gully: The Last Rainforest* (20th Century Fox)
I-E	Comparing cats to dogs	*Cats Do, Dogs Don't* by Norma Simon
I-E	Introduction to pandas	*Pandas* by Norman S. Barrett
I-E	Animals wearing clothes	*Animals Should Definitely Not Wear Clothing* by Judith Barret

26 UNDERSTANDING ECOLOGY AND NATURE

		Book
I-E	Ducklings' adventure	*Make Way for Ducklings* by Robert McCloskey
E	Stuffed animal becomes real	*The Velveteen Rabbit* by Margery Williams
E	Portrayal of creative ideas about ecology	*Everybody Needs a Rock* and *When Clay Sings* by Byrd Baylor
E	A basic ecological principle: everything goes somewhere	*When the Wind Stops* by Charlotte S. Zolotow
E	Activities to help heal the environment	*Earth Book for Kids* by Linda Schwartz
E	Bird science	*Feathers for Lunch* by Lois Ehlert
E-M	Our environment	*The Desert Is Theirs* by Byrd Baylor
E-M	The world before pollution	*The Zabojaba Jungle* by William Steig
E-M	Humans' negative effects on the environment	*The Great Kapok Tree* by Lynn Cherry
E-M	Benefits animals give humans	*Whales* by Gail Gibbons
E-M	Starting the day productively	*The Way to Start a Day* by Byrd Baylor
E-M	Desert inhabitants	*Desert Voices* by Byrd Baylor
E-M	Dinosaurs	*Living with Dinosaurs* by Patricia Lauber
E-M	Solving pollution problems	*Garbage* by Karen O'Connor
E-M	Recycling	*Recycle! A Handbook for Kids* by G. Gibbons
E-M	Weather	*Weather* by G. Jeunesse and P. de Bourgoing
E-M	Living in harmony with nature	*Hawk, I'm Your Brother* by Byrd Baylor
E-M	Conserving the rain forest	*The Great Kapok Tree: A Tale of the Amazon Rain Forest* by Lynne Cherry
E-M	Seeds and plants	*Little Green Pumpkins* by Christa Chevalier
M	Harvesting	*Corn Belt Harvest* by R. Bial
M	Respect for nature	*The Whale's Song* by Dyan Sheldon
M	The loon	*Great Northern Diver: The Loon* by Barbara Esbensen
M	Wild animals need freedom in their environment	*Trumpet of the Swan* by E. B. White

		Book
M	Impact of a volcano on plant and animal life and on the future	*Volcano: The Eruption and Healing of Mount St. Helens* by Patricia Lauber
M	An A–Z list of inspiring ideas about ecology	*Going Green: A Kid's Guide to How to Save the Planet* by Billy Goodman
M	Native American concepts of ecology	*Our Voices, Our Land* by Christine Price
M	Poems about the natural world from thirteen Native American cultures	*Thirteen Moons on Turtle's Back: A Native American Year of Moons* by Joseph Bruchac and Jonathan London
M	From how we got into this mess through suggestions for good ecological practices	*Going Green: A Kid's Handbook to Saving the Planet* by John Elkington, Julia Haile, Douglas Hill, and Joel Makower
M	A basic ecological principle: everything goes somewhere	*When the Wind Stops* by Charlotte Zolotow
M	Recycling and new products from it	*Recycling: Meeting the Challenge of the Trash Crisis* by Alvin, Virginia, and Robert Silverstein
M	Recycling	*The Mushroom Center Disaster* by N. M. Bodecker
M	A school adopts a stream	*Come Back Solmon* by Molly Cone
M	Earth Day activities	*Celebrating Earth Day: A Sourcebook of Activities and Experiments* by Robert Gardner
M	Birds' poetry	*Bird Watch* by Jane Yolen
M	Cleaning the river	*Riverkeeper* by George Ancona

Activities to Use with Quotes and Books

Opening the School Day Discussion

Write a new quotation on the board each day of this unit. Ask students to identify an area of their environment that they want to improve individually and collectively during this unit's study.

An ecology class project. Have students design a class ecology project, or select one of the following options:

1. The class will brainstorm about different ideas they could use to advertise their environmental campaign to the school and to beautify a section of the schoolyard.

2. Ask students to devise a poster or banner to hang in the school or other common location. Then have students formulate a slogan and a design for their posters or banners.

3. Contact a guest speaker from an advertising agency to speak to the class about advertising.

4. Have a recycling campaign to pick up the schoolyard, or design a campaign for a schoolwide awareness project. Have one group go to library and get information on recycling, and make posters.

5. *Social Studies.* This group finds ways to help ecology. Projects can be completed by the entire class or as individual actions, such as writing members of Congress.

6. *Math.* A math problem could be derived according to age and ability: How long will it take to fill a landfill? How long until the ozone layer is in danger? How long until air and water pollution are severe in this state?

Winter survival. Talk about how animals survive in winter, and share the following information: Animals need more food in winter to give them energy to maintain their body temperature. Despite the snow and ice covering the feeding grounds and the death of many plants, animals have survived through such adaptations as migration, hibernation, thicker fur, and fur that changes colors. Allow the children to make a three-column chart of animals, showing how the animals they select adapt to winter and how these adaptations can be used by humans.

Crystal Christmas tree. Discuss how trees are affected by extreme cold. Then have students trace a tree and cut it out. Allow them to design the colorful "ornaments." Next, mix a quart of water and one-half to three-quarters cup of epsom salts, and have students brush "crystals" on the trees. Let students record in their science logs what happened to the epsom salts, describe how snow-capped trees have a similar appearance, and describe the effects of snow on trees.

Resources to Which Students Can Write to Obtain More Information about Actions They Can Take to Improve the Environment

Friends of the Earth (Conservation)
218 D Street S.E.
Washington, DC 20003
(202) 544-2600

Works on local, national, and international levels to protect the planet; preserve biological, cultural, and ethnic diversity; and empower citizens to have a voice in decisions that affect the environment.

Center for Environmental Information (CEI)
46 Prince Street
Rochester, NY 14607-1016
(716) 271-3550

Members are interested in helping to preserve the environment. Disseminates information on environmental issues. Holds conferences and educational programs.

Environmental Action Foundation (EAF)
6930 Carroll Ave, 6th floor
Takoma Park, MD 20912
(202) 745-4870

This is an environmental research and educational organization that provides resources for concerned citizens and organizations in the area of energy policy, toxic substances, and solid waste reduction.

National Recycling Coalition (Waste) (NRC)
1101 30th Street N.W., Suite 305
Washington, DC 20007
(202) 625-6406

This is a coalition of individuals and environmental, labor, and business organizations to encourage the recovery, reuse, and conservation of materials and energy. Its benefits in the areas of recycling are widely known.

Others:

Citizens for a Better Environment
924 Market Street, Suite 505
San Francisco, CA 94102

Earth Birthday Project
183 Pinehurst #34
New York, NY 10033

Clean Water Action
317 Pennsylvania Avenue, S.E.
Washington, DC 20003

The Institute for Earth Education
P.O. Box 288
Warrenville, IL 60555

Institute for Environmental Education
32000 Chagrin Boulevard
Cleveland, OH 44124

Keep America Beautiful
9 West Broad Street
Stanford, CT 06892

National Arbor Day Foundation
100 Arbor Avenue
Nebraska City, NE 68410

(JW) *Journal writing.* Write the words to "Old MacDonald Had a Farm" on the board and have students sing the song into a tape recorder. Guide them to learn to read animal names. Students will enjoy listening to their singing as you replay the tape and point to the words they sang on the tape. After singing, have the children write about (or draw) an animal that they would most enjoy taking care of and write (or tell) why they would enjoy caring for that animal. On a subsequent day, read trade books from the list in this unit about the animals they selected. Last, have students describe or draw items and activities that show how animals need to be cared for properly.

Animal act. Hand out strips of paper with sentences that contain animal names. Sentences could come from *Big Ones and Little Ones* by Zara Habon or *Animals Should Definitely Not Wear Clothing* by Judith Barret, which you read to the class. Then give one sentence to each student. Have students read their sentence to themselves or, for younger students, you can whisper the words to individual students so they can hold up their sentence and read it to the class after they have enacted the animal and meaning of the sentence. After each student enacts the meaning on his or her sentence, ask classmates to guess what each sentence said. Then have students read their sentences out loud and tell one way that animal could receive proper care.

Our trees. Ask a nursery to donate several small tree sprouts to your class. Have students work in small groups to plant the trees on the school grounds. Tell each group they must water and care for their trees. Be sure the trees are about 8 feet apart. Discuss good places to plant and why they are good.

Nature blooms. Read *The Reason for a Flower* by Ruth Heller. Introduce the topic of flowers discuss and tell students the benefits they provide. See what flowers the students have in their yards or houses.

Multicultural Emphasis: Facts about Understanding Ecology and Nature That Come from Other Cultures

Ask students to divide into groups. Each group chooses one culture from those discussed here. Give each group the following information about their cultural group and ask them to collect additional research to share with the class concerning the methods of maintaining the environment that are practiced in their respective cultures.

Native Americans. Native Americans believed that the land, like the sun and the wind, could not be owned. They used the earth's resources for shelter; for material to make weapons; for game to eat; for minerals and metals to make pottery, furniture, toys, jewelry, and woodwork; and for canoes to travel. Have students research what natural resources would be provided to make each of these things that Native Americans use, and read one of the following:

- *Our Voices, Our Land* by Christine Price. Describes Native American beliefs about ecology.
- *Thirteen Moons on Turtle's Back: A Native American Year of Moons* by Joseph Bruchac and Jonathan London. Poems telling stories of the natural world from thirteen different Native American cultures.
- *Desert Giant* by Barbara Bash. A story of the giant saguaro cactus and its life-giving properties for the Tohan O'Odham Indians and the creatures of the desert.
- *Everybody Needs a Rock* and *When Clay Sings* both by Byrd Baylor. Two excellent books for creativity.

Animals were essential to survival for Native Americans' survival. Animals provided food, skins for clothing, materials for weapons and tools, coverings for their houses, and so on. When Europeans introduced horses into Native American culture, Native Americans traded their handicrafts for horses, which soon became regarded as a priceless treasure. The horse gave them fast transportation so they could travel farther on hunting trips, and ways to carry heavy things. To this day, Native American cultures hold animals in very high esteem.

Japan. The Japanese celebrate Vernal Equinox Day in the spring as a special day to praise nature and their love for all living things.

Africa. Take a safari trip to Tanzania with Caren Barzalay Stelson's book *Safari.* See the animals in national wildlife parks, and meet some Masais. Then read *Where the Forest Meets the Sky,* by Jeannie Baker, a book about the Australian wilderness and a good one to compare the two wildernesses. Last ask students to read *African Journey,* by John Chiasson, which describes how the environment influences the lives in Africa, or share the following story with them.

Bringing the Rain to Kapiti Plain by Verna Aardema tells of a boy who brought rain during a severe drought so his herd of cows would be able to graze. A full-page painting shows the abundance of plants and wildlife living on the Kapiti Plain in Africa. The environment is threatened by nature and by humans, much like what is happening to rain forests today.

The Arabian camel is used for travel in the Sahara Desert because it can go for days without drinking water. Among the most common animals in their stories are gorillas (the largest apes) and chimpanzees (the smallest) because they live in the rain forest. Africa, the second largest continent, has the lion, tiger, elephant, giraffe, and hippopotamus, to name a few. Share with students that most people in Africa consider Africa's wildlife to be their greatest national treasure. You and students can read many trade books from the list in this unit that describe these animals.

Switzerland. The Swiss love to hike in their beautiful mountains and valleys. A typical Swiss walking stick is curved like a cane and decorated with badges depicting the different places the hiker has been. On a nature field trip, each child could find a stick on the ground to use as a cane. When the children get back, they could make their own badge to put on the stick to represent their field trip.

Caribbean Island. Flambozan by Arnold Adoff is a perfect book to introduce children to the Caribbean. It's about a young girl, named after the tree, who shares her appreciation of her natural world. Have the students compare their habitat to hers.

Japan. Japanese authors use animals symbolically in their tales to communicate themes and characteristics like the following.

- The dragon is the most important beast in folk literature. Legend has it that the dragon, or king, lives in a palace on the bottom of the sea.
- The fox is a symbol of abundance in some stories and a mischief-maker in others.
- The cat is a symbol of friendliness, welcome, and prosperity.
- Many buildings and homes are decorated with the monkey because it is believed to protect children.

Thailand. Traditional Thai beliefs about animals are told in folktales and stories. In the folk literature of this culture, animals are almost human, with each representing a specific trait: the water buffalo is docile but fierce, yet trust small children; the rabbit is a hero or a trickster; and the parrot with his mimicry is not his own person.

Turkey. Turkey has a horse population of several hundred thousand. These horses run wild, as do other types of wild game, including bears, gazelles, boar, deer, pheasants, and quail. As you introduce these game animals, show pictures and read details from trade books or encyclopedia.

Yugoslavia. A local breed of sheepdogs has helped shepherds for centuries. It is said that a single dog can fight several wolves at once and go away the winner. Similarly, it takes only two dogs to tend as many as two thousand sheep.

Your Own Additions to the Unit

27 Understanding Science and Health

Learning Objectives   This unit introduces students to the systematic body of knowledge about science and health derived from observation, study, and experimentation. The quotations, activities, and books are also designed to increase students' appreciation of scientific disciplines.

Resources   *Select a different quotation to discuss and write on the board each day of this unit's study.*

When I go to bed at night,
I don't wake until the light.

What was it like so long ago
and what did it take to make it so?

Rainbow in the sky,
Why do you arch so high?

Rain, go away, so I can go out to play.

The clouds could bring showers.
That's O.K. It's good for trees and flowers.

Water is a wondrous thing.
It's so good for everything!

Eating right can make you bright
If I had what I wanted to eat,
Would I be healthy from head to feet?

Clean nails make pretty hands.

Hands, when dirty, make clothes not pretty.

Eating wrong can't make you strong.

A tree can be so straight and tall,
It is even pretty in the fall.

The sun is so pretty and bright
It makes me feel that all is right.

Summer, Winter, Spring, and Fall—
I can't choose. I like them all!

When the sun goes down in the West,
It is time for me to go and rest.

It's amazing to see how all the
Animals live in the sea.

Appreciate the wonders of the world.

Finding the Right Book Concerning Understanding Science and Health to Meet Students' Needs

Difficulty code: I = Introductory; E = Easy; M = Medium

		Book
I	Your foot	*The Foot Book* by Dr. Seuss
I	Seasonal activities, mostly in pictures	*All Year Long* by Nancy Tafun
I	Your eye	*The Eye Book* by Dr. Seuss
I	The dentist	*The Dentist and Me* by Joy Schalebin Lewis
I	Loose tooth	*Little Rabbit's Loose Tooth* by Lucy Bate
I	Exploring the dentist's office	*I Know a Dentist* by Naomi Barnett
I	Pros and cons of taking a bath	*I Hate to Take a Bath* by Judith Barrett
I	Pros and cons of going to bed	*I Hate to Go to Bed* by Judith Barrett
I		*Teeth* by Wonder Starters
I	Verses about the body	*All about Me* by Leland B. Jacobs
I	Adjusting to AIDS	*Alex, the Kid with AIDS* by Linda Girard Walvoord
I	Living with asthma	*All about Asthma* by William and Vivian Ostrow
I	All about diabetes	*Even Little Kids Get Diabetes* by Connie Pirner
I	Nutrition, health and hygiene, reducing diets, and exercise	*Slimming Down and Growing Up* by Neva Cozle
I–E	Sun	*Shine, Sun* by Carol Greene
I–E	Making something	*Make Mine a Peanut Butter Sandwich and a Glass of Milk* by Ken Robbins
I–E	Light and shadows	*Light and Shadow* by Barbara Rogasky
I–E	Making cornmeal	*Corn Is Maize: The Gift of the Indians* by Aliki
I–E	Flowers	*Reason for Flowers* by Ruth Neller
I–M	Distances, directions, and locations	*The Wonderful World of Maps* by James Madden
I–M	Why we use maps	*What's in a Map?* by Sally Cartwright
I–M	Changes in the environment over the past twenty-five years (pictures only)	*Window* by Jeannie Baker

		Book
E	Sun	*Sunshine* by Jan Ormerod
E	Studying fossils	*Dinosaur Bones* by Aliki
E	Cheyenne legend of the creation of the Big Dipper	*Her Seven Brothers* by Paul Goble
E	Planets	*Space Probes to the Planets* by Fay Robinson
E–M	Desert life	*Cactus Hotel* by Brenda Guiberson
E–M	Common lies about animals	*Lies (People Believe) about Animals* by Susan Sussman and Robert James
E–M	The ocean floor	*The Magic School Bus on the Ocean Floor* by Joanna Cole
E–M	Way of life	*Before You Came This Way* by Byrd Baylor
E–M	Aquatic mammals	*Going on a Whale Watch* by Bruce McMillan
E–M	Snakes	*Take a Look at Snakes* by Betsy Maestro
E–M	Moon	*Moonlight* by Jan Ormerod
E–M	Hatching eggs	*All about Eggs* by Millicent Selsam
E–M	Observing with a microscope	*Greg's Microscope* by Millicent Selam
E–M	Growth/development of animals	*When an Animal Grows* by Millicent Selsam
E–M	Birds' way of life	*Album of Birds* by Tom McGowen
E–M	Sea life—jellyfish	*Down in the Sea: The Jellyfish* by Patricia Kite
E–M	Sea life—octopus	*Down in the Sea: The Octopus* by Patricia Kite
M	Killer bees' danger and safety tips	*Here Come the Killer BEES* by Laurence Pringle
M	A soothing bedtime rhyme	*Goodnight Moon* by Margaret Wise Brown
M	How earth gave life to the Tohan O'Oldham Indians	*Desert Giant* by Barbara Bash
M	How the planet functions	*The Kids' Earth Handbook* by Sandra Markle
M	Japanese: The role of the willow in life	*The Gift of the Willow* by Helena C. Pittman
M	Six natural habitat exhibits	*Windows on Wild Life* by Ginny Johnston

Activities to Use with Quotes and Books

Opening the School Day Discussion

Write a quote on the board, and discuss it. Ask students what they wonder about the world. Plan experiments during the week to answer their questions.

Daily schedule. Each student will devise a schedule for himself to keep at home in the bathroom to aid in good hygiene (e.g., times when you wash your hands, brush your teeth, comb your hair, and wash your hair, take a bath, and put on clean clothes).

Healthy foods. Play the alphabet-memory game in which one student says a healthy food to buy that begins with *A* (e.g. "I went shopping and bought *ap*ples"). A second student says, "I went shopping and bought *a*pples and *b*eans"), and so on.

Peanuts for protein. List vocabulary words from the book *A Weed Is a Flower: The Life of George Washington Carver*. Encourage students to listen for the words as you read. Discuss the meanings of the words within the context of the story. On a map of the United States, help students locate the four states described in the book. Discuss why peanuts are so healthful.

A meal in itself. Put students in charge of bringing a healthful food to class. Then have them work in groups of four to create a food dish and its name. Before you begin, ask students to write the foods they are going to bring on a slip of paper so that no one can see. The day before the activity begins, have them pass these slips to you so you can form groups of students whose foods will make a dish. For example, you might put students who bring bread, peanut butter, and jelly in one group. When students arrive at their groups, they have to decide what dish they want to make. Be sure no foods need to be cooked.

> ***Examples***
>
> *Salad:* Stuff celery with peanut butter or cream cheese.
>
> *Entree:* Spam macaroni and cheese—1 can of low-fat Spam, 2 cups of cooked macaroni, soft processed cheese. Spam can be cut into bite-size pieces with a table knife. Place into a bowl of cooked macaroni and stir in cheese (just enough to cover the pieces slightly). Serves 6 or more, depending serving size.
>
> *Dessert:* Apple or pear slices wrapped with American cheese.

The day before the activity begins, demonstrate how dishes can be made. In small groups make a healthful snack, like "Bumps on a log," made of celery, apples, peanut butter, and raisins. Students make their own snacks and compare the dishes they have made.

(JW) *Eat for strength.* After introducing the quote, "Eating wrong can't make you strong," read or tell the story of "Popeye, the Sailor Man." Explain that Popeye ate spinach, a healthful food, and that he credited this food with making him strong. Ask students to identify foods that they think would make them stronger. Next, read *Gregory, the Terrible Eater* by Mitchell Sharmot to introduce the quote, "If I had what I wanted to eat, would I be healthy from head to feet?" Then have students write three junk foods and three healthy foods.

I lost a tooth. Read *Little Rabbit's Loose Tooth* by Lucy Bate. You might show the children a note you wrote to the tooth fairy when you were a child. Have students draw a picture or write about a time when they lost a tooth.

Changes in nature. Tell students they are going to prove that water evaporates. On each table, place a container of water. In small groups, have them mark the water level on the container and label it "Before." Have them take the containers outside or to a windowsill. Later in the day, have students bring them inside, mark the new water level, and then write the word "After." Call the experiment "Evaporation." Discuss what happened.

Our weather person. Have a meteorologist come to class and bring maps, discuss rain, and explain the rain cycle to students. The next day have the students write a thank-you note to the weather forecaster. In the letter have them include drawings and new words they learned about weather.

Over the rainbow. Take students outside to show them that although sunlight looks white, it is really made up of many colors. Use prisms to produce beams of color from the sunlight. Discuss rainbows. Explain that raindrops are like prisms that make visible all the beautiful colors in sunlight. When you return to the classroom, have the students draw a picture of a rainbow and write the names of the colors in their rainbows.

My sunshine. Give each child a piece of paper in the shape of the sun and have them write inside that shape the things they most enjoyed learning about the sun. When finished, they may share their writings with the class or hang them around the classroom.

(RRG) *Scientific interests.* Make a photocopy or overhead transparency of the books and topics listed in this unit. Then, ask each student to select a different topic about science to study, using the ideas stimulated by a discussion of the book list. Next, have students keep a learning log as they read three or more books about their topics. As they read, ask them to create three possible solutions to the problem they are examining. After one week's reading, ask students to share their work in small groups. Each group will choose a recorder and write solutions on posterboard. Last, have the group report their work to the class and discuss ecological improvements they can make.

The Man in the Moon. Introduce *Goodnight Moon* by Margaret Wise Brown and have the students tell what they think the story is about. Read the book and ask students to use science books to find out why there appears to be a Man in the Moon. Discuss this concept.

The human body. Have students touch and move parts of their body—stretch, touch their head, bow from the waist, and so on. Students can also follow a record that tells them how to *move* and *dance,* such as *Creative Movements—Kids in Motion—Body Talk* by Steve and Gregg (Young Heart records).

My hands and feet. Make sure students know there is a right and left hand and that hands come in all shapes and sizes. Have them sing "This Old Hand" to the tune of "This Old Man" (*Theme-A-Saurus,* by Jean Warren, Warren Publishing House, 1989). Read *The Foot Book* by Dr. Seuss. Have students complete a sheet of patterns by matching different types of feet. Then instruct them to trace and label their right and left hands and feet on butcher paper, which will be hung up so the class can compare and contrast classmates' different hands and feet. Last, discuss how everyone is unique and how each hand/footprint is different.

(JW) *My senses help me learn.* Students visit five centers, one for each sense:

> *Center 1:* Nose/smell
>
> *Center 2:* Ears/hearing
>
> *Center 3:* Mouth/taste
>
> *Center 4:* Hands and feet (skin)/touch
>
> *Center 5:* Eyes/seeing

Each center will contain a book about one of these senses: *The Nose Book, The Tooth Book, The Foot Book, The Eye Book.* Students read each book, discuss what they have learned, and write or draw the most important concepts in their own learning logs.

The amazing creature and me. Say to students, "Think of the most amazing living creature you can." Then, using a variety of materials (magazine pictures, colored paper, cotton balls, crayons, paint, etc.), have them create their own amazing creature. It can be as large or small as they desire. Have them think of a name for it and prepare to share it with the class. Have them share what it does and why they like it. Tell students to base their description on information they gained from a book listed in this unit. Their creatures will be a result of their imagination combined with facts about the animal they studied.

Star gazing. Ask the children why they think they see stars only at night. Then ask two or three children to stand away from the group, and give each a flashlight that has been turned on. Ask these two students to shine the light toward the ceiling. Next, turn on all the lights on in the room. Ask the group if they see the lights from the flashlights. Gradually darken the room and ask the students: "What happens to the light coming from the flashlights?" "Does it become easier or harder to see?" This will help students to understand that just as they can't see the light from the flashlights when the room lights are on, they can't see the lights from the stars when the sun is shining.

The sun. Recite the following poem with children, letting them take turns filling in the blanks.

> The morning sun peeked through the trees.
>
> To kiss the _____ and the honey bees.
>
> It danced by the _____ and the fields of hay.
>
> Until it reached the _____ where it stayed all day.

Sun, Sun, don't you run.

Stay with me and have some fun

Shine on the _____, shine on me.

Shine on the _____, shine on the tree.

Shine on the _____, shine so fair.

Shine on the _____, shine everywhere.

Multicultural Emphasis: Concepts about Science and Health from Other Cultures

Share the following activities with students. Each relates to scientific or nutritional concepts and teaches students about customs in other parts of the world.

Native American. Read *Corn Is Maize: The Gift of the Indians* by Aliki. Long ago Native Americans used a *metate* and *mano* to grind corn. Secure these tools or show students a picture of them. Next, provide two stones for grinding corn. Let children remove kernels of dried corn from the cobs. Then put the corn in a bowl, cover it with water, and leave it to soak overnight. Last, have students take turns grinding the corn until it becomes meal. Take the cornmeal home, make cornbread, and let students taste it.

China. Tree rubbings is a modern term for the Chinese art of *t'ai-pen* or "ink squeezing." The earliest recorded Chinese rubbings were made in 7 A.D., using dampened rice paper pressed onto an object. These rubbings were used to duplicate and preserve a pattern. By preserving the intricacy of a tree bark pattern in a rubbing, children can begin to appreciate the textural beauty and individuality of each tree. Remind them that bark is part of the tree just as skin is part of our bodies.

>   *Time:* 15–30 minutes
>
>   *Materials:* 5 sheets of lightweight white paper per child
>   Brown or black chalk or charcoal
>   Masking tape
>
>   *Method:*
>
>   1. Walk to a wooded area. Let the children find a tree that is pleasant to touch. Let them feel its bark. Is the bark rough or smooth?
>
>   2. Find a tree with rough bark. Tape a sheet of paper over the bark and rub colored chalk onto the paper. A pattern emerges.
>
>   3. Do another rubbing with a second sheet of paper on another part of the bark. Compare rubbings. Note that each pattern is as individual as a fingerprint.
>
>   4. Have each student select a tree and complete a rubbing. Students compare their rubbings to their classmates' when they return to the room.

Native American. Perhaps because of its color and because it comes into leaf early, the birch tree is often called the "tree of spring." Years ago, birch bark canoes and baskets were made from the bark of fallen trees. Today these crafts are still practiced by many Native Americans. Let the children try painting these birch bark designs, ideally outdoors near the birch trees that inspired them.

> *Time:* 15–30 minutes
>
> *Materials:* 1 circle of white construction paper per child
> 1 pine tree branch per child
> Black tempera paint
> Clear adhesive tape
>
> *Method:*
>
> 1. Dip the needles of the branch in the paint, then drag the needles across the paper. This produces a striped effect that makes the paper resemble birch bark.
>
> 2. When the paper is dry, roll into a cone and tape it closed like a *muhkuk,* the Ojibwa birch bark cone. Use this cone to hold rocks, sand, or pine cones.

Greece. Fishing is a major industry in Greece. Today, however, fishermen are having problems because of the pollution in the Mediterranean Sea.

Switzerland. Switzerland, 130 million years ago, was under the Tetlys Sea. It was all water, with none of the mountains or flat land that appears today. As the earth moved, solid rock was pushed above the water. Geologists can tell the period of time by studying the layers of limestone exposed on the rocks' surfaces.

Popcorn blossoms. Have students make flower blossoms with tinted popcorn that depict typical flowers in their countries. Have them shake the popped popcorn with powdered tempera paints in brown paper bags. Let the children glue tinted popcorn onto small twigs glued onto construction paper. They may create group poems about their blooming trees.

Seed collection. Have children bring in different seeds to make a collection. The seeds may be placed on a bulletin board or chart along with a picture of the fruit each one produces. Children may also place seeds in envelopes with pictures of fruit on the outside, along with pertinent information on planting. These seeds and fruits are those that are native to their homelands.

Fruit salad. Prepare a fruit salad. One of the activities is to locate all the different types of seeds found in the fruit. Allow children to sort and graph seeds by color, texture, size, and shape. Children may write the recipe as the salad is prepared.

Your Own Additions to the Unit

28 Valuing School

Learning Objectives The purpose of this unit is to increase students' value for and positive response to school. Many young children are inhibited in their ability to draw and do other artistic projects. These quotations, activities, and books illustrate several benefits students can receive from studying content disciplines.

Resources *Select a different quotation to discuss and write on the board each day of this unit's study.*

Wasted time is not worth a dime.

*When time goes by slow
I wonder why—I don't know.*

*I need to save the time it took
to find my pencil, paper, and book.*

*When you use time well,
Things work out swell.*

*A student in the know
Will stay in school and grow.*

School is your opportunity to grow.

*I can draw what I'm thinking
and make the picture to my liking!*

Coloring is so much fun to look at when it's done.

I can color my book so pretty that all will want to look.

With my colors I can show a picture you are sure to know.

Art is "I," science is "We."
—Mr. Bernard

We can all take a part in the class we call art.

Music inspires the heart and causes joy to start.

When I work with clay, my hands get to play.

Math is the stairsteps to the world.

With your imagination you can write.

Bring your thoughts alive with your pen.

Experience rhapsody and harmony in Language Arts.

A student in the know will stay in school and grow.

*Use the diversity of your experiences—
when you write there is paradise.*

The desire to write grows with writing.
—Erasmus

*Writing is a deliberate act.
One has to make up one's mind to do it.*
—James Britton

Writing is like a signature of your thoughts and spirit.

Errors count but not as much as most English teachers think.
—Mina Shaughnessy

*When you're sad—reach for knowledge;
Where there is a tree of knowledge, there is paradise.*

*The problem with writing is not poor spelling,
punctuation, grammar, and handwriting.
The problem with writing is no writing.*
—Donald Graves

The principal goal of education is to create men who are capable of doing new things, not simply of repeating what other generations have done—men who are creative, are inventive discoverers. The second goal of education is to form minds which can be critical, can verify, and not accept everything they are offered.
—Jean Piaget

Finding the Right Book Concerning Valuing School to Meet Students' Needs

Difficulty code: I = Introductory; E = Easy; M = Medium

		Book
I	Value of school	*Louis James Hates School* by Bill Morrison
I	Lovable elephant's busy day from 8 A.M. to 8 P.M.	*Around the Clock with Harriet: A Book about Telling Time* by Betsy and Giulio Maestro
I	A little bear doing something each hour of a day	*Bear Child's Book of Hours* by Anne Rockwell
I	Telling time	*What Time Is It, Mr. Bear?* by Lizzy Pearl
I	About the color red	*Who Said Red?* by Mary Serfono

28 VALUING SCHOOL

		Book
I	Mouse collects colors and has colorful seasons	*Frederick* by Leo Lionni
I	Different colors	*Dinosaur Days* by David C. Knight
I	Different colors	*Little Blue and Little Yellow* by Leo Lionni
I	Colors and shapes	*What Comes in 2's, 3's, and 4's* by Suzanne Akers
I	Introduction to art	*Anno's Alphabet* by Mitsumasa Anno
I	Introduction to colors and color vocabulary	*Do You Know Colors?* by J. P. Miller and Katherine Howard
I	Colors and animals	*Brown Bear, Brown Bear, What Do You See?* by Billy Martin, Jr.
I	Introduces colors to describe life beside a bay	*Beside the Bay* by Sheila White Samton
I	Introduces ten basic shapes	*Shapes* by Rosalinda Kightley
I	Numbers (1–10), colors, and modifiers	*One Fish, Two Fish, Red Fish, Blue Fish* by Dr. Seuss
I	A record album	*Color Me a Rainbow* by Sharon Lucky
I	Colors	*An Apple Is Red* by Nancy Curry
I	Time passing slowly	*That Dreadful Day* by James Stevenson
I	Waiting	*Not Yet, Yvette* by Helen Ketterman
I–E	Birthday far away	*Will It Ever Be My Birthday?* by Dorothy Corey
I–E	History of time telling	*Anno's Sundial* by Mitsumasa Anno
I–E	Answer to a little boy's question	*A Little at a Time* by David Adler
I–E	Folk song names days of week and steps in harvesting	*Busy Monday Morning* by Janina Domonska
I–E	Sequence of months and holidays	*Over and Over* by Charlotte Zolotow
E	Totem poles	*The Legend of the Indian Paintbrush* by Mischa Damjam
E	About going to school	*Timothy Goes to School* by Rosemary Wells
E	Colorful photographs	*Our Money* by Karen Spies
E	Reading and mathematics	*My Mother Sends Her Wisdom* by Louise McClenathan
E	An ebullient introduction to shapes	*Shape Space* by Cathryn Falwell

		Book
E	Scenes of India in a diary entry of a trip	*Anni's India Diary* by Anni Axworthy
E	The importance of the buffalo to the Indians	*Buffalo Hunt* by Russell Freedman
E–M	What aging means	*A Look at Aging* by Rebecca Anders
E–M	Magical lands and times	*The Lion, the Witch, and the Wardrobe* by C. S. Lewis
E–M	Nineteenth-century event	*Ox Cart Man* by Donald Hall
E–M	A good model for children to use in writing postcards	*Stringbean's Trip to the Shining Sea* by Vera and Jennifer Williams
E–M	Colloquial language	*Air Mail to the Moon* by Tom Birdseye
E–M	Developing memory through math, finger dexterity, etc.	*Razzle Dazzle! Magic Tricks for You* by Laurence B. White
E–M	Colorfully illustrated	*Our Constitution* by Linda Carlson Johnson
E–M	Historic photographs	*Our Declaration of Independence* by Jay Schlirfer
M	Mixing art and science	*Gee, Wiz* by Linda Allison
M	Biographical information on people of 1775 with detailed map of the famous ride	*Paul Revere's Ride* by Henry Wadsworth Longfellow
M	A Thai girl seeks education	*Sing to the Dawn* by Minfong Ho
M	A girl discovers a unique family and a fountain of youth	*Tuck Everlasting* by Natalie Babbitt
M	A distortion in time	*Singularity* by William Sleator
M	Shared dreams create a mystery	*Into the Dream* by William Sleator
M	Science fiction about time	*A Wrinkle in Time* by Madeleine L'Engle
M	Invention of a time machine	*Time Machine* by H. G. Wells

Activities to Use with Quotes and Books

Opening the School Day Discussion

Before you write a quote on the board, ask students to write the thing they most value about school. Make an overhead transparency of all the quotes in this unit and display it for the class. Ask the class to describe other values of school that these quotes call to mind.

Where do I use math? Have students list places where they use math (not in school) or where they see numbers. Set a time limit on it and then see who has the most. Have students read their lists to the class for corrections and discuss their answers.

(RRG) *Math fun.* Divide the class into five groups and assign one number per group, using the numbers 2 through 6. With the number that each group is given, they are to think of different things (objects) that come in that number (e.g., the number 2—two arms, two legs, two wheels on a bike). Then have each group think of as many things as possible that can be characterized by that number. Add up the total numbers of objects, multiply by the number they were given, then take one-half of it and see if each one in the group comes up with the same answer. Last, read aloud to the whole class the book *Take a Number* and discuss students' responses.

(JW) *Journal writing.* Have students write a quote in their journals and tell what they think Mr. Bernard meant when he said, "Art is 'I,' science is 'we.' " Ask volunteers to share why they think art is an individual activity and science is a group activity. Then have students brainstorm ideas and form a semantic map on the chalkboard (or ask each group to make its own semantic map) that combine all the quotations in this unit in a creative way.

Noble works. Have kids brainstorm about books they could read that are considered "noble works"—for example, *The Secret Garden.* Then divide students into groups and have them research the author and the era in which the book was written.

Books about school. Ask students to select one of the books listed in this unit to teach the most important concepts to a small group. After all students have taught, ask them to assess their teaching abilities and to analyze if they would enjoy teaching as a profession.

Teaching students to increase the value they place on school. Share the story of the life of Helen Keller, which shows why education helps people to achieve their potential. At the age of seven, Helen was isolated from the rest of the world because she could not speak, hear, or see. Through schooling, however, she eventually graduated with honors from Radcliffe College and became a renowned speaker and author. Ask the class to answer the following questions on a piece of paper:

1. Did this story help you to value your school more?
2. How much do you value school? Is this enough to receive all it has to offer? Why or why not?
3. What could you do to make school more important in your life?
4. What would have to occur before you could bring more desire and/or determination to school? How can you make this occur?

(BLM) *Recognizing leadership skills.* Divide the class into groups of six and cut out each piece of the squares on Blackline Master 38 (in BLM section). Then put three pieces in each of six different envelopes, being sure that no envelope has two pieces from the same square. Next, distribute six envelopes to each group and instruct each group to form six squares of equal size. As each group completes their squares, distribute a sheet with the following questions for them to answer:

1. Did a leader of your group emerge? Why or why not?
2. What was it about your leader that caused him or her to emerge as the leader?
3. Ask the leader of your group why he or she assumed the leadership role and what this person thinks causes leaders to emerge.
4. Ask group leaders what they did that was most effective, and compare this answer to those given by other group members.

Last, call all the groups together and discuss what they learned about the types of thinking effective leaders do.

Imaging. Give students a piece of paper with an abstract ink blot on it and ask them to transform this blot into an object (e.g., a monster, an animal, a person).

Classroom mural. Cut a long piece of butcher's paper. The students work together to create a classroom mural of a topic of choice by painting pictures and writing descriptions. Then display it outside the classroom for the whole school to admire. In the mural, students also write all the quotes they've learned.

(JW) *Improving my drawing.* Students draw a picture in their journal before studying the quotes in this unit. At the end of the unit, they draw a second picture and compare it to see if their ability to draw has improved.

Color wheel. Have children pick their favorite colors. They are to "be" that color. Have colors red and yellow form a circle around orange to show that red and yellow make orange. Continue, using all the colors in the class. If some color combinations are not used, discuss and show the mixed colors to the class. For advanced students, have them act out what they feel that color would be like. The class can guess which color is being depicted from the students' actions.

(BLM) *Our new class schedule.* Small groups meet to discuss ideas for a class schedule that could avoid wasting time. Each idea must show how it will save time. You can use Blackline Master 22 (in BLM section) for this activity.

Let's make time. Read *Tick Tock, Let's Read the Clock* or another book about time listed in this unit. Then ask students to take turns lying on the floor so that their bodies' positions form a specific time (i.e., two students become the hands on the clock while the other children sit cross-legged in a circle to represent the numbers on the face of the clock). Practice several different times, allowing students to change roles.

What time is it? Read *What Time Is It, Mr. Bear?* or another book listed in this unit. Show children how to make spinners with the face of a clock, perhaps out of two bobby pins. Have the students put the numbers on the clock face. Call out times and have them mark each time on the "clock." On a second day, pair up children with partners. One calls out a time, the other marks the spinner, and then they switch roles.

Good morning and good night. Teach A.M. and P.M. Give situations such as, "You're asleep in bed at night. The clock says 9:00. Is it A.M.? P.M.?" Have children make up riddles and questions to say to classmates.

The speed of time. Write the quote, "When time goes by slow, I wonder why—I don't know." Read *That Dreadful Day* by James Stevenson or another book from the list in this unit. Tell students to visualize why the time might have passed slowly and to picture the characters in the story. Have students share a personal experience about time and discuss why it seems as if time goes slowly.

Multicultural Emphasis: Value of School in Other Cultures

Mexican American. The following books describe the values many Mexican Americans place on schooling. *Family Pictures/Cuadros de Familia* by Carmen Lomas Garza has a personal bilingual focus with illustrated paintings. *Pueblo Storyteller* by Diane Hozt-Goldsmith can be read as a model.

Thailand. Thai children learn the following poem in their schools about the value of schools:

> When you are young, you should learn and study.
> When you are grown, you will use the knowledge you
> have learned to earn your living.
> If something is useful and worth learning, you
> should pay attention.

Thai proverbs about colors are: If you wear the following colors during these days of the week, you will be successful and lucky. Sunday—red, Monday—yellow, Tuesday—pink, Wednesday—green, Thursday—orange, Friday—blue, and Saturday—violet.

Japan. The Journey: Japanese Americans, Racism and Renewal, a five-panel mural by Sheil Hamanaka, can be used to inspire students to create their own murals reflecting their understanding of the topic or can be compared to the book *Journey to Topaz* by Uchida.

Vietnamese. Families who follow Confucian philosophy value education and help children to want to learn. Elementary school lasts five years and runs four hours a day, six days a week, all year long. Secondary school is four years long. Then students take an examination and, on the basis of the results, can go on to high school, vocational-technical school, or directly to work. High school lasts three years, and students who pass the examination at the end receive a diploma. A diploma means increased respect and high-paying jobs.

Native Americans. Native Americans traditionally value colorful decor created with natural sources of color such as clay dug from creek beds and vegetable coloring for dyeing cloth. They use bright colors feathered headresses, to decorate weapons, and to paint totem poles made from big trees or rocks. *The Legend of the Indian Paintbrush* by Mischa Damjam can be read to illustrate the high numerous types of Native American values for fine arts.

Hawaiian. Hawaii Is a Rainbow by Stephanie Feeney will show students vivid colors in the natural environment and the diversity of the Hawaiian people. Its photography highlights the colors of Hawaii.

Asian American. Compare Allen Say's illustrations in the book *The Boy of the Three-Year Nap* by Diane Snyder or *Who's Hiding Here?* by Yoshi to the work of some American illustrators.

Indonesia. Indonesians take a flexible view of time; punctuality is less important than in the United States. This value arose because, in an agricultural society like theirs, the changing of seasons is the important marker of time, not minutes and hours. For this reason, some Indonesian children may need to learn about punctuality.

Mexican American. The following two books can be incorporated into a unit on dinosaurs. Students will enjoy comparing and contrasting the interpretations of prior periods in history by English-speaking and Spanish-speaking cultures.

> Cedar, Sally. *Cuidado, un Dinosaurio!* Spain: Ediciones S. M., 1985. Dini, a dinosaur born fifty million years too late, is adopted as a pet by a friendly family but finds it difficult to adapt to modern life.
>
> Hoff, Syd. *Danielito y el Dinosaurio.* New York: Harper and Row, 1969. Danielito goes to the museum and meets a real dinosaur. Together they visit the city and have a wonderful time.

Students may also enjoy having situations such as the following posed for class discussions: *Si ustedes quisieran que sus mamas tuvieran mas tiempo para divertirse, como las ayudarian?* ("If you wanted your moms to have more time to have fun, how would you help them?")

Switzerland. The Swiss are known worldwide for their watches. Daniel Jean Richard created the first Swiss watch in 1679. Seven out of ten watches ever made in the world originated in Switzerland.

Albert Einstein studied and taught in the Federal Institutes of Technology in Zurich, a world-famous school of higher education.

Your Own Additions to the Unit

29 Venturing

Learning Objectives The purpose of this unit is to increase students' ability to take calculated risks, to venture into new learning opportunities, and to use their imagination to increase their learning. Quotations, activities, and books demonstrate techniques students can use to increase the challenges they set for themselves.

Resources *Select a different quotation to discuss and write on the board each day of this unit's study.*

He who does not venture,
does not cross the sea.
—Rosemary Holman

Reach and achieve.

The world is filled with wonder.

Creating is good imagination at work.

Search to discover.

Imagine that _____.

Let's use our imaginations.

Dreams that come true begin with you.

The gift of imaging
Is like another school.

Want no fortune beyond the opportunity.

It is fun to use my imagination.

There is no learning without
some difficulty and fumbling.
If you want to keep on learning,
you must keep on risking failure—all your life.
It's as simple as that.
—John Gardner, *Self-Renewal*

Finding the Right Book Concerning Venturing to Meet Students' Needs

Difficulty code: I = Introductory; E = Easy; M = Medium

		Book
I	Waking up with surprise	*Imogene's Antlers* by David Small
I	Human qualities in nonhuman things	*Mud Puddle* by Robert Munsch
I	A city attacked by food	*Cloudy with a Chance of Meatballs* by Judi Barrett
I	Teddy bear's adventures in a store	*Corduroy* by Don Freeman
I	Fantasy	*Miss Hickory* by Carolyn Bailey
I	Exploring an imaginary place	*Where the Wild Things Are* by Maurice Sendak
I	Folk songs and nonsense verses	*I Know an Old Lady Who Swallowed a Fly* by Nadine Bernard Westcott
I	Playing alone, using your imagination	*Come Away from the Water, Shirley* by John Mackintosh Burningham
I	Using your imagination	*The Amazing Pig: An Old Hungarian Tale* by Paul Galdone
I	Poetry with imagination	*The Ice Cream Store* by Dennis Lee
I	Rainy day imagination	*One Monday Morning* by Uri Shulevitz
I–E	Stimulating your imagination	*Imagine That!! Exploring Make Believe* by Joyce Strauss
E	Imagination from shadows	*Henry and the Dragon* by Eileen Christopher
E	Daydreaming	*Daydreams and Night* by Elisabeth Nardine
E	Nothing really happens except in the present	*The Trip* by Ezra Jack Keats
E	When a child believes, magical things can happen	*The Snow Angel* by Angela McAllister
E	Tales of adventure	*Children of the Wild West* by Russell Freedman
E	Tales of the Wild West	*Cowboys of the Wild West* by Russell Freedman
E	The bittersweet feelings of moving day	*The Leaving Morning* by Angela Johnson
E–M	Adventure	*Jumanji* by Chris Van Allsburg
E–M	Frontier man	*Daniel Boone* by Laurie Lawlor
E–M	What wondering can do	*Incredible* by Kevin McFarland

		Book
M	A girl must decide between her heritage and contemporary Eskimo ways	*Julie of the Wolves* by Jean George
M	The search for self	*Dogsong* by Gary Paulsen
M	Gaining a better sense of yourself through competition	*Black Star, Bright Dawn* by Scott O'Dell
M	Two rodents seeking adventure	*The Down Seekers* by Carol Hamilton
M	Travel adventures of two orphans	*The Magic Hat of Mortimer Wintergreen* by Myron Levoy
M	Adventure to save father	*North of Danger* by Dale Fife
M	Exploration	*The Remarkable Voyages of Captain Cook* by Rhoda Blumberg
M	Adventure	*A Wrinkle in Time* by Madeleine L'Engle
M	Ocean explorations	*Exploring an Ocean Tide Pool* by Jeanne Bendick
M	Travel before and after the railroad	*Tracks across America: The Story of the American Railroad 1825–1900* by Leonard Everett Fisher
M	The four voyages of Columbus	*Christopher Columbus: Voyager to the Unknown* by Nancy Levinson
M	Imaginary adventure with English and Spanish words	*Abuela* by Arthur Dorros
M	A covered wagon adventure	*Addie: Across the Prairie* by Laurie Lawlor
M	Seeking adventure	*If You Seek Adventure* by Fulvio Testa
M	Steps to interviewing	*Innovations in Interviewing* by Allen Ivey
M	Taking risks to achieve	*Nothing's Fair in Fifth Grade* by Barthe De Clements

Activities to Use with Quotes and Books

Opening the School Day Discussion

Each day, write a quote and discuss its meaning. Ask students if they agree with it, and have them rewrite it in their own words. Then have volunteers read their quotes to the class.

(JW) *How should it end?* Read *Fortune* by Diane Stanley aloud to the class. Talk about Omar's greed and the trouble it caused him. Have individuals or pairs rewrite the ending of *Fortune* and share it with the group.

(BLM) *Venture into writing.* Explain that before a journey begins, you must have a map. Prewriting is such a map for the journey of writing. Then have students brainstorm a list of topics about which to write; this can be done as a whole classroom or on an individual basis. As a group, record student input on an overhead projector and leave the list on display as a resource for the class. Alternatively, on an individual level, have students write topics that are of interest to them. Then, have students write a brief description of what they will be writing about, and then list descriptions, details, plot, and so on to be followed in their papers. Reiterate that using these thought processes will enable students to know where they are going in their written expressions in the future. Blackline Master 34 (in BLM section) is to be used with this activity.

Teaching students to venture. Present the following steps as ways to add positive adventure to students' lives. Then have them discuss or write how they can apply the steps to their lives and how they will know that they have done so.

1. Don't be afraid to begin something because of the fear that you may make a mistake.
2. Plan well, and then make as many mistakes as it takes to learn as much as you need to know to succeed.
3. Be aware that failure and success come together in most projects.
4. Mistakes are the stairsteps to growth. When Thomas Edison was asked, after about 25,000 documented mistakes in the process of inventing an electric storage battery, how it felt to be a failure, he responded: "Failure? I'm not a failure! I now know 25,000 ways not to make a battery."*
5. Be willing to make a fool of yourself to get started. The real fools will be the ones on the sidelines.

School dreams. Ask students to answer this question: "If you could have anything at all that would increase learning at school, imagine what you would like." Then have them form groups, select the idea the group thinks is best, and tell why.

Sky creations. Have the children go outside and see what their imagination can do with the white clouds in the sky. Be the first to show what you expect from the experience. Do not let any child's comments be invalidated. Have children explain the figure in their cloud. Some students may be shy at first. Tell those who haven't been able to find a cloud to see if they can do it after school. They can draw what they see and bring it to class to share the next day.

---

*Taken from Dan Zadra, *There Will Never Be Another You* (Creative Education Publishers, p. 43).

Multicultural Emphasis: Concepts of Venturing That Come from Other Cultures

Native American. Share the following legend and ask students to imagine the story and tell what it explains about Native American culture.

Hanuman, the Monkey God

Hanuman, the Monkey God, once had a craving for hot, spicy food. He became so hungry for it that he turned to the sun and swallowed the sun whole. With the sun inside him, Hanuman grew hotter and hotter, while the people on earth became colder and colder. The flowers died and the trees lost their leaves. Snow fell during the dark days and the dark nights. The birds went away, for there was no sun to warm them, and the animals hid in their caves. The people grew sad and wondered what they could do to bring back the sun.

Then a child suggested, "Let's make Hanuman laugh! He will laugh until he spits out the sun. Then we will be warm again."

The people thought about this and said, "Yes, that is a good idea! But how can we do this?"

They thought. Someone suggested telling Hanuman a funny story, but they knew he was too hot to listen. Someone else suggested painting a funny picture, but they knew he wouldn't look. Then a child said, "I know. We can paint one another!"

"What?" said the people. "That is a silly idea." Then they began to laugh. Someone picked up some red dirt and put it on a neighbor's head. Someone else threw blue powder over all the adults. Oh, how funny they looked. The colors flew and mixed, and the people laughed and laughed so loudly that Hanuman looked down.

"What is this?" he bellowed. Then he saw the blue, orange, purple, and green people and he smiled. He giggled. One huge laugh fell out and another, until Hanuman was rolling with laughter. He laughed so hard that tears came to his eyes. At last, out popped the sun.

"Hurrah!" said the people. "The plan worked." Then they, too, started to laugh as they felt the world become warm and sunny. Every year on Holi they remember Hanuman and throw colored powders over one another to make the Monkey God laugh again!

Mexican American. Stories about Mexican-American culture follow:

Gispert, M., and C. Peris. *Martin Quiere Leer.* Spain: Editorial Teide, S.A., 1984. Martin's love for books causes his imagination to run wild with story characters. One day his home town is flooded and his favorite book is ruined. This misfortune is sad, but a new friendship emerges because of it.

Wylie, Joanne, and David Wylie. *Un Cuento de un Pez Grande.* Chicago: Children's Press, 1984. A nicely illustrated story of an imaginary fish.

Gerson, Sara. *Castillos de Arena.* Mexico: Editorial Trillas, S.A., 1986. The wonderful experience of building a sand castle stimulates Diana's imagination.

Caribbean. Many Caribbean people left their island homes to seek a new life in the United States. Eve Bunting presents their story in a picture storybook called *How Many Days to America? A Thanksgiving Story*. After you read this book to the class, ask students to read about how other cultures ventured to America and how the people had to persevere to make the trip. Break the class into several small groups, each with a different culture, and entitle the unit "Coming to America." Students can use Blackline Master 3 (in BLM section) to record their journey's route and findings.

Your Own Additions to the Unit

30 Verifying What Is Real through the Senses

Learning Objectives Students are often pressured to accept false goals, appearances, dialogues, and demeanors. The quotations, activities, and books in this unit build students' observation skills and their ability to discern shallow from deeper, more meaningful aims. Moreover, students increase their ability to use their senses to gain new information.

Resources *Select a different quotation to discuss and write on the board each day of this unit's study.*

*I look to see
if its real to me.*

You can see without your eyes.

*Use your senses and it will show
you many things that are there to know.*

*There won't be learning fences
If you just use your senses.*

*It is funny how realness and fakeness
can be felt between people.*
—Janet Lynn

*Fakeness is not really felt because
it is emptiness and incompleteness.*
—Janet Lynn

*Realness is everything done in love,
and fakeness is everything else.*
—Janet Lynn

Realness is felt with fullness and completeness.
—Janet Lynn

*You must mix well
look, taste, and smell
and hear and feel
to know what is real.*

Finding the Right Book Concerning What Is Real to Meet Students' Needs

Difficulty code: I = Introductory; E = Easy; M = Medium

		Book
I	Observing nature	*Walk with Your Eyes* by Marcia Brown
I	Finding a bear	*Where Is the Bear in the City?* by Bonnie Larkin Nims
I	Observing surroundings	*Brown Bear, Brown Bear, What Do You See?* by Bill Marten
I	Identifying	*Take Another Look* by Tana Hoban
I	Identifying	*26 Letters and 99 Cents* by Tana Hoban
I	Pictures	*A, B, See!* by Tana Hoban
I	Finding a caterpillar	*One Bear at Bedtime* by Mick Inkpen
I	Looking and seeing	*Amazing Look-through Book* by Ed Emberley
I	Looking for things	*The Turnaround Wind* by Arnold Lobel
I-E	Noticing things	*Everyone Is Going Somewhere* by Suzanne Rosenblatt
I-E	Hidden objects to find	*I Spy* by Jean Marzollo
I-E	Seeing beauty	*At Christmas Time* by Valerie Worth
I-E	A visual delight	*The First Christmas* by Francis Lincoln
I-E	Predicting	*Look Again* by Tana Hoban
E	Learning about the sense of smell	*Breathtaking Noses* by H. Machotka
E	In life and nature	*Bambi* by Felix Salten
E-M	Learning about the senses	*The Science Book of the Senses* by N. Ardley
E-M	An imaginary place	*Where the Wild Things Are* by Maurice Sendak
E-M	Wishing to be someone else	*Sometimes I Wish I Were Mindy* by Abby and Sarah Levine
E-M	Finding out what was in a lot that appeared to be empty	*The Empty Lot* by Dale H. Fife
E-M	Learning the fundamental science principles in each trick	*Shozan! Simple Science Magic* by Laurence B. White
E-M	Realizing that TV is not life	*The TV Kid* by Betsy Byars

		Book
E-M	Definition of "realness"	*The Velveteen Rabbit* by Margery Williams
E-M	A vision of peace	*The Fragile Flag* by Jane Langton
E-M	What is real and what is thought to be real	*Lies (People Believe) about Animals* by Susan Sussman and Robert James
M	A best friend's sudden death causes a sense of loss and guilt	*A Taste of Blackberries* by Doris Smith
M	Visible traits are not always the most important ones	*Growin'* by Nikki Grimes
M	Capturing a butterfly, then letting it go	*The Butterfly Hunt* by Yoshi
M	Character, not appearances, is real	*The Paper Bag Princess* by Robert Munsch
M	Civil War period	*The Long Road to Gettysburg* by Jim Murphy
M	A child with AIDS	*Alex, the Kid with AIDS* by Linda Walvoord Girard
M	Money—often the root of problems	*Silver* by Norma Fox Mazer
M	How history repeats itself (Japanese folklore)	*The Wave* by Margaret Hodges
M	Native American changes	*Choctaw Boy* by Paul Conklin
M	Human variety	*Why Am I Different?* by Norma Simon
M	Learning that truth may not be the same as fact	*The Facts and Fictions of Minna Pratt* by Patricia MacLachlan

Activities to Use with Quotes and Books

Opening the School Day Discussion

Before quotes are introduced, discuss that *realness* can be defined as love and things in life that they can depend on. Last, discuss each quotation in the context of the "real things" in their lives.

Realness and fakeness. Discuss the quotation, "Realness is everything done in love and fakeness is everything else." Then break the class into two groups with smaller groups within them: Half the small groups will list situations that seem real to them. The other half will list situations that seem fake. Put a time limit on this activity. Then have one group read each situation they listed as "fake" and have the "real" identify a way to change each situation to make it more "real" and more valuable. List all the suggestions for changing "fakeness" to "realness" on the board, and discuss their commonalities at the end of the activity.

How does it feel? Begin by discussing the quote, "It is funny how realness and fakeness can be felt between people." Read the familiar story *The Velveteen Rabbit* by Margery Williams or a book listed in this unit. Ask students to discuss how the story illustrates the quote and things they have learned that help them discern phoniness in their lives.

What is real and magical. Ask students to discuss how David Copperfield and other magicians convince people that something is real when it isn't. Then ask students to apply the strategies these magicians use to their own lives. Discuss how people might use similar tactics to misrepresent things. Then divide the class into small groups to complete a science experiment in which they fill a beaker with a colored liquid (vinegar and food coloring) but are not told the ingredients, only that the liquid contains "magical qualities." Then ask students to sprinkle a "special potion" (baking soda) into the beaker. When the powder enters the beaker, the liquid will begin to bubble, foam, and expand until it erupts from the beaker. Ask students to explain what happened. Last, ask them what they will think in the future when they witness or hear about phenomena that doesn't seem possible or real.

Teaching students that somethings may seem real in life but are not. Tell students that judging what is real, true, or of value often cannot be done just by observing surface facts. Ask them to prove, for example, how many people in their city were arrested for stealing that day, by referring to their evening news broadcast or daily newspaper. Share the following example. There is so much good news in the world today that we tend to overlook or fail to report it. Newspapers cover the exceptions, and bad news is the exception. That's one reason we see so much of it in the headlines. Ask students for other examples of having to "look deep" before truth, "realness," or value can be discerned. Last, have students share what they have learned from this activity, either orally or in writing.

(JW) *Journal writing.* Have the group imagine something they could see but have never seen in the zoo, park, playground, or on vacation. Have them write a story or draw a picture of their image and tell why it is likely to be there.

(BLM) *Imaging.* Put on the board or transparency a big outline of something (e.g., a cat face, a flower) (see Blackline Master 39 (in BLM section). Then have the class look at it for one minute, close their eyes, and ask them if they can still see the picture in their mind. Ask them what they saw. Next, use bright-colored posterboard and have the students draw a picture of what they saw in their mind. You may want to bring other optical illusions to class.

The mind's eye. Have each small group of students list things they can "see" without their eyes—for example, memories, or what is likely to be happening in a place they are not, such as in the lunchroom. Ask them what it is like to see without using their eyes.

Buddy group. Go outside with the entire class "buddied up." Have them look at things in the school hall, yard, or playground and ask questions of each other (e.g., "Feel the leaf of this tree. Does it need water?" "Is the hall or yard clean? Why is it important that it is?" "What is happening in an anthill?" "Take a deep breath, what do you sense?") When they return, ask them what noise they could identify? Conclude by discussing whether asking questions improved their observation skills and how. How did their senses make things real for them?

Multicultural Emphasis: Concepts about What Is Real Using the Senses to Learn

(BLM) *Europe.* In the 1800s, Europeans became fascinated by optical illusions. Use the book *Take Another Look* to introduce optical illusions. Blackline Master 39 can be the first one students try to see.

Mexican Americans. The following English and Spanish books are grouped by the sense they describe. Students benefit from reading one book in English and one book in Spanish about each of the senses. After both books are read, ask students to list the similarities and differences between the uses of senses that were conveyed between the English-speaking and Spanish-speaking cultures.

The Sense of Touch

Kline, Suzy. *Don't Touch.* Illinois: Albert Whitman, 1985.

Brighton, Catherine. *My Hands, My World.* New York: Macmillan, 1984.

Parramon, J. M., and J. J. Puig. *El Tacto.* Illustrated by Maria Rius. New York: Barron's Educational Series, 1985. Illustrates and describes the different textures we find in the world.

Smith, Kathie Billingslea, and Victoria Crenson. *Coleccion Mil Preguntas: Tocando.* Argentina: Editorial Sigmar, 1988. The sense of touch is explored through questions and answers with interesting explanations and illustrations.

The Sense of Taste

Gardner, Beau. *Guess What?* New York: Lothrop, Lee and Shepherd, 1985.

Flores, Rosa. *Caracolitos: Lo Sabroso Sabrosito.* Oklahoma: Economy Company, 1979. All of the different tastes that our tongues can distinguish are depicted with illustrations of children and food.

Lasa, Maite. *Voy a Cocinar.* Mexico: Sistemas Tecnicas de Edicion, S.A. de C.V., 1988. Recipe book for children with recipes that are culturally appealing.

Parramon, J. M., and J. J. Puig. *El Gusto.* Illustrated by Maria Rius. New York: Barron's Educational Series, 1985. Beautifully illustrates all the different tastes.

Rodriquez, Ana, and Jorge Blanco. *Cocinar Es un Juego Muy Sabroso.* Venezuela: Ediciones Maria Di Mase, 1982. A beautifully illustrated cookbook with recipes that are very appealing to children.

Smith, Kathie Billingslea, and Victoria Crenson. *Coleccion Mil Preguntas: Gustando.* Argentina: Editorial Sigmar, 1988. The sense of taste is explored through questions and answers with interesting explanations and illustrations.

The Sense of Sound

Alexander, Martha. *Pigs Say Oink: The First Book of Sounds.* New York: Random House, 1978.

Colleccion Piñata: Ritmos y Sonidos. Mexico: Editorial Piñata, 1985. The wonders of sounds.

Parramon, J. M., and J. J. Puig. *El Oido.* Illustrated by Maria Rius. New York: Barron's Educational Series, 1985. This book illustrates the most enjoyable sounds in the world.

de Podendorf, Illa. *Sonidos.* Illinois: National Textbook, 1979. An interesting presentation of sounds and how they are a part of our daily lives.

Smith, Kathie Billingslea, and Victoria Crenson. *Coleccion Mil Preguntas: Oyendo.* Buenos Aires: Editorial Sigmar, 1988. The sense of hearing is explored through questions and answers with interesting explanations and illustrations.

Wolf, Bernard. *Ana y Su Mundo de Silencio.* New York: J. B. Lippincott, 1979. A true story of Ana's daily life as a deaf child.

The Sense of Sight

Martin, Bill Jr. *Brown Bear, Brown Bear, What Do You See?* New York: Holt, Rinehart and Winston, 1970.

Parramon, J. M., and J. J. Puig. *La Vista.* Illustrated by Maria Rius. New York: Barron's Educational Series, 1985. This book explores, through beautiful illustrations, the wonders of our sense of sight.

Smith, Kathie Billingslea, and Victoria Crenson. *Coleccion mil preguntas: Viendo.* Argentina: Editorial Sigmar, 1988. The sense of sight is explored through questions and answers with interesting explanations and illustrations.

The Sense of Smell

Pluckrose, Henry. *Smelling.* New York: Franklin Watts Inc., 1986. Additional titles are available for the other senses.

Allington, Richard. *Smelling.* Wisconsin: Raintree Publishers, 1980. Additional titles are available for the other senses.

Parramon, J. M., and J. J. Puig. *El Olfato.* Illustrated by Maria Rius. New York: Barron's Educational Series, 1985. This book vividly illustrates the most memorable smells in life.

Smith, Kathie Billingslea, and Victoria Crenson. *Coleccion Mil Preguntas: Oliendo.* Argentina: Editorial Sigmar, 1988. The sense of smell is explored through questions and answers with interesting explanations and illustrations.

All Five Senses

Aliki. *My Five Senses.* New York: Harper & Row Junior Books, 1962.

Tymme, Jean. *I Like to See: A Book of the Five Senses.* Wisconsin: Western Publishing Company, 1978.

Broekel, Ray. *Tus Cinco Sentidos.* Chicago: Children's Press, 1988. The book explores the five senses through photographs and answers questions posed by the author.

Murphy, Chuck. *Tus Sentidos.* Colombia: Editorial Norma S.A., 1986. This pop-up book of the senses describes the location of each of the senses and how each helps us know our world.

Native American. A plant discovered by Native Americans called *Abrus precatorius* has roots that have been used as a substitute for licorice, even though they contain poisonous resins. The poisonous red and black seeds are used to make necklaces and as weights.

Indian henys is a perennial herb. Its stem fibers are used to make matting and ropes. The dried roots also have medicinal properties that Indian used for healing. Ask the class to find other natural elements that are important in many ways. Contrast these items to products that are marketed with false claims of their benefits.

Mexico. The gum tree (*arbol gomifero*) grows in the forests of Mexico. The sapodilla tree is used to make chewing gum. How do you suspect Mexicans first discovered the values of the gum tree, jumping beans, and sand clay?

Jumping beans: This bean is known in Mexico as the "leaper." A full-grown larva of the moth lives inside the bean, which moves when its "tenant" moves. More information can be found in *Jumping Bean* by Edna Miller. Ask students what makes a jumping bean "real" and not magical.

Sand clay: This material was wonderful for building the Mexico adobe houses and the pyramids of the Zapotec Indian civilization. A sand clay recipe students may want to try is this: Use 1 cup of cornstarch, 2 cups sifted dry sand, and 1fi cups of cold water. Mix the cornstarch and dry sand together. Add the water and stir until smooth. Place in an old electric skillet and cook over medium heat, stirring constantly, until mixture is very thick and holds its shape, which will take about 5–10 minutes of cooking time. Place the clay on a plate and cover it with a damp cloth. When it is cool enough to handle, knead thoroughly until pliable. Doubling the recipe will make enough for 15 students. If you are not going to use the clay right away, after it cools, store in a tightly covered container. It can be stored for several days, but knead well before using.

Your Own Additions to the Unit

BLACKLINE MASTER 1
Conducting Successful Interviews

Name _____ Date _____

Steps for Conducting Effective Interviews

1. State the purpose of the interview first. Tell the Interviewee the purpose. The purpose is: _____

2. Begin with a question that seeks background information about the topic. This question builds trust between two people and increases the chances that they will better understand each other.

3. Next, ask for a description of an experience that led to the present problem. This description will be better if follow-up questions are used that begin with the following words:

   How _____
   When _____
   Where _____
   What _____
   Who _____
   Why _____

4. Then, ask the person to give an example. This example will ensure that you understand the intent of the speaker.

5. Paraphrase what the person says if you aren't sure you understand what was said.

6. Ask for an interviewee's definition of simple words that could mean different things, such as *difficult, happy,* and *good.*

7. Listen carefully so you can follow up with a question that begins with one of the words in #3 above.

8. Spend at least 30 minutes reading information about the topic before you go to your interview.

9. Take notes in the spaces directly below each question so the interviewee will not have to wait too long while you write.

10. You may want to use a tape recorder, but first ask the interviewee if it is acceptable.

11. Write a thank-you note as a follow-up to the interview.

12. After each interview, critique yourself and find ways you can improve.

Copyright © 1995 by Allyn and Bacon

BLACKLINE MASTER 2
Learning to Appreciate Individual Differences

Name _____ Date _____

Stress Situation	*Solution:* **Quotation and outline for role plays**
Accepting and appreciating differences between ethnic groups	
A classmate is trying to become a member of your small group of friends, and your initial reaction is not to add any new people to the group.	

Copyright © 1995 by Allyn and Bacon

BLACKLINE MASTER 3
Strategies for Overcoming the Negative Effects of Peer Pressure

Name _____ Date _____

Type of Peer Pressure	Pros/Cons	Strategies for Overcoming Cons

Directions:
1. List the type of peer pressure you face in the left-hand column.
2. Think of all the pros and cons you face or positive and negative effects of each type of peer pressure in the middle column.
3. Write the strategies you will use to overcome the "cons" or negative effects by using quotations and activities from this unit. List these strategies in the right-hand column.
4. Keep this Blackline Master as a personal record for your further reference so you can evaluate how often you used each strategy to overcome peer pressure's negative effects.

BLACKLINE MASTER 4
How to Make an "Easy Slit Book"

Name _____   Date _____

Use two sheets or more of 8½ × 11" paper.
The more sheets used, the more pages will be in the book.

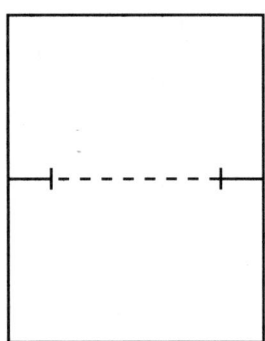 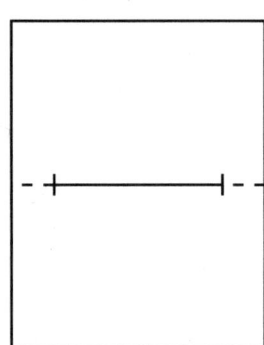 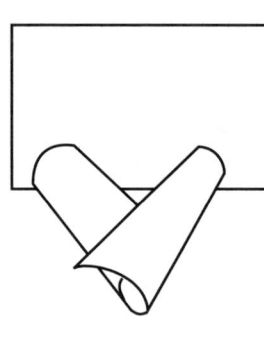 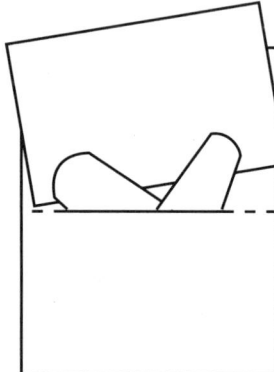

1. Fold one sheet horizontally. Take your ruler and cut 1½" in from each folded end as shown above.

2. Fold second sheets. Measure 1½" from each end and cut between the marks as shown.

3. Gently roll the edges of one half of the first sheet toward the center.

4. Slip the rolled edges through the cut in the second sheet. Cut and insert more of the pages described in #1 to make a book with more pages.

Modified from an original version described in *Managing the Whole Language Classroom* (Creative Teaching Press, p. 39).

Copyright © 1995 by Allyn and Bacon

BLACKLINE MASTER 5
How to Make Personalized Bookmarks

Name _____   Date _____

Materials Needed:
  Light cardboard (white)
  Glue
  Ribbon (optional)
  Scissors

Step 1: Choose the design you desire for the top of your bookmark from Blackline Master 6.

Step 2: Cut one bookmark, as shown to the right.

Step 3: Cut two of the design you choose from Blackline Master 6.

Step 4: Glue one design on the front of the bookmark, placing the bottom of the design on the dotted line.

Step 5: Place a second design on the back of the bookmark and glue it together to the matched design on the front, with the bookmark between the two designs.

Step 6: (Optional) For goal Marking: If ribbon is used, glue it between the two designs at the top. Use the ribbon to mark the place where you stopped reading yesterday. Place the bookmark at the page you set as your goal to read for today's reading.

Step 7: Decorate the front of the bookmark by using favorite quotes or names of books read.

Ribbon   Cut One Bookmark

Copyright © 1995 by Allyn and Bacon

BLACKLINE MASTER 6
Bookmark Designs

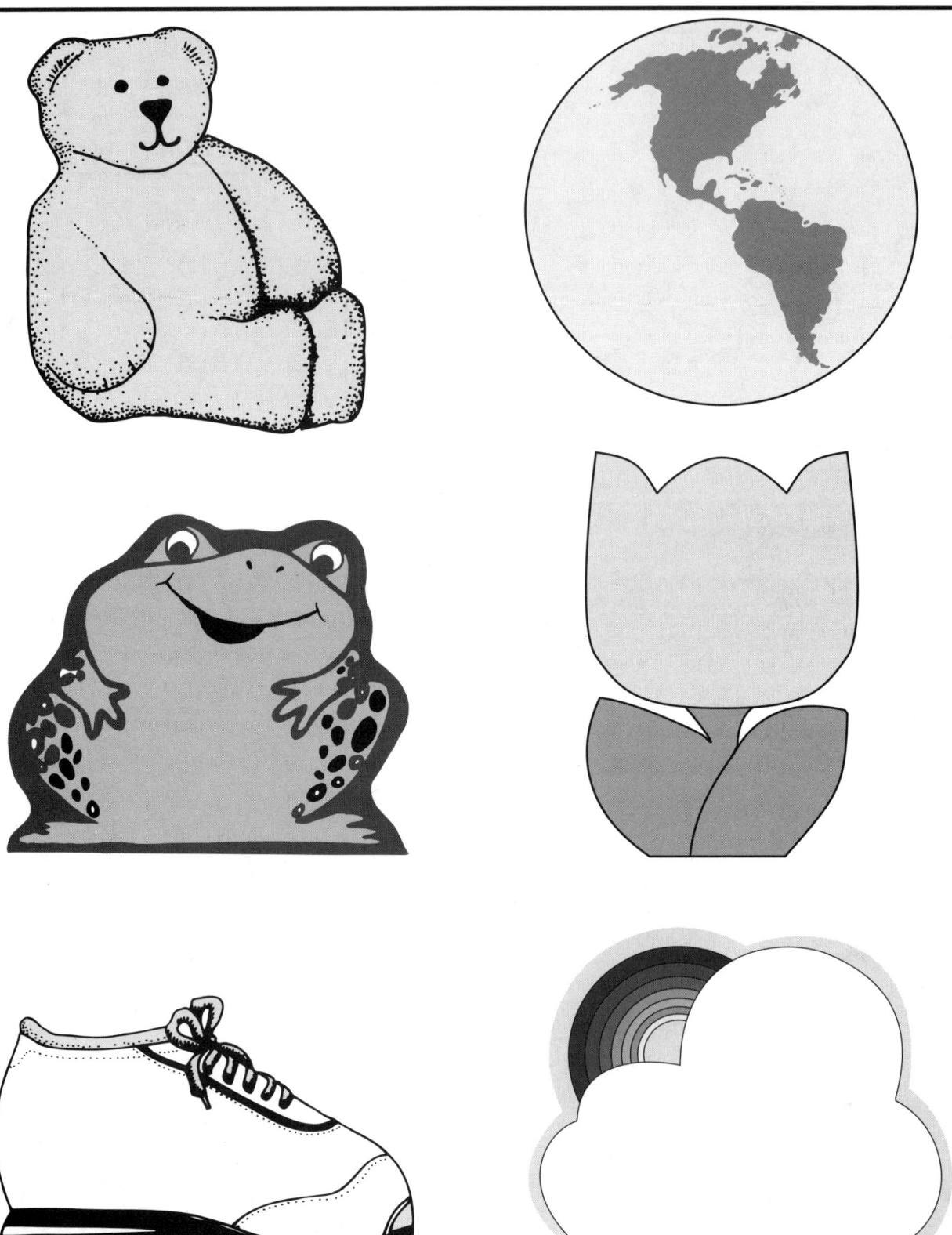

BLACKLINE MASTER 7
My Friend the Author

Name _____ Date _____

	Date Read	Author's Name	Title of Book
1.			
2.			
3.			
4.			
5.			

Qualities Liked   How Qualities Were Shown in the Book

1.

2.

3.

4.

5.

6.

7.

BLACKLINE MASTER 8
Learning New Words by Rhyming

Name _____ Date _____

(1)
1. old
2. age
3. day
4. boy
5. cub
6. beat
7. long
8. all
9. know
10. out

(2)
1. fold
2. page
3. say
4. coy
5. tub
6. seat
7. wrong
8. fall
9. snow
10. shout

(3)
1. bold
2. cage
3. bay
4. toy
5. rub
6. neat
7. song
8. ball
9. show
10. pout

(4)
1. mold
2. sage
3. pay
4. joy
5. sub
6. feat
7. thong
8. mall
9. blow
10. bout

BLACKLINE MASTER 9

Thinking Processes That Build My Creativity

Name _____ Date _____

Directions: Under the dotted line, make a design, drawing, diagram, or story that will help you remember the SCRAMBLIN' creative thinking processes. When you finish, share and explain your creation to a friend or the class. Remember to use SCRAMBLIN' thinking processes as you make your creation.

Substitute an entirely new idea for a commonly used idea.

Combine two unlike ideas.

Rearrange sections or reorder the steps normally taken.

Adapt by changing one detail of the first idea.

Minimize by taking away one part of an idea.

Bigger—make idea better by adding something new to an original idea.

Linking—brainstorm ideas by listing as many different examples as possible.

Invent by trying to think of all the reasons the original idea won't work.

Newness—stimulate new ideas by asking, "What is an original and better way to *(first idea)*." --

BLACKLINE MASTER 10
Please and Thank You Records to Improve Manners

These record forms can be used to chart students' progress in many different areas by changing the title written above each record form. "Please" and "Thank You" are used as examples.

Please	Thank You
Name _____	Date _____

Please	Thank You
Name _____	Date _____

Please	Thank You
Name _____	Date _____

Please	Thank You
Name _____	Date _____

BLACKLINE MASTER 11

Adding to My Train of Knowledge

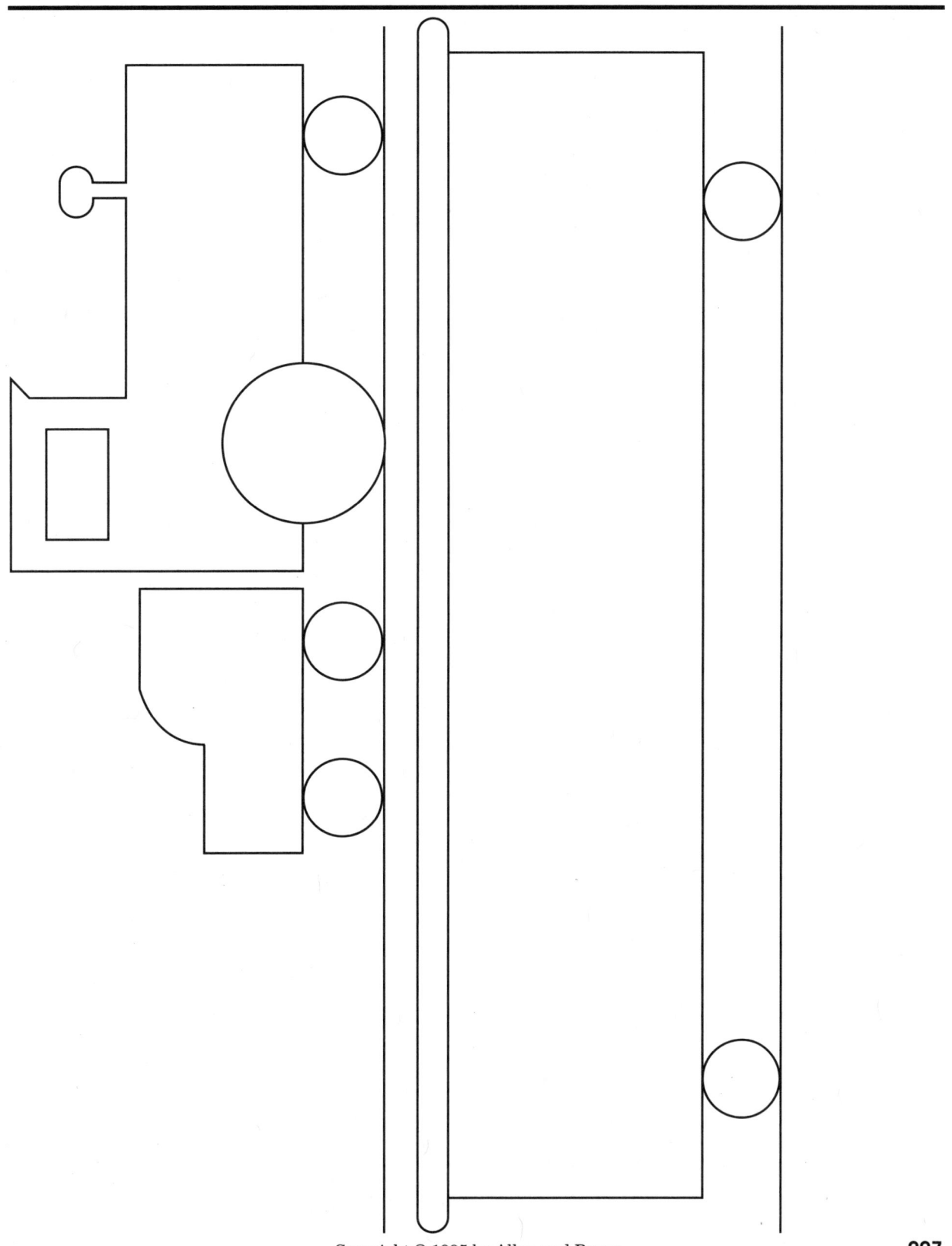

Copyright © 1995 by Allyn and Bacon

227

BLACKLINE MASTER 12
Individualized Instruction to Eliminate Excuses

Name _____ Date _____

Excuses	Reason for	Strategy to Overcome

BLACKLINE MASTER 13
Game Board

Glue game board and game pieces on cardboard or use game board as a transparency. Game board can also be enlarged and traced on posterboard. Use the instructions given in the units for which the game is to be used, as this game board can be used with activities from many different units. Also, you and/or the students can invent their own rules and use this game board to review concepts in many content disciplines.

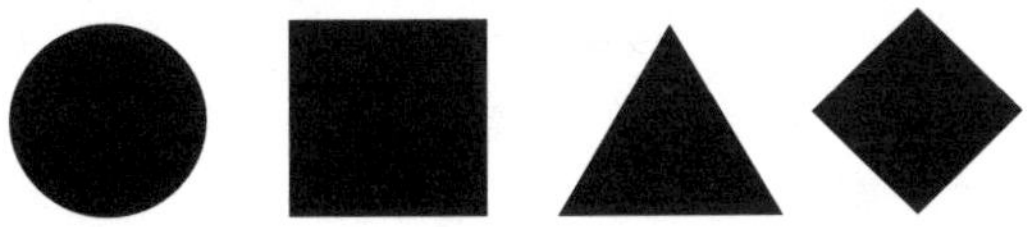

GAME PIECES   3" by 5" index cards to be used during the game

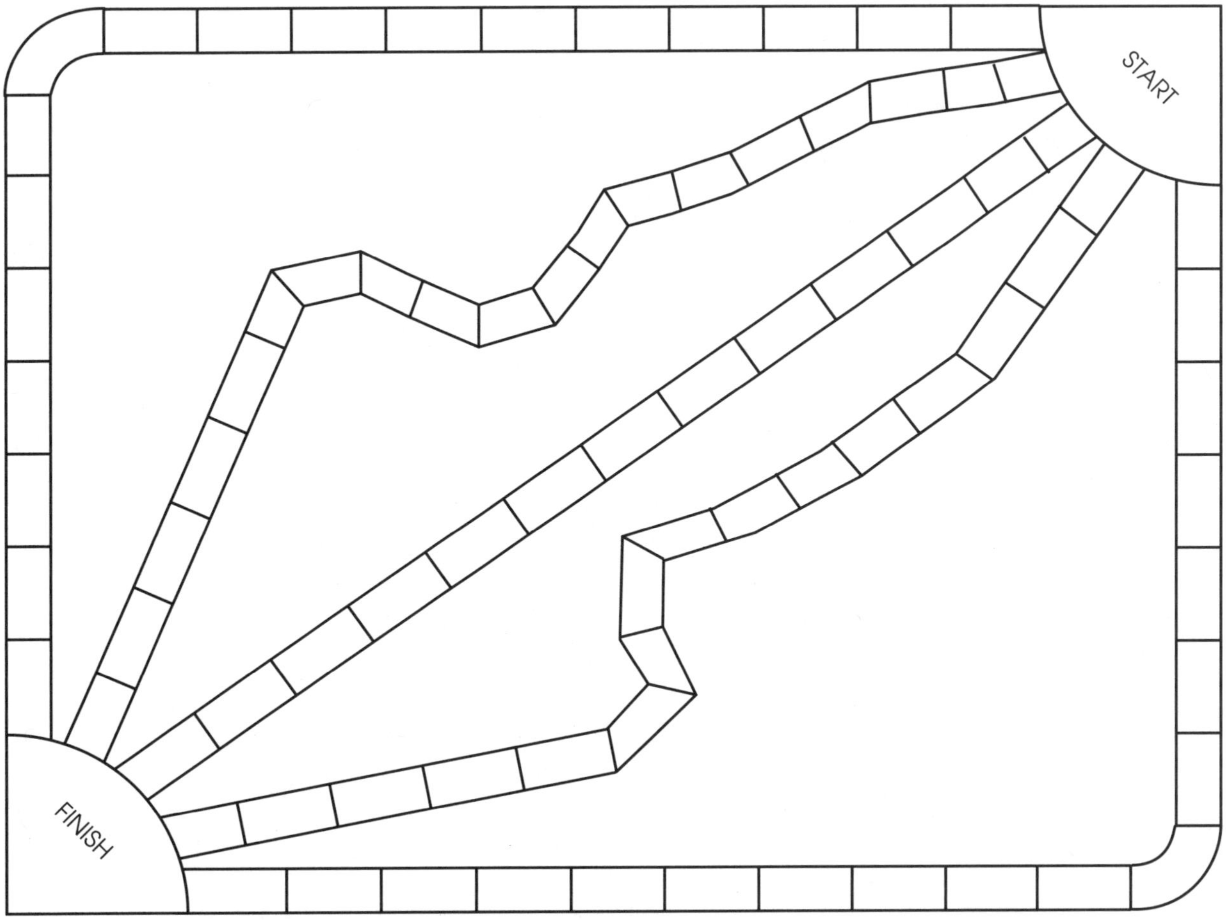

GAME BOARD

Copyright © 1995 by Allyn and Bacon

229

BLACKLINE MASTER 14
The Spinning Game

Materials Needed:
- 8.5" x 11" white cardboard or posterboard
- Brad
- Scissors

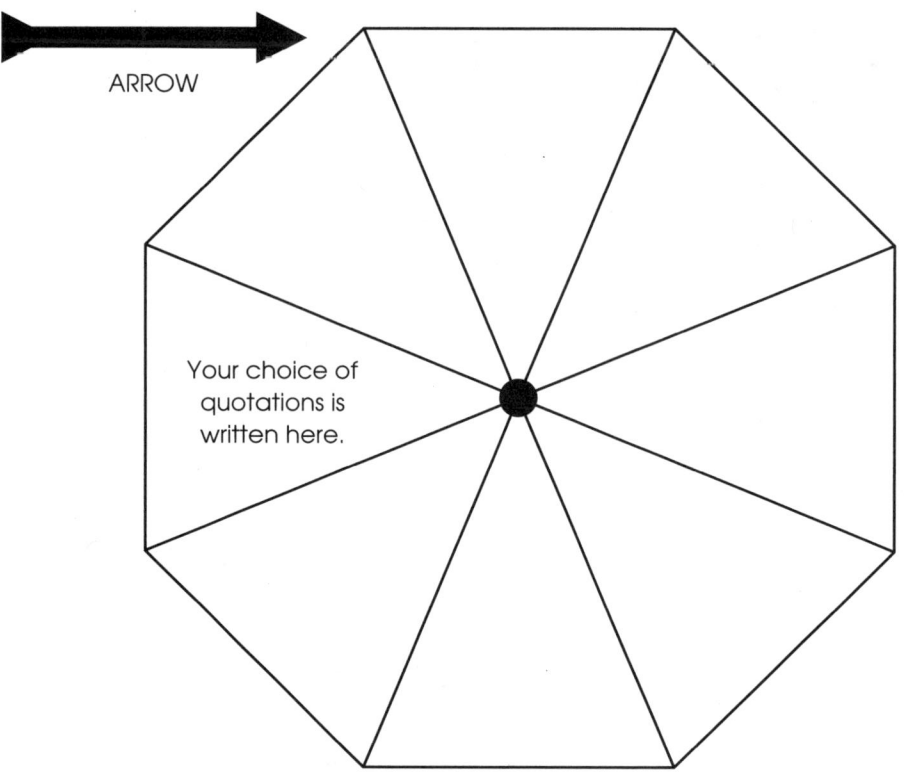

1. Place one (1) quotation or concept in each section of the above spinner.
2. Follow the instructions for this game, as they appear in individual units.

How to make:
Place the above figure and the arrow on cardboard and cut both out. Glue the figure to cardboard. Make a slit through the small circle and the arrow. Connect the arrow to the figure with a brad just tight enough so arrow will be able to spin.

BLACKLINE MASTER 15
Parents' Strategies to Overcome Mistakes

Mistakes Made	Strategies Used to Overcome Mistakes

BLACKLINE MASTER 16
How to Write a Play

Decisions to be made are: roles or identity, place or situation, focus or issue, and order in which they appear.

To create a workable drama, write your ideas for three parts of a drama, which you will combine to make your original play.

Roles people will play	*Places scenes will occur*	*Focus or moral of each scene*
a.	a.	a.
b.	b.	b.
c.	c.	c.

Identity they desire	*Situations*	*Issues resolved about life*
a.	a.	a.
b.	b.	b.
c.	c.	c.

Conclusion:

Who are you?	Where are you?	What are we concerned about?

Examples for opening scene:

A soldier:	at a railway station:	becoming anxious because of the lateness of the train.
A farmer:	at a market:	complaining to others of the price of fertilizer.
Pirates:	on a ship:	lost.

BLACKLINE MASTER 17
Using a Venn Diagram to Compare and Contrast

Name _____ Date _____

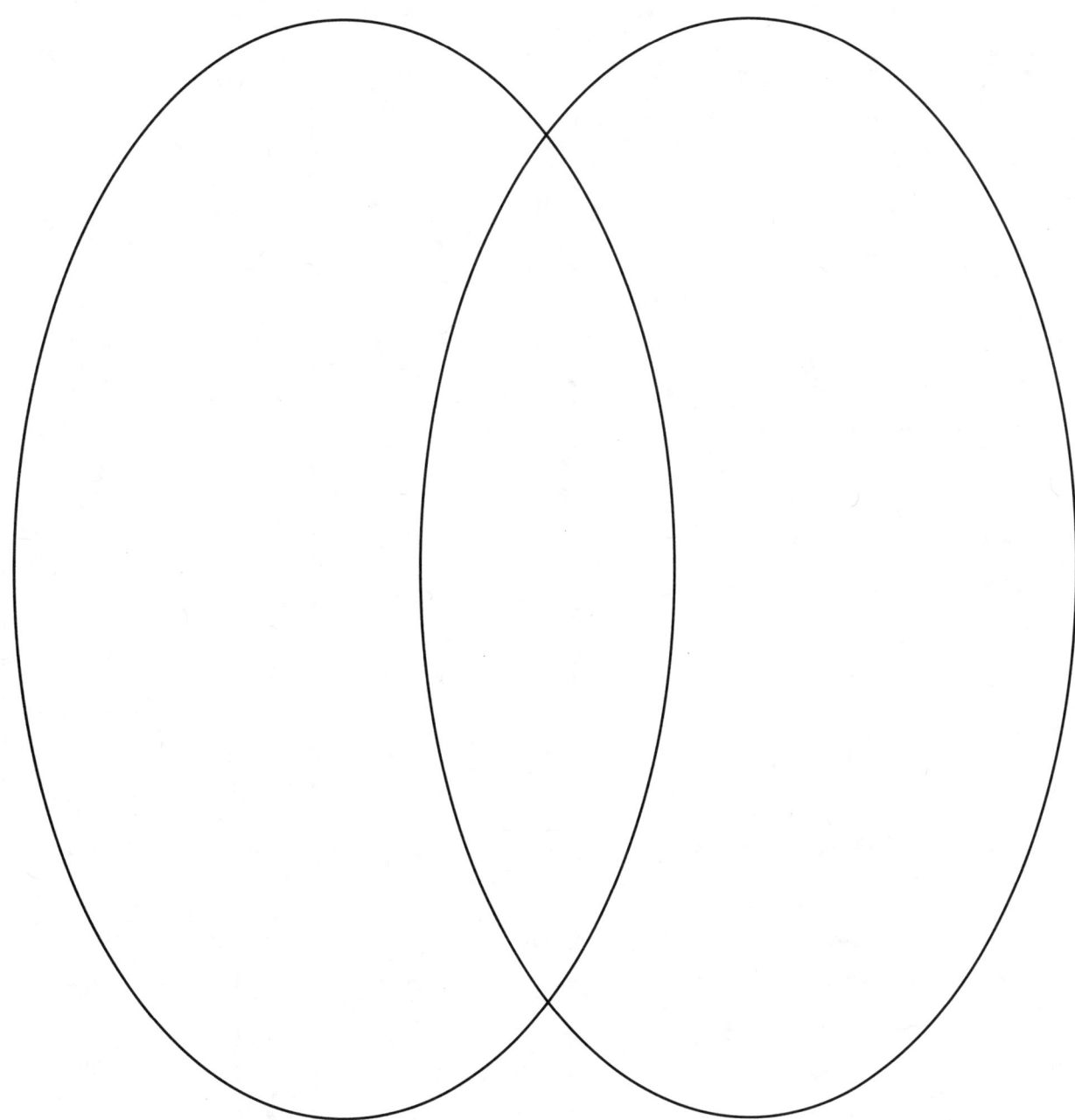

BLACKLINE MASTER 18
Creating Words Game

A	A	A	A	U	U	V
B	B	Q	S	Y	Y	Y
C	C	C	W	X	Z	P
D	D	D	K	K	K	K
E	E	E	E	E	L	L
F	G	G	H	M	N	P
I	I	I	I	I	I	J
O	O	O	O	O	O	O
R	R	R	R	R	T	T
P	A	A	T	S	N	O

BLACKLINE MASTER 19
Room Floor Plan

Name _____ Date _____

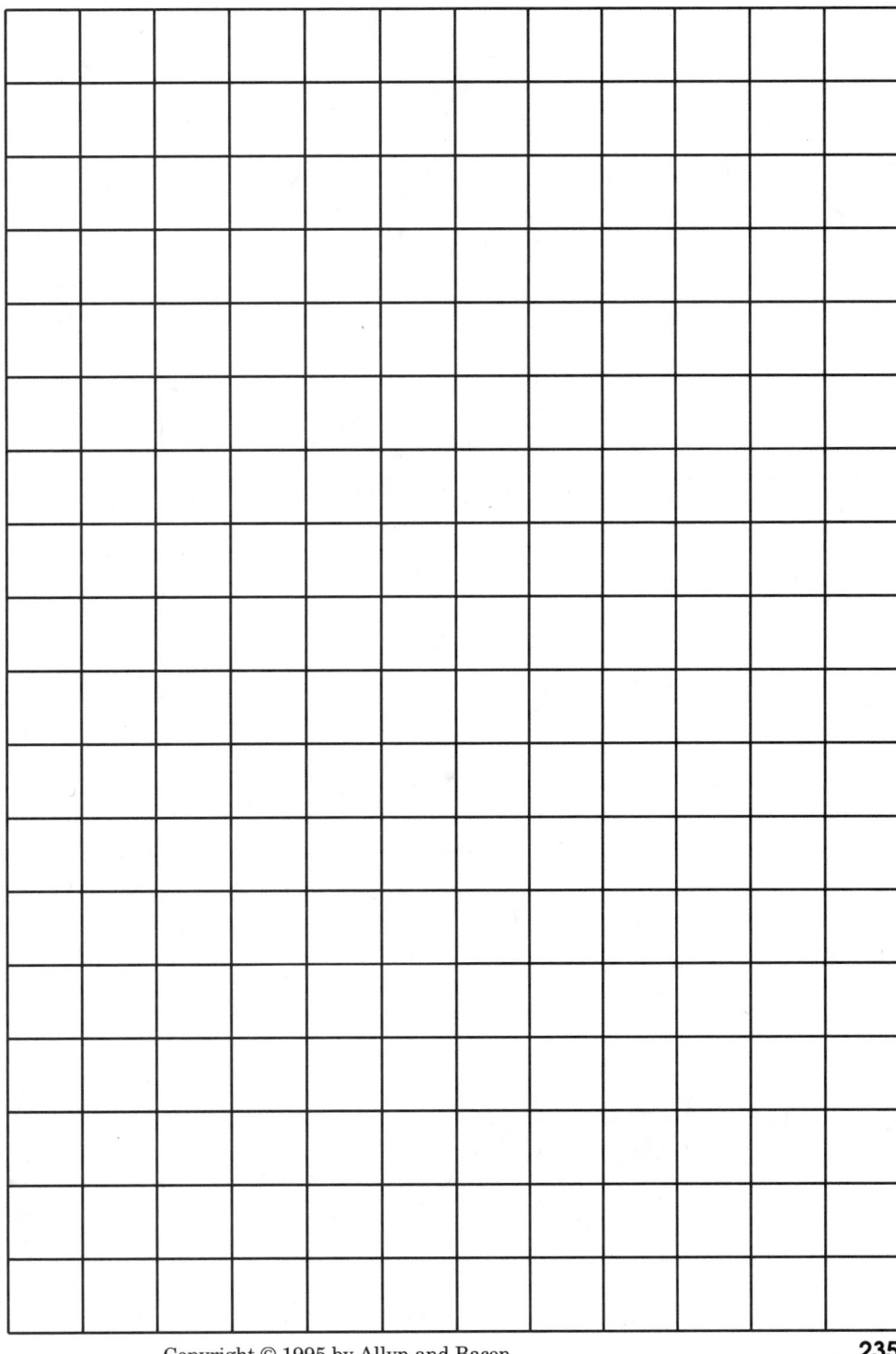

BLACKLINE MASTER 20
Your Room Furniture

Measure your room. Use Blackline Master 19 as your floor plan (each square = 1 foot). On the floor plan, mark where the window(s) and doors are. Now you are ready to rearrange your room. Cut out the pieces below that you have in your room, or make a place on the floor plan for the furniture you have by showing the space it takes up in a room.

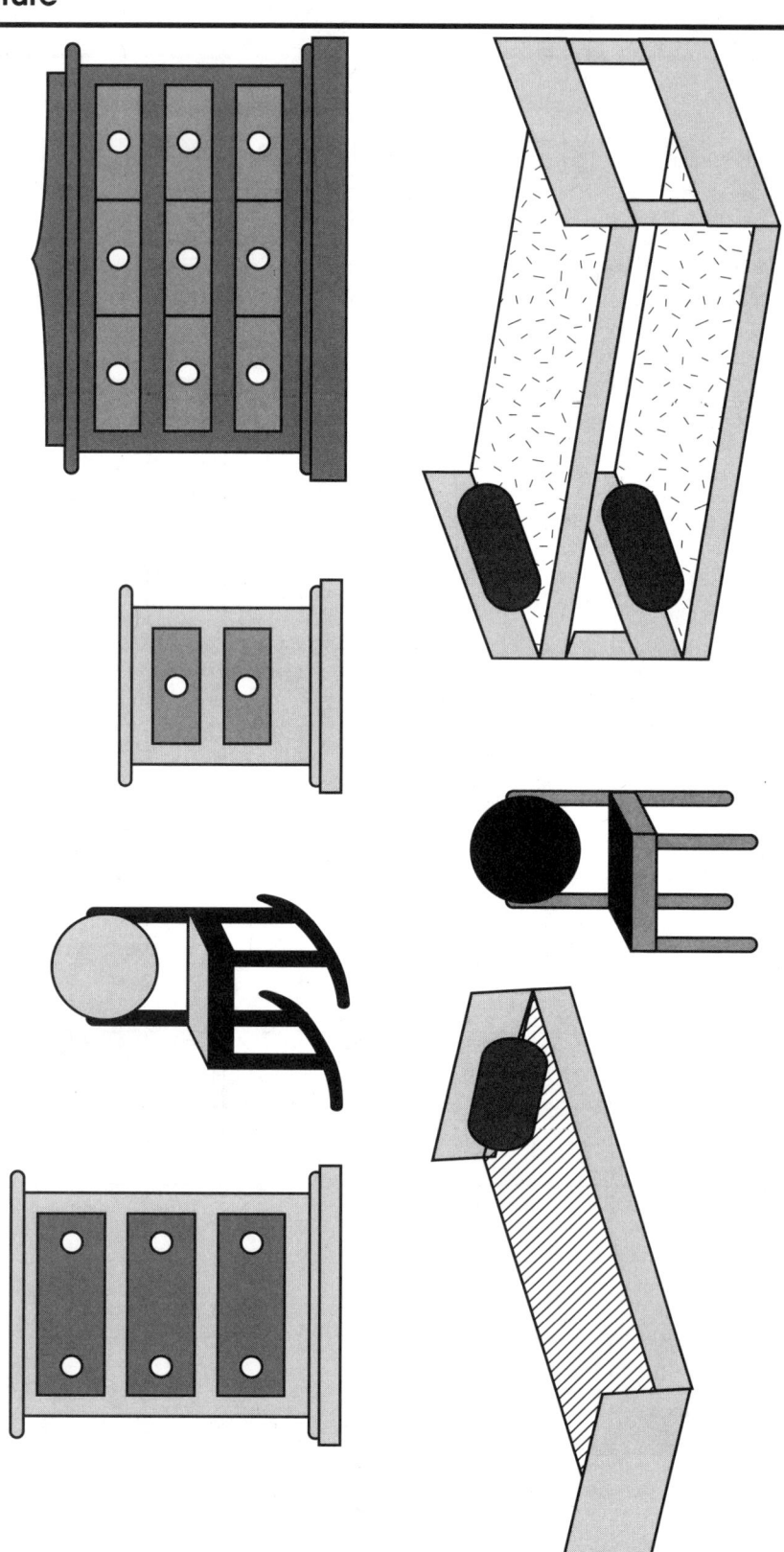

BLACKLINE MASTER 21
Schoolroom Furniture

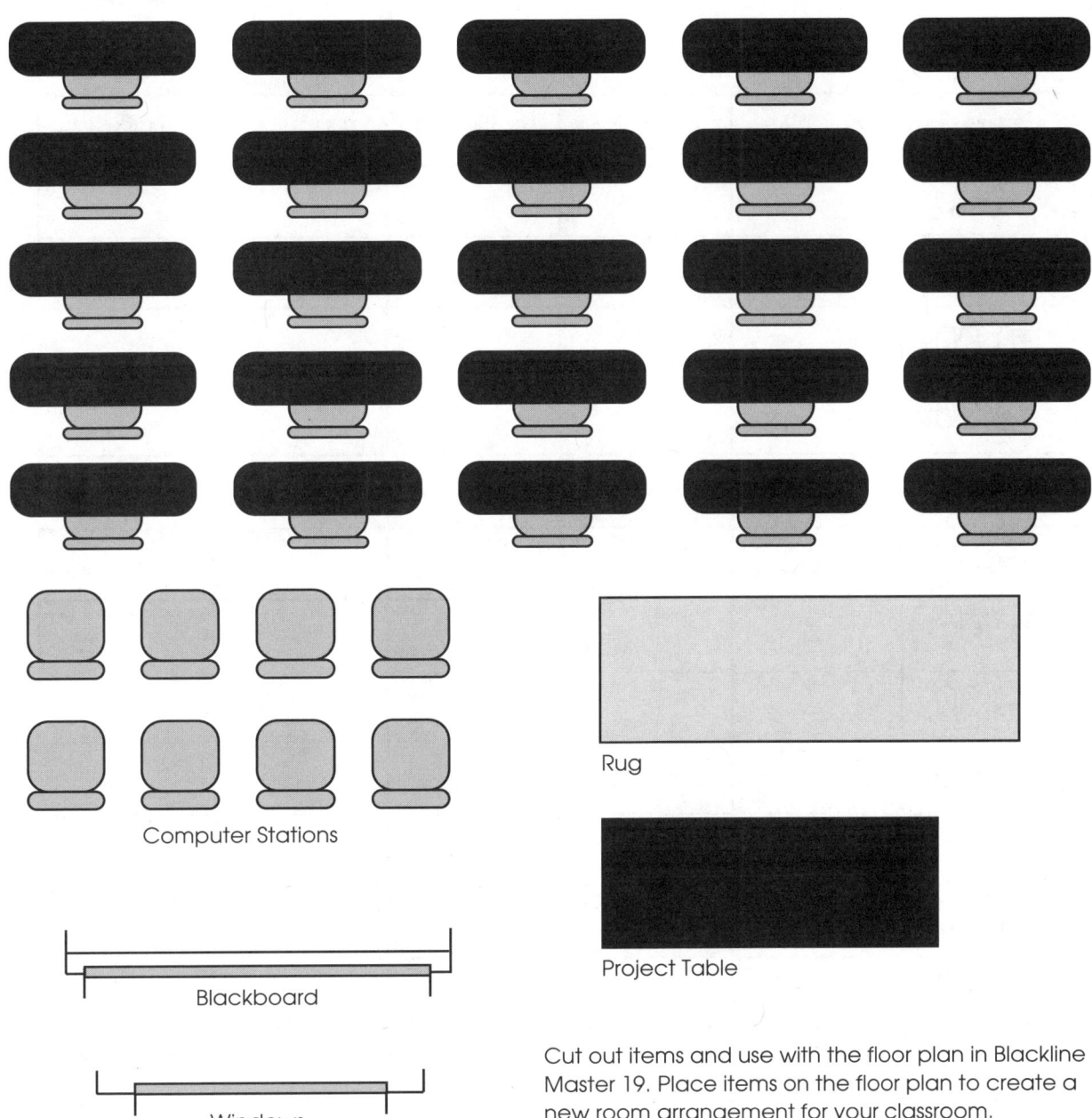

Cut out items and use with the floor plan in Blackline Master 19. Place items on the floor plan to create a new room arrangement for your classroom.

BLACKLINE MASTER 22
School Time Diary

Name _____ Date _____

TIME	MONDAY	TUESDAY	WEDNESDAY	THURSDAY	FRIDAY
7:00					
7:30					
8:00					
8:30					
9:00					
9:30					
10:00					
10:30					
11:00					
11:30					
12:00					
12:30					
1:00					
1:30					
2:00					
2:30					

Copyright © 1995 by Allyn and Bacon

BLACKLINE MASTER 23
After School Time Diary

Name _____ Date _____

TIME	MONDAY	TUESDAY	WEDNESDAY	THURSDAY	FRIDAY
2:30					
3:00					
3:30					
4:00					
4:30					
5:00					
5:30					
6:00					
6:30					
7:00					
7:30					
8:00					
8:30					
9:00					
9:30					
10:00					

Copyright © 1995 by Allyn and Bacon

BLACKLINE MASTER 24

Webbing to Learn New Concepts

BLACKLINE MASTER 25
Writing Evaluation Form

EDITING CHECKLIST   NAME _____

AUTHOR _____ DATE _____

TITLE _____

_____ SPELLING   (It was a (speceli) shirt.) *special*

(Watch for homonyms; (Wear) should I (where) it?) *Where ... wear*

_____ CAPITALIZATION   (I looked good. let's go! I'm ready to visit doctor collins.)

(Watch for out of place capitals; We went to the /School.)

_____ PUNCTUATION   (The sentences all end with punctuation marks⊙ I've checked for

appropriate use of commas⌄ for example⌄ in listing and for sentence clarity.

Apostrophes are used to show possession and as part of a contraction⊙)

_____ PARAGRAPH IDENTION   (¶Another idea for.....) *and that is the best...*

_____ MARGINS   (→|then... / |and so...)

_____ COMPLETE SENTENCES   (Then ∧ went home.) *we*

_____ CLEAR MEANING   (They then went to MacDonalds after practice.) *band ... ⌄'*

_____ WHAT COULD MAKE THIS PAPER BETTER? _____

_____

_____

_____

⬭	Spelling or word choice	⊙	Add period	¶	New paragraph
=	Capitalize	∧	Add comma	⌃	Insert
/	Don't capitalize	⌄	Add apostrophe	ℓ	Delete

Copyright © 1995 by Allyn and Bacon

241

BLACKLINE MASTER 26
Telephone Etiquette

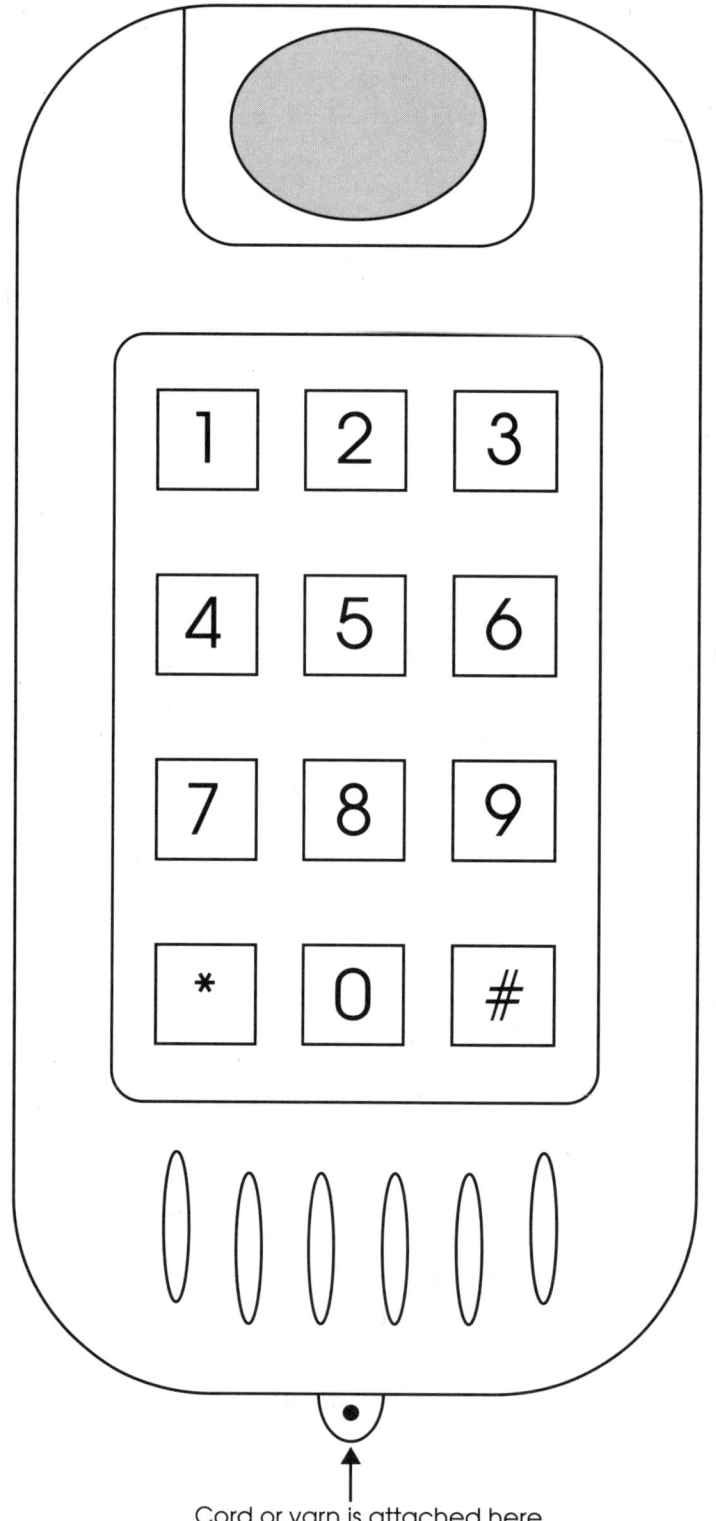

Cord or yarn is attached here

BLACKLINE MASTER 27
Six Steps to Improving Listening Skills

In the future, you can improve your listening ability by doing these six things:

1. As soon as you start to listen, try to find the sentence that tells what the subject is by asking yourself what the focus of the person's talk is.

2. Pay close attention to all words that tell directions and describe objects, such as *north, south, east, west,* or *up, down, here, there, over, under, above, man, baby,* and so on. As soon as you hear such words, picture the topic in your mind.

3. Listen for the words that signal order, such as *first, second, last, after, before,* and *also.* Then put yourself in the place of the person speaking, and, in your mind, perform the order of the activities he or she describes.

4. As you listen, picture details of what is described. This mental picutre will help you distinguish the most important details and how they relate together. As you hear each detail, tie it to the detail immediately preceding it. The person talking had a very important reason for putting these details together, and you try to guess what that reason was as you listen.

5. Pay special attention to words such as *and, or, but, yet,* and *because.* These words tell you how two ideas are related.

6. Ask questions of the person talking to clarify the points being made.

To practice using these good listening skills, find a picture in your textbook and describe it to your partner. Your partner will do the same for you. Draw what is described and then compare to the original picture to determine how well you listened.

BLACKLINE MASTER 28
Native American Symbols

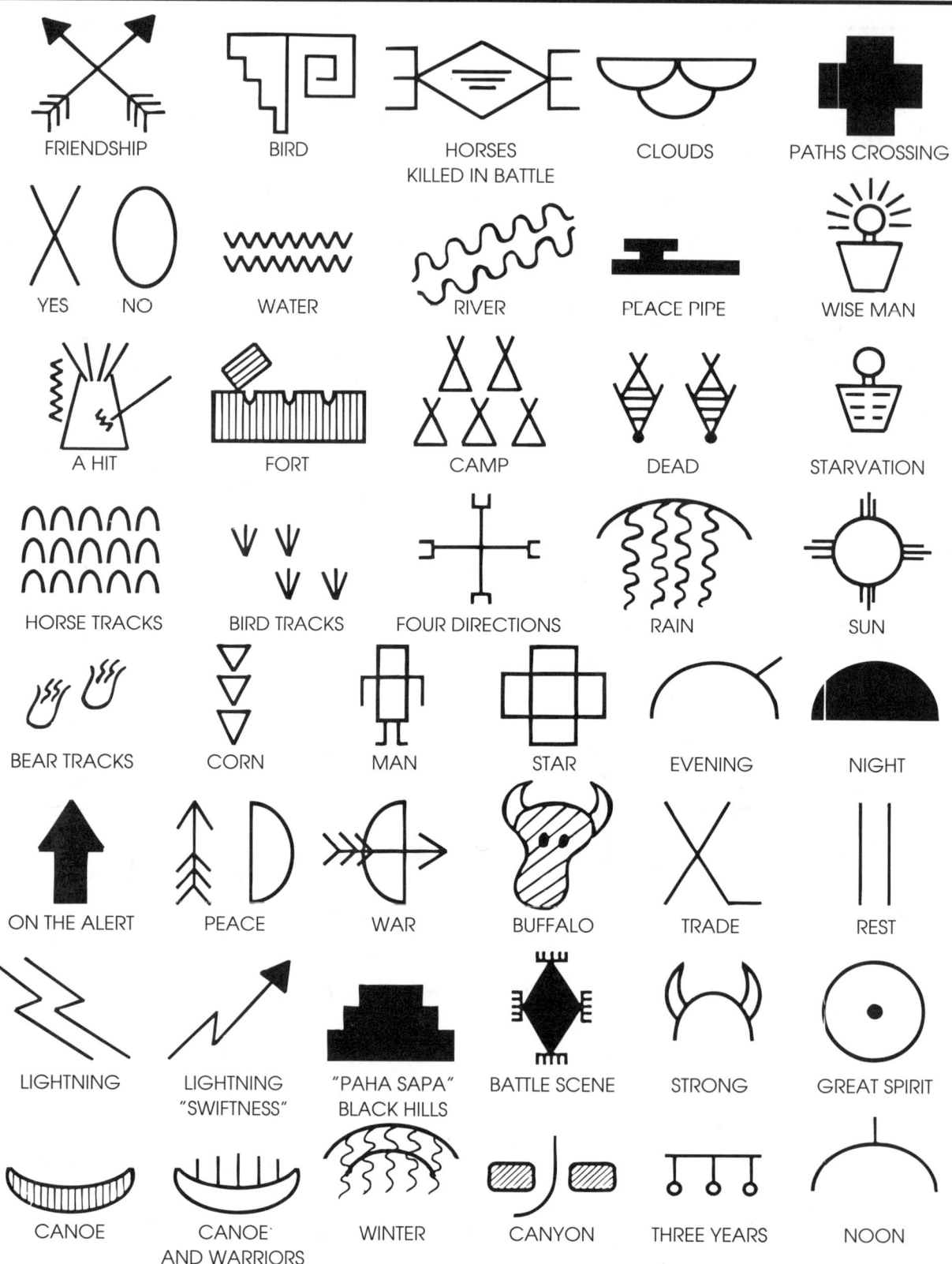

BLACKLINE MASTER 29
Learning to Make Good Decisions

Name _____   Date _____

Qualities of Good Decision Makers	Characters in Literature Who Demonstrated This Quality and How They Demonstrated It
1. Anticipate the consequences of alternative actions before making a decision.	
2. Use outside resources and solicit advice from other people before making a decision.	
3. Have a positive attitude and are fair to all sides when making a decision.	
4. Seek the truth and objective evidence before making a decision.	
5. Listen to various points of views before making a decision.	
6. Recognize propaganda and inconsistent application of standards.	
7. Consider the well-being of those who will be affected before making a decision.	
8.	
9.	
10.	
11.	

BLACKLINE MASTER 30
Map of Africa

BLACKLINE MASTER 31
I Persevere

Name _____ Date _____

1. Place the task you want to achieve on the top dome of the Perseverence Tower.

2. Put the first action you will take to achieve this task on the bottom step of the tower.

3. Continue to list your persevering efforts by placing one on each upward step. Write each action after you complete it.

4. GIANT STEPS ARE ALLOWED!!

Copyright © 1995 by Allyn and Bacon

BLACKLINE MASTER 32
Methods of Resolving Disagreements as Depicted in Literature

Name _____ Date _____

Book Title	Disagreement Featured	Resolution

Refer to this record if you need to resolve a difficulty. The methods literary characters used may assist you.

BLACKLINE MASTER 33
The Reading Wheel

BLACKLINE MASTER 34
Story Map

Name _____ Date _____

The Setting:
Characters: Time: Place:

↓

The Problem:

↓

The Goal:

↓

Main Action/Climax:

↓

The Outcome

BLACKLINE MASTER 35
Map of the World

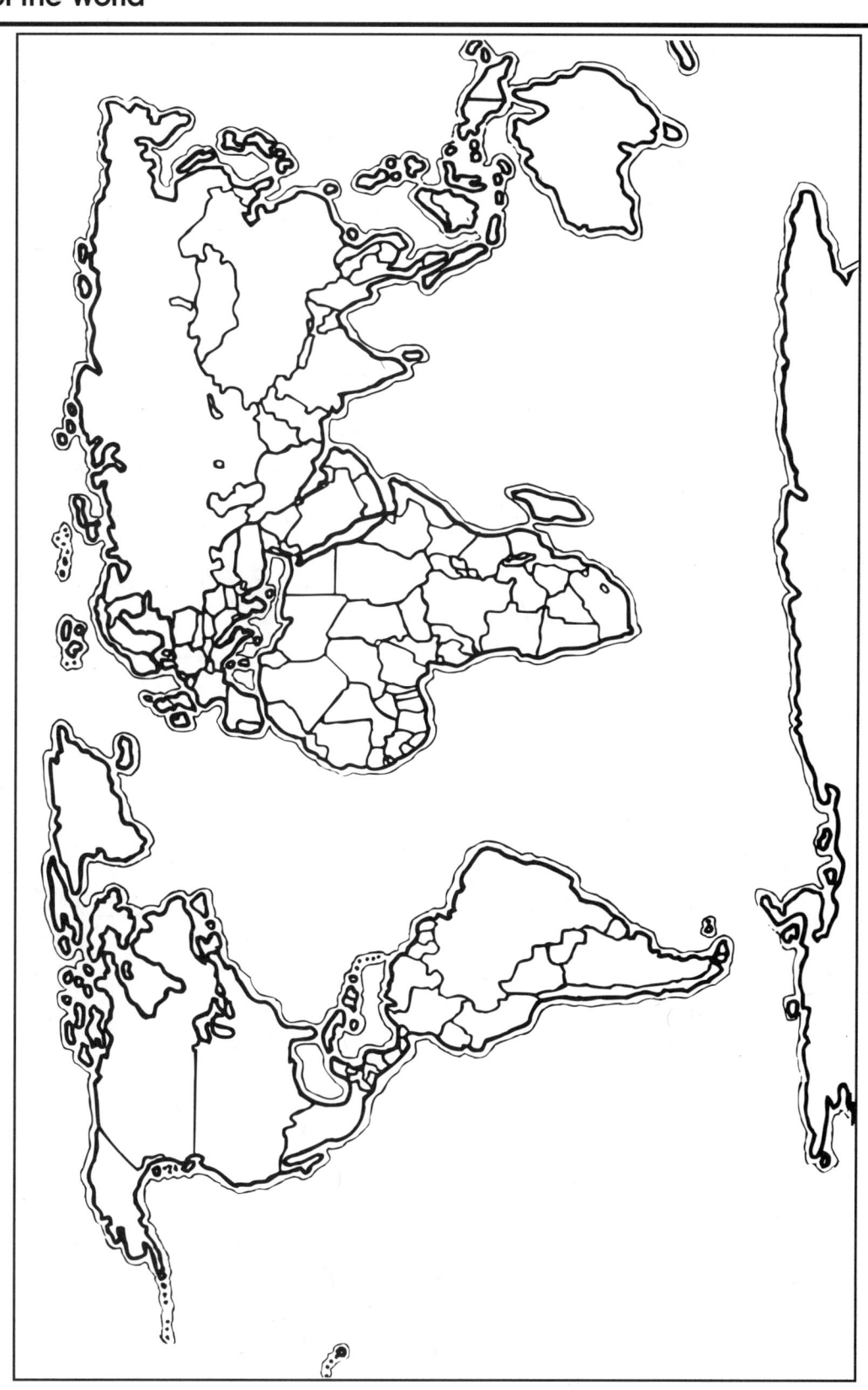

BLACKLINE MASTER 36
Puzzle Me

DIRECTIONS: There are many different types of word puzzles. The ones here allow you to use any letters you wish to complete each diagram. But be careful — they're not as easy as they look!

Name _____

Date _____

1.
2.
3.
4.
5.
6.

*Taken from *The Gifted Reader Handbook,* Copyright 1988, Scott, Foresman, and Company by Anthony D. Fredericks, Glenview, Illinois.

BLACKLINE MASTER 37
Finger Puppet Pattern

1. Cut out puppets and circles marked "cut out."
2. Insert your fingers into the holes you cut out.
3. Hold up the puppets on an index card.
4. Present your puppet play, talking as if you are the puppet you made.

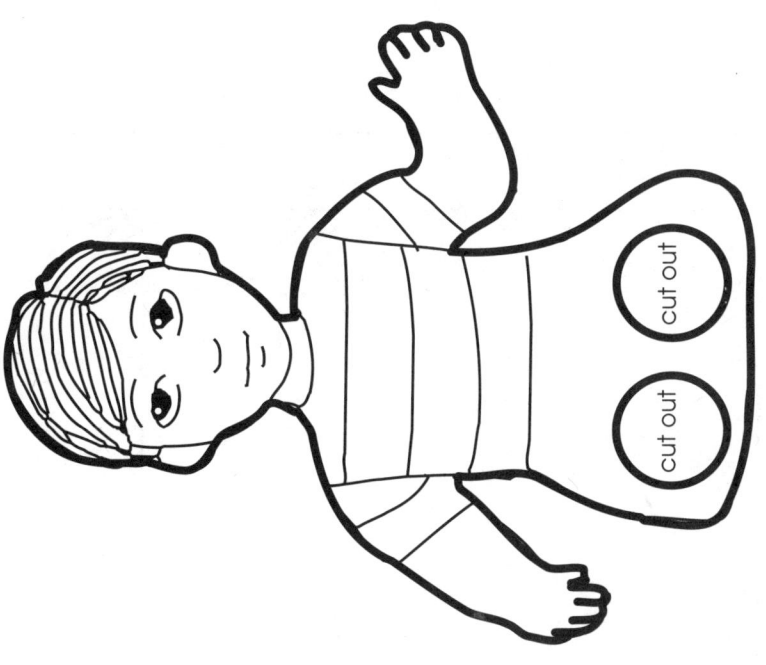

BLACKLINE MASTER 38
Block Puzzle

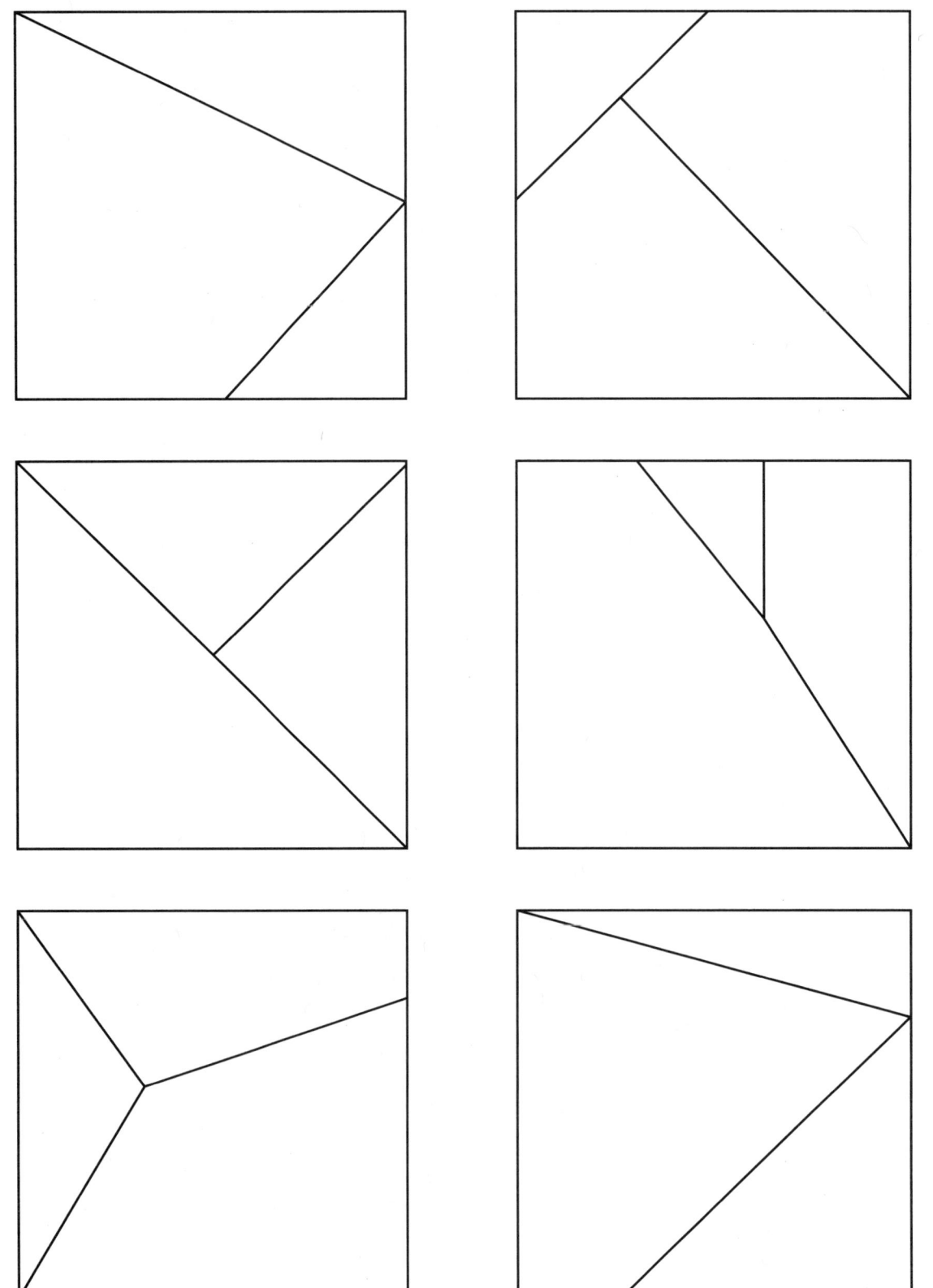

254

BLACKLINE MASTER 39
What Do You See?

Cut off the answer before giving Blackline Master 39 to students (*Answer:* vase or two people).

Copyright © 1995 by Allyn and Bacon